INSEAD Business Press Series

J. Frank Brown
THE GLOBAL BUSINESS LEADER
Practical Advice for Success in a Transcultural Marketplace

Lourdes Casanova
GLOBAL LATINAS
Latin America's Emerging Multinationals

David Fubini, Colin Price & Maurizio Zollo
MERGERS
Leadership, Performance and Corporate Health

Manfred Kets de Vries
SEX, MONEY, HAPPINESS & DEATH
Musings from the Underground

Manfred Kets de Vries, Konstantin Korotov & Elizabeth Florent-Treacy
COACH AND COUCH
The Psychology of Making Better Leaders

Juliette McGannon & Michael McGannon
THE BUSINESS LEADER'S HEALTH MANUAL
Tips and Strategies for Getting to the Top and Staying There

Renato Orsato
SUSTAINABILITY STRATEGIES
When Does it Pay to be Green?

James Teboul
SERVICE IS FRONT STAGE
Positioning Services for Value Advantage

Jean-Claude Thoenig & Charles Waldman
THE MARKING ENTERPRISE
Business Success and Societal Embedding

Rolando Tomasini & Luk van Wassenhove
HUMANITARIAN LOGISTICS

The Business Leader's Health Manual

TIPS AND STRATEGIES FOR GETTING TO THE TOP AND STAYING THERE

Juliette McGannon

Co-Founder and Managing Director of The McGannon Institute of Proactive Health (MIPH), and Director of the Business Leader's Health Program (BLHP) at INSEAD

and

Michael McGannon

Specialist in Preventative Medicine, Co-Founder, The McGannon Institute of Proactive Health (MIPH), and Medical Director of the Business Leader's Health Program (BLHP) at INSEAD

INSEAD
Business Press

palgrave
macmillan

First published 2009 by
PALGRAVE MACMILLAN

Palgrave Macmillan in the UK is an imprint of Macmillan Publishers Limited,
registered in England, company number 785998, of Houndmills, Basingstoke,
Hampshire RG21 6XS.

Palgrave Macmillan in the US is a division of St Martin's Press LLC,
175 Fifth Avenue, New York, NY 10010.

Palgrave Macmillan is the global academic imprint of the above companies
and has companies and representatives throughout the world.

Palgrave® and Macmillan® are registered trademarks in the United States,
the United Kingdom, Europe and other countries.

ISBN 978-1-349-30474-5   ISBN 978-0-230-24041-4 (eBook)
DOI 10.1007/978-0-230-24041-4

This book is printed on paper suitable for recycling and made from fully
managed and sustained forest sources. Logging, pulping and manufacturing
processes are expected to conform to the environmental regulations of the
country of origin.

A catalogue record for this book is available from the British Library.

A catalog record for this book is available from the Library of Congress.

10 9 8 7 6 5 4 3 2 1
18 17 16 15 14 13 12 11 10 09

This book is dedicated to our ancestors,
Don and Patty McGannon, models of love
and loyalty, and our sons, Kevin, Jules and Seàn
in gratitude for helping us to become worthy ancestors

Contents

The authors

Juliette McGannon, RM, CFI, is the Managing Director of the McGannon Institute of Proactive Health (MIPH), based in Nice, France, as well as the Director of the Business Leader's Health Programme (BLHP) at INSEAD. She received her training in California in nutrition and physiology, her field of expertise being fitness prescription and effective stress management. She is a Reiki Master, a Professor of Yoga, and the innovator of the SMART (Stress Management And Relaxation Techniques), the Forest and Paris Expeditions (Team Building) and Yoga for Managers modules. These modules have been enjoyed by over 75,000 international managers from over 40 countries. Her audio CD, *Managing Personal & Professional Balance during Life's Hurricanes,* has brought welcome relief to tens of thousands of managers. Her present research project is focused on the techniques that optimally balance the left and right brains during stressful moments.

Dr. Michael McGannon, MD, is a specialist in proactive medicine, particularly as it applies to business life. He holds a doctorate in medicine from Georgetown University (Washington, DC, US) and a postdoctoral research fellowship in gastroenterology (digestive diseases) from Stanford University Medical Center (California, US). He has also written extensively at the health/business interface for such international publications as *The International Herald Tribune* (Paris), *The Financial Times* (London), *L'Impresa* (Milano), and *The Business Times* (Singapore) among others.

This is their third book, after *Urban Warrior's Book of Solutions* (1999) and *Fit for the Fast Track* (2002). They are presently developing their Business Leader's Health Program (BLHP) on the Second Life platform.

Making contact

Run your own Business Leader's Health Programme and witness the dramatic difference in your organization.

Our contact addresses:

At INSEAD (European Business Institute): Boulevard de Constance, 77305, Fontainebleau Cedex (France). Tel: +33 160724161. E-mail: juliette.mcgannon@insead.edu, michael.mcgannon@insead.edu

At MIPH (McGannon Institute of Proactive Health): 20 Quai Lunel, Impasse de la Marine, 06300, Nice (France). Tel: +33 608925800 Or 334+93310987. E-mails: juliette.mcgannon@orange.fr, michael.mc-gannon@orange.fr

Foreword

It is essential for today's leaders to be nimble not only in mind, but also in body. In a constantly changing global landscape, executives encounter numerous challenges and opportunities that require such flexibility – from adapting to fluctuations in the economy and assessing risk profiles to expanding into new markets and achieving sustainable growth. The *Business Leader's Health Manual* proves that in order to prosper under these conditions, leaders should place further emphasis on their overall health in addition to their careers. Finding a balance between work and life is necessary to achieve lasting success.

The McGannons' expertise in leadership and health has been instrumental to the participants in our executive education programs. At INSEAD, we take a holistic approach to developing leaders. While business and financial acumen are critical, leaders must also adopt a global, socially responsible mindset and a healthy lifestyle. The McGannons' manual will be an extremely valuable guide for any executive who wants to maximize their effectiveness in work and life. As careers and schedules become increasingly demanding, health management will become part and parcel to every leader's toolkit.

J. Frank Brown
Dean of INSEAD

Introduction

Life moves so much more rapidly now than it did before ...
the huge acceleration in the rate of growth of facts, of knowledge, of
techniques, of inventions, of advances in technology ...

To put it bluntly, we need a different type of human being ... able to live in a world that changes perpetually, which doesn't stand still, who don't need to staticize the world ... to freeze it and make it stable, who don't need to do what their daddies did, who are able to face tomorrow not knowing what's going to come, not knowing what will happen, with confidence enough in ourselves that we will be able to improvise in that situation which has never existed before.

The society which can turn out such people will survive;
the societies that cannot turn out such people, will die.

Abraham Maslow, *The Farther Reaches of Human Nature*

The term *leader* has evolved and transmuted over time, often idealizing, even romanticizing, military aspects of leadership to fire up the troops to want to follow their bellicose leader. But leadership is far more than glorifying the hell of war, as we have seen throughout history and very recently again.

> *True leadership starts precisely with a minority of ONE.*
> *That is, all leaders lead themselves first and foremost,*
> *knowing full well that in doing so, others want to follow their lead.*

To get a better idea what sort of aspirations are held by today's business leaders, we simply asked the managers as part of their participation in the Leaders' Health Programme the following two questions (the responses are given in order):

1. **What are the top 10 leaders of all time?**
   1. Mahatma Gandhi
   2. Jesus Christ
   3. The Prophet Mohammed
   4. The Buddha
   5. Martin Luther King, Jr.
   6. John F. Kennedy
   7. Nelson Mandela
   8. Lee Kuan Yew
   9. Sir Winston Churchill (as wartime leader)
   10. Ernest Shackleton, Irish explorer

2. **What are the top five personal qualities of truly great leaders?**
   1. Courage (Hans in Chapter 1)
   2. Fairness (Isabelle in Chapter 2)
   3. Commitment (Fadi in Chapter 3)
   4. Confidence (Rachel in Chapter 4)
   5. Humility (Miguel in Chapter 5)

The objective of this manual, full of tips and solutions, is to assist business leaders in their climb to the top of life's mountains. Each and every one of these leaders finishes their stories by owning their **CORE** Assets (health and sanity). Their new power is in their focus on the three Pillars of Life, without which leadership is impossible:

- Health (mental and physical)
- Family and friends
- Job

All three of these Pillars must be in optimal shape through evaluation and maintenance.

At the end of the day or life, a leader is one who hears the wake-up calls in life in their myriad forms and has the courage to begin their own Journey of Awakening. Each of these leaders within has overcome his or her personal challenges, crossed the Valley of Darkness and emerged whole and intact because they realize that self-mastery is the only game worth playing.

JULIETTE AND MICHAEL MCGANNON
November 2008
Nice, France

The heart of the matter: from ticker to timebomb ... and back!

1

chapter

In this chapter, you will learn, by illustrative example, how to first get it wrong and then get it right by:

1 Understanding heart disease, and thereby avoiding it
2 Being free of the abdominal obesity associated with heart disease and Alzheimer's disease
3 Understanding the role of insulin and sugar in the metabolic syndrome
4 Controlling your cholesterol without drugs
5 Discovering BURST walking to achieve total fitness

Abbreviations and acronyms that you will need to read this chapter smoothly include:

AGE	Advanced glycated end-product
ALA	Alpha-linolenic acid
BMI	Body mass index
BP	Blood pressure
CAD	Coronary artery disease
CCU	Coronary Care Unit
EFA	Essential fatty acid
GI	Glycemic index
HAP	Health Action Plan
HDL	High-density lipoprotein
HS-CRP	High-sensitivity C-reactive protein
LA	Linoleic acid
LDL	Low-density lipoprotein
SAD	Standard American diet
TGs	Triglycerides
WHR	Waist-to-hip ratio

INTRODUCTION

My name is Hans. My home base is in The Netherlands, but I have lived in the US and Asia for stints of 4 years apiece: I am truly a world citizen.

My Journey of Awakening started out with an anatomy of a health bankruptcy leading to a serious heart problem. It is a still photograph of the "me" before I woke up from a nightmare. Before my heart problem, I had been very proactive and faithful to a healthy profit margin at work ("the bottom line"), but, with regard to my core assets – my spouse, my family, my health, sanity, and happiness – I had been very reactive and negligent. By most standards, I had been living the "good life," and things seemed to be going just fine on all fronts, except for that nagging ear ticking that sometimes kept me awake at night.

A few years ago, I started as a real time bomb, but I just couldn't hear the ticking … not yet. Let me share my journey of awakening with you.

PROFESSIONAL LIFE

My university education was intense yet smooth, aside from the untimely death of my father at the early age of 54 years from "some heart problem." My mother subsequently became depressed, gained weight, and developed mild diabetes. Curiously, since the death of my father, I myself had developed a bizarre ear problem, a ticking, that affected my balance from time to time. I actually used that as an excuse to stop my jogging program.

I had developed, several years after my MBA, my own version of "hero": the fellow who would put in a full 16-hour day of negotiations in our Hong Kong office, jump on a plane for 14 hours to London, arrive at 8 a.m., shower, and hit the ground running to put in a 14-hour working day. Wow! High blood pressure and a bit of a big tummy seemed to me to be a small price to pay for such collective adulation. I am now the Vice President in charge of design development for a company specializing in machine parts. In the early days, my management philosophy in business was: If it ain't broke, don't fix it. I applied the same philosophy to my health.

After many brief discussions with my family, and with my wife Elke's tacit consent, I had decided to assume an even heavier workload, with lots of travel to the Far East (about 150 days per year) in order to achieve personal and professional objectives.

PERSONAL LIFE

I am now 46 years of age, about 10 years younger than my father was when he had his heart attack. After 21 years, I was (and still am) happily married to Elke, the mother of our four children: Cornelius aged 18, Emma, 15, Jan, 11, and little Henk (our son with special learning needs), who is 7. We live in a small city in The Netherlands. I play tennis on the weekends, when it is warm enough.

The intimate aspects of my relationship with Elke had, in a word, been better before all this happened. She worked off and on and seemed content with her ladies groups' meetings. But my long hours and business trips had stolen something special away from our relationship. We drifted apart and had discussed separation, and even the "D" word, on numerous occasions when we argued.

I thought for sure that the children had everything they needed or wanted. Sure, sometimes they would whine and complain: Cornelius about my missing his football games and judo tournaments, and Emma about her piano recitals. But they had everything they really needed to survive.

The worst part of the week was, of course, Saturday mornings. There was always a little tension as if we needed some time to reacquaint ourselves, lots of pregnant, sometimes painful, silences. The whole family would make legitimate claims on my time and energy. Unfortunately, at a time when they needed my energy and attention the most, I was in need of being left alone to read my paper in the garden, answer mails, take some calls. Some day, I thought, they'll understand.

This is my story of how I was forced to get back to basics of life, backing away from the brink.

HEALTH PROFILE

Slowly, imperceptibly, starting in the late 1980s, I put a few inches around my waist (as if my whole metabolism was slowing down), my blood pressure started climbing, and I got out of breath more easily. Elke didn't seem to care too much about my widening girth (perhaps because she also had been gaining weight herself). In an effort to forestall blood pressure issues and diabetes, we had tried *everything*, including sweaty jogging suits, herbal diets, low-fat diets, and all the fad diets that Elke could find.

Until 1999, I had a life that followed fairly traditional values of hard work, sacrifice, and advancement through the ranks of my company, more or less in the way I had predicted when I graduated from business school. And I did very well. After 2001, the global markets opened up and I found myself traveling incessantly to China, the US, and India, much to my delight.

NUTRITION

One word could best describe what and how I used to eat: rich. Lots of cakes, biscuits, pastries, chips, fatty meats like T-bone steaks, pork chops, bacon, and lamb at will. I'm not that keen on salads or vegetables (I could never tell exactly what fibre was), especially since my bout of "the runs" during my last trip to India the previous year. When I thought about it, I would take a one-a-day multivitamin.

Slowly but surely, various imbalances that I had thought improbable in my own life took hold. I had had a weight gain of roughly 1 kilogram (kg) per year over the past 7 years. My physical form, which I had since stopped checking in the morning mirror, went from svelte to bloated, amorphous. I used to say that I was "big boned," but now my children would only laugh at that euphemism. At their insistence, I had tried the endless stream of "new diets" without any real success. I generally ate a late dinner, drank about 45 drinks (15 half-pints of beer, 25 glasses of wine, and about 5 glasses of scotch a week – often more), and smoked the occasional cigarette. I thought I was "in touch" with my body, mind, and feelings.

PHYSICAL ACTIVITY

Although a very active athlete (I adore football and tennis) as a university student, physical activity for me had been something of a luxury: restricted to an occasional game of tennis or golf on weekends, but only if and when time permitted. Even our once regular family hikes in the countryside had been phased out.

Once an avid reader of everything from spy novels to political analyses, I had been unable to get in any real reading since my last brief vacation 18 months before, when I had read half a novel. I probably read too many daily newspapers and management books and watched too much TV.

Most important leadership quality	Courage

My idea of great leaders	• John Fitzgerald Kennedy • Mahatma Gandhi • Martin Luther King, Jr.

My most inspiring quotation

The stories of past courage can define that ingredient – they can teach, they can offer hope, they can provide inspiration. But they cannot supply courage itself. For this each man must look into his own soul.

John F. Kennedy, *Profiles in Courage*

MY FIRST WAKE-UP CALL

The first check-up

I never had much cause for concern or reflection. Sure, there was an occasional heart attack or cancer victim at work. Although I cannot pinpoint the exact time, I found myself gradually to be more withdrawn and drinking more alcohol, both alone and after work with colleagues. I had slowly and methodically isolated myself from those things I loved. I was rapidly changing for the worse, and I did not want to hear about it. Although my family said that they understood my frequent absences, I still felt bad about being a "phantom father and spouse" and about my half-hearted attempts to spend more time at home.

Things began to change rather quickly in my life as I turned 44 years of age, head of an international division of a multinational company. Eventually, just for some peace, I succumbed to my wife's and kids' pleading to go for a medical exam, a check-up. After all, I reasoned, if I do it with my car, why not my body? Maybe they would find out what this annoying ticking in my ears was. Going into this check-up, I was obviously well aware of the fact that I had many of the telltale signs and symptoms of someone who had been neglecting his body. Joking about it had become a ritual. I dutifully presented myself to Dr. Nekkers, an old friend and tennis partner, with the usual list of complaints: I slept poorly and always felt tired; my libido was shot to hell; chronic backaches and headaches plagued me with increasing frequency; as I usually bolted my food, I had dreadful heartburn and bloating; and lastly, mild depression struck me from time to time. (I used to think too much.)

I had been certain that, despite these nuisances, everything would be decreed more or less "normal" and that the same old lecture from Dr. Nekkers was as customary as my complaint list: lose some weight, stop smoking and drinking so much, watch your diet, get some more exercise, and so on. Though an excellent doctor and good friend over the years, Dr. Nekkers was not a particularly good actor. As he performed my physical exam, his bushy eyebrows perked up and frowned, as if in disbelief and dismay. He hummed and hawed as he jotted these findings into my medical dossier: he seemed in his own little world. Just as he was finishing his entry, his nurse poked her head into the office and announced, somewhat out of breath, "Excuse me, Dr. Nekkers, your 11 o'clock appointment is here and requires your immediate attention: blood pressure at rest is 220 over 115 and he has severe headaches ... ." He was up and out the door before he could reply.

"Wow, that must be serious," I thought, without really knowing what those numbers implied. Curious to find out something about myself, I leaned over his desk and read his last note in my chart:

History: 44-year-old male, senior manager, family history of heart disease and diabetes, here today for a routine check-up. Sedentary. Appears tired (?depressed). Complains of poor sleep and backaches.

No medications.

Physical exam: Obese male, mild sweating, poor dentition.

Rectal exam: haemorrhoids, no occult blood, prostate: normal, no nodules.

Assessment
Health risk level: High for diabetes and heart attack.
Health age: 61.8 years of age!

Plan: (tough case!)
- Health issue 1: Elevated blood pressure – learn to relax, control stress, reduce alcohol/coffee intake and start meds.
- Health issue 2: Excess weight (refractory), inactive. Low-fat diet.
- Health issue 3: Cholesterol imbalances: start med.

- Health issue 4: Early diabetes: start oral meds.
- Health issue 5: Homocysteine elevation: ???
- Health issue 6: Resting heart rate of 80 beats/min: *extremely* unfit

Follow-up:

Borderline laboratory values. Return to clinic in several months for follow-up. Start medication for blood pressure, diabetes, and cholesterol. Probable metabolic syndrome?

Hans' baseline health and fitness report

	NORMAL/IDEAL RANGE	ME
Actual age (years)		44
Health age (years)	Actual age (or less)	61.8
Blood pressure (mmHg)	< 135/85	165/105
Resting heart rate (beats/minute)	< 60	80
Weight (kg)		98
Body fat %	< 20% men, < 23% women	35%
Body fat weight (kg)		34.3
Lean weight (kg)		63.7
Waist-to-hip ratio	< 0.90 men, < 0.80 women	1.10
Total cholesterol (g/L)	< 2.00	2.90
LDL cholesterol (g/L)	< 1.30	1.85
Triglycerides –TGs (g/L)	< 1.40	3.50
HDL cholesterol (g/L)	> 0.50	0.35
TGs:HDL ratio	< 1	10
Fasting blood sugar (glucose) (g/L)	0.70–1.20	1.25
Homocysteine[1] level (micromoles/L)	7.0–10	96.6
High-sensitivity C-reactive protein (HS-CRP[2]) (mg/L)	Less than 1 mg/L	Not done

g, gram; L, litre; mg, milligram; mmHg, millimetres of mercury.

When Dr. Nekkers returned, slightly out of breath, I was amazed to see he was able to pick up right where we had left off: "Hans, I see that you've read my note. I calculated your health age to be *61.8 years*!" That is, I had the same health risks as someone 61.8 years of age. (But I was only 44 at the time – I had beaten my father's record!) The overall assessment was: watch out for heart attack or metabolic syndrome.

"These figures, Hans, are handy statistical ways of letting you know that, healthwise, you are not really getting away with your lifestyle, and these medications are only delaying the inevitable," Dr. Nekkers explained. "In a word, based on your lifestyle and family history, your body is aging a lot faster than a normal person of the same 44 years. In fact, you are a pretty good candidate for nasty problems, like diabetes or a heart attack."

I began to feel my face flushing warm and beads of sweat on my brow. My only real objective at that time was to merely resume work at a high level and carry out my professional responsibilities. As he seemed to drone on, I interrupted, exasperated: "Doc, let's be straight here. Won't these pills you prescribed for me take care of these minor problems? You know, one of modern medicine's magic bullets?" I could feel an angry voice swelling up inside. Must restrain these bad emotions, I thought. Let's go back to work.

"Hans, don't you read the papers? Haven't you heard about prescription drugs? Don't think for a minute that the side effects are not dangerous,"[3] he admonished me for my attitude and ignorance. I knew that there had to be a quick way out of this one. While packing his doctor's bag, he responded, "You will receive your whole report in several weeks, complete with my full recommendations regarding exercise, stress, and diet. The usual, right? This time try to take them a little more seriously or you may find yourself looking down the barrel of a loaded gun. His last words stuck a long time with me:

> *"If you decide to do nothing about your health, your next call shouldn't be to your doctor, but to your lawyer."*

I was starting to feel very adolescent and exposed without my denial to cover me. "Yeah, Doc, I know and I really *do* care, but I am pushing for that promotion I mentioned to you and time is short. It's not just that, but exercise is boring, diet foods are boring, losing weight is hard work." Although I was a little proud of my fast-track macho arrogance, I started feeling like a pampered celebrity: boring, boring, boring!

"Oh, is that it, Hans? You want to talk about something boring?! Try spending 5 days in the local hospital like a caged animal recuperating from a heart attack. Now, that's *real* boredom!"

I walked into the parking lot stunned – more so than with my usual anxiety and irritation that accompanied these visits – not just because of my deteriorating health, but also because of the tone of Dr. Nekkers's voice: he was actually giving up on me. I'm losing an ally and a friend at the same time, I thought. As I drove back to the office, I decided that it was high time to finally get myself back into what I called "fighting shape." This was it! No more fooling around. Today was the day. I was definitely *not* going the way of my father!

I made a mental checklist of the possible outcomes to my type of "reactive" behaviour pattern and checked off the ones that I had even seen colleagues in my company succumb to:

1. A heart attack – the BIG one, as I called it.

2. A stroke.

3. Various cancers.

4. Mental breakdown/depression.

5. Ulcers, alcoholism, diabetes . . . . .

6. Overall poor life quality (divorce, kid trouble, no free time).

There was a check mark by each of the conditions!

But, alas, the impetus to change for the better created by the anxiety in Dr. Nekkers's office quickly wore off as I dove headlong back into my work and slipped back once again into my reactive mindset. I didn't even open the finalized report from Dr. Nekkers; I already knew enough. I let the fuse burn down yet a little more.

But, finally, in combination with the three medications that I was ordered to take (one for blood pressure, one for cholesterol, and a pill for diabetes), I bit the bullet and started a low-fat diet, switched from red meats to fish, and took reluctantly to low-fat everything, from salad dressings to diet sodas. Then a couple of years later, while closing some deals for my company in Hong Kong, it came: my next wake-up call finally came.

MY SECOND WAKE-UP CALL

Aside from the extra travel and the new "prosperity tissue" around my waist, the only thing in my life that had changed since my check-up was that my memory had started slipping, ever so slightly. Everything else had seemed more or less under control.

After a series of critical negotiations for my company in Hong Kong that continued nearly non-stop until 10 p.m., I had finally dragged my weary body back to the hotel (they're always *so* friendly here, my home away from home) for a night-cap and some much-needed sleep. Picking up the phone, I dialled 15 for the concierge: "Yes, please, a wake-up call at 6.30 tomorrow sharp. Thank you." Ready for another round tomorrow, then home on Wednesday. Exhausted, I fell asleep, comfortably anaesthetized by the alcohol and mulling over the day of work that awaited me.

In the middle of the night, I noticed a vague pressure sensation (it was not really pain), which impaired my breathing. At first, it was a gnawing pain on my left side and jaw, but it then progressed to a severe crushing pain across my chest that made me feel like vomiting. This was most certainly not my usual type of indigestion. It felt as though someone was sitting on my chest, pinning me to the bed. I could not move!

Then a wave panic seized my mind, and thoughts of the family raced through my head: This is the strongest case of heartburn I have ever had. Am I suffocating? Is this the BIG one? It cannot be all that serious. What should I do? Should I call my wife? Where are my children right now? This cannot be happening! In my panic, my priorities seemed to shift so suddenly and so drastically, just as they had after Dr. Nekkers' check-up a couple of years before. All I wanted to do was to speak with my wife and children. I now realize, in retrospect, that this was the beginning of my "awakening."

Groping for my eyeglasses on the night table, another wave of panic came over me: What should I do? Sit tight? Call someone? Who should I call for help? What if this is nothing, a little asthma or bronchitis (my wife had become accustomed to my minor breathing problems and would know precisely what to do now). While leaning back in bed waiting for the concierge to answer, I thought of how I really should have paid more attention to Dr. Nekkers about the weight, the stress: so many "shoulds." Oh, well, too late for that now.

"Hello, concierge here. How may I help you, Sir?" he asked cheerfully.

"Well, you see, I'm having this little problem with indigestion that's keeping me awake ..."

I proceeded to explain my symptoms and what I thought was happening. As I told my story, I detected during our conversation that an increasing tone of alarm had broken through his normally calm voice. Apparently, this type of thing was not at all new to him. He suggested calling an ambulance "just to be safe, Sir." In the meantime, he was going to send someone to my room to help gather my personal belongings. I couldn't believe that this was happening to me.

The waves of pressure in the chest came and went, increasing in severity and frequency, and sometimes moving across my chest and up to my jaw. I was still quite lucid, and the only memory I had of the ambulance arriving was how sweaty and cold I felt, and how suddenly helpless I had become. As they loaded me into the ambulance, I could feel a tear tickle my cheek as I thought of how many things in my life I would never get around to doing: obviously, this is more than heartburn. Whatever it may be, please, dear God, save me. I promise to get it right this time. What about Elke? Should I call her? I really miss her now!, I thought as they loaded me into the back of the ambulance. *Best to not scare her.*

It is just not supposed to happen this way. The kids hadn't even graduated from secondary school yet. A condensed surrealistic version of my life flashed before me like a very clear fast-forward movie: my stellar university years, my corporate combats and victories, happy courtship scenes from my marriage with Elke, the birth of Cornelius, Emma and Jan. My thoughts raced. Where were the golden years, the payoff for all the sacrifice: my hobbies, golf, the farm, sailing, the grandchildren? What meaning did all this have? All of the rhetoric seemed to evaporate .in front of me as I was totally and utterly engaged in one of the biggest battles of my life.

Amidst the panic, I could not help but notice how remarkably well equipped the interior of this ambulance was. I had an oxygen mask on now, intravenous lines, a urinary catheter, and monitor lines, all beeping and hissing. Would all this be enough to save me? I felt very helpless and scared about what was happening: this was definitely not being treated as a routine case of indigestion!

"We could even do minor surgery and deliver babies, if those situations arose," chatted one of the two paramedics. I could see that he, although competent and professional, seemed a little nervous every time he glanced up at the portable heart monitor. In contrast to the hyperalert demeanour of the paramedics, however, was the calm demeanour of the doctor riding in the ambulance: his eyes almost closed, he seemed asleep. The morphine shot had made me very comfortable but could not completely block the pain from breaking through. Somehow I was strangely free of panic; I was floating freely. Was I having one of those celebrated "out-of-body" experiences? Had I died?

Day One

The ambulance jolted to a halt in front of the Emergency Room entrance. Amidst the noise and chaos, I remembered seeing the ambulance doctor now actually sitting quietly in a dark corner of my room in the Intensive Care Unit, apparently uninvolved with my care, just watching. It struck me that his serene demeanour and behaviour seemed inappropriate for part of a medical team. Who could he be? Just as my attention was drawn to a vertical scar on his chest, peeking just above his surgical shirt, he started to speak. His voice, although soft, was easily heard above the background din. "The sad part of all this, Hans, is that it should NOT really have to happen like this." Then he winked at me. "Talk to you later once you're all settled in the hospital ..."

I had heard and read of near-death experiences but always wrote them off as fantasies of a fevered, repressed or drugged mind. Strangely now, however, I felt at warm peace amidst this tense atmosphere, given-up control and surveillance for the moment. With every wave of pain, I felt snapped back inside my body, until the morphine and nitroglycerine permitted the pain to disappear and I was floating, unanchored above my body, unaffected by the flurry of activity below.

The last memory I had in the wee hours of that morning was that my condition had been stabilized long enough to schedule an emergency angiogram or cardiac catheterization. This is a procedure by which the medical and surgical teams can determined precisely to what extent certain heart arteries are blocked, by injecting radio-opaque dye into the arteries of the heart. Judging by the remarks made by the doctors at the "cath," I understood the stakes and realized that my life was, for that moment, in the hands of Dr. Jason Lee, chief of cardiovascular surgery. I fell asleep, exhausted and scared, with the help of painkillers and sleeping pills, until noon.

I wasn't a particularly good patient: I don't like having to have myself cleaned and wiped (especially after being given a laxative to prevent any strain on the heart due to difficult bowel movements), having my bedpan cleaned, my intravenous lines changed, my catheter sites checked for bleeding.

The Coronary Care Unit (CCU) itself reminded me of a battlefield hospital that we might see on TV: wheeling in the endless procession of the "wounded." The staff seemed to have that knowing look in their eyes that I had been brought back from the "great beyond." In a very real sense, I was a victory for them and I was determined right then not to let them down.

Curiously, I had never felt more "awake" in my life nor more alive. It's true what they say that you don't know what you have until it's gone. My cynical attitudes about the medical community started to melt and give way to an admiration and compassion. Elke, for now, was the only person whom I desperately wanted to see and touch. Never feeling quite so alone, I wanted desperately to hear her sweet voice.

Dr. Lee, my cardiologist, came by to explain to me, "I have looked over your admission report. Your condition should be stable enough for the next couple of days to walk around the hospital hallways on this level by tomorrow afternoon, when I am going to place a stent to clear the artery. But don't worry about anything, you will be tethered to the portable heart monitor that sends signals from your heart to a master control panel here in the CCU so we will be able to know not only your whereabouts, but also how your heart is healing and beating. If your heart starts any strange rhythms or whatever, we'll know about it before you will.

"If you take a walk about 25 metres down this hall here, you will find the hospital library. I would like you to meet our chief hospital librarian, Dr. Charles, who is a retired internist and a very special man indeed. He is one person here at the university hospital that commands everyone's respect. He runs our very unique cardiac rehabilitation program, which we, unlike many other places, start as early as possible, even before the procedure. That way, we know we have your undivided attention. People have a way of paying close attention just before stent surgery. You'll discover all that tomorrow. Just get some rest for now."

Hans' second health and fitness report

	NORMAL/IDEAL RANGES	ME (FIRST CHECK-UP)	SECOND CHECK-UP, THE HEART ATTACK
Actual age (years)		44	46
Health age (years)	Actual age (or less)	61.8	59.5
Blood pressure (mmHg)	< 135/85	165/105	155/95
Resting heart rate (beats/minute)	< 60	80	84
Weight (kg)		98	104
Body fat %	< 20% men, < 23% women	35%	37%
Body fat weight (kg)		34.3	38.5
Lean weight (kg)		63.7	65.5
Waist-to-hip ratio	< 0.90 men, < 0.80 women	1.10	1.30
Total cholesterol (g/L)	< 2.00	2.90	2.15
LDL cholesterol (g/L)	< 1.30	1.85	1.70
Triglycerides – TGs (g/L)	< 1.40	3.50	2.40

	NORMAL/IDEAL RANGES	ME (FIRST CHECK-UP)	SECOND CHECK-UP, THE HEART ATTACK
HDL cholesterol (g/L)	> 0.50	0.35	0.39
TGs:HDL ratio	< 1	10	6
Fasting blood sugar (glucose) (g/L)	0.70–1.10	1.25	1.1
Homocysteine[1] level (micromoles/L)	7.0–10	96.6	50.7
High-sensitivity C-reactive protein (HS-CRP[2]) (mg/L)	Less than 1 mg/L	Not done	15.2

Day Two

The next morning, to make room for more "wounded," I was moved out of the CCU into a step-down unit by 10 a.m. There I had a quiet room with three roommates and a phone by my bed. The hospital administration had even gone to the trouble of placing a large poster above the TV monitor: "No portable phones, please."

My first call was to my local office to let them know why I had not come in that morning. Already after 24 intense hours, it seemed to be weeks since I had been to the office; it was a million miles away. Replacing the receiver, I was suddenly gripped by a feeling of fear about the prospect of making an infinitely more difficult call: to Elke and the kids. What should I say? How detailed should I be? What if nobody answers; should I leave a message? Will they say, "We told you so, Dad"? Will I be a burden to them for the rest of my life? I picked up the receiver and replaced it, hesitating and paralysed by these nagging questions.

"I know the feeling," a voice came from the adjacent bed. "Pleasure to meet you. I'm Raymond Young, call me Ray. Are you one of Dr. Lee's patients?"

"Yes, I am. I came in early yesterday morning," I replied.

I swallowed hard, sipping on the ice chips in front of me, searching for the words and courage to call her. "Uhhh, hello, Elke?" There was a terrible echo on the line. "This is Hans. Am ... am I waking you up. No? ... great. Uhhh ... listen, Elke ... uhhh ... something has happened to me ... No, honey, I'm fine but ... uhhh ... I'm in the local university hospital, St Andrew's. I had a heart attack last night.

"No, no, honey, calm down now. Everything is just fine ... they're really good and professional here. And I'm in good company. I had no idea how busy these places were. Me? Ohh, I'm OK, but I will need an operation ... a stent placement ... yes, that's right, a heart stent." I wasn't doing very well to reassure her.

"Listen, Elke, tell the kids that everything is just great. Don't let them worry ... when this whole thing is over ..." I attempted a brave front but I felt a lump in my throat which told me that I was close to tears. "Anyway, I really miss you and I'll call as things develop after I've spoken to the chief cardiologist again." I needed to wrap it up; it was too hard to speak.

Dr. Nekkers was right: this was really boring! I certainly had plenty of time to reflect about myself and my life. I was fed up allowing my fear or denial or whatever it was to stop me from learning about my body. I decided right there to use my time until my operation reading about my condition, to educate myself, for real this time.

After having spoken to Elke, I had to get out of that room and move around a bit. After a light lunch, I checked in with the head nurse in the step-down unit and attached my portable heart monitor, known on the CCU as the "Executive's Walkman." As I made my way down the hospital corridor in bathrobe and slippers towards the library, I realised that the annoying ticking in my ears had finally stopped. Strange and lovely silence!

Once at the library, I knocked faintly on the door and poked my head in timidly. There was a man in about his mid-60s, talking on the phone. He gestured to me to come in. On the wall above the black board was written:

> ### The Future of Medicine
> The doctors of the future will give no medicine but instead will interest his patients in the care of the human frame, in diet, and in the cause and prevention of disease.
>
> Thomas Edison

"Hello. Come in, please." That voice sounded vaguely familiar. "Dr. Richard Charles, MD," the name tag read.

"Don't I know you?" I queried. I wasn't exactly sure, but it seemed that this was the same fellow that I had exchanged several words with in the ambulance.

"Dr. Dick Charles, at your service," he smiled. "Yes, indeed. We met briefly the night you came in. Glad to see you made it. You see, I'm a retired internist, and I split my time between riding ambulances and running this place. Now, how may I help you?"

"First of all," I asked, " what's the fastest way out of here? Nothing personal, but spending more than a day or two here will get me seriously depressed. It has already started."

"Alright, let's be straight." His voice immediately took a firmer tone at this point. "You have had a heart attack, and while we can together put a Health Action Plan (HAP) to keep those "new" arteries clean, you have got to be very vigilant about depression. You will do your part by reporting to me any feelings of depression – excessive fatigue, any feelings of withdrawal or just a case of the "blues" – and I shall do my part here in the classroom."

What I found out over the next hours and days astounded me: there was virtually no real consensus between governmental health organizations and various medical academic associations on issues of health, life, and death. That is, we were so very far from any *real* understanding of what my disease was – coronary heart disease, which kills thousands of people in their prime every day worldwide.

Deep down somehow, in the chaos of my situation, I sensed an opportunity of a lifetime: to get to know myself better and, in doing so, to lead myself from the inside out. As I was trained as an engineer, I can distinguish a weak bit of science from the real thing. Most importantly, in a flash, it became clear to me that my Journey of Awakening had just begun.

THE JOURNEY OF AWAKENING BEGINS WITH A NEW VIEW OF HEART DISEASE

Day Three: morning session – first truth

The next day started as intensely as the first 2 days there had, with all prospective members of the "Zipper Club" (that's the name given, as the bypass scar resembles a zipper of sorts) convening just outside Dr. Charles' classroom. As we filed into the classroom, I noticed a sign above the blackboard that would come to symbolize Dr. Charles' approach:

> The tragedy of science is the slaying of a beautiful hypothesis by an ugly fact.
>
> **T.H. Huxley**

Dr. Charles took center-stage, his hand already dusty with chalk. I immediately enjoyed his no-nonsense approach and "just the facts" style, punctuated with winks and smiles. He pushed on.

1. "The first truth is that the process that leads to a heart attack – **arteriosclerosis** – is NOT just a blockage of a garden hose. In this classroom, there is a new view of this killer that almost got you all.
2. "The second truth is that most if not all of you have a little-known, yet life-threatening syndrome, called **metabolic syndrome**. Even my fellow doctors are not using this term yet.
3. "The third truth is that **weight control** has little to do with the fats you have grown to love, and everything to do with insulin, which is raised by sugar intake. In fact, the fats we eat can actually prevent the disease or even cure it. These types of fat are called essential fatty acids (EFAs).

"Now, I'm sure you are all wondering if I have mistaken you all for a class of medical students, but no, I haven't. This is the material which, had you mastered it *before* your heart attacks, might well have helped you prevent that event. Let's face it, folks, you are the lucky ones who actually made it to the Emergency Room; now is the time to assume responsibility for the care of your bodies."

A hush fell over the class. That comment alone managed to rivet our attention on the doctor and the blackboard for over 3 hours, without a break, until lunch.

Truth 1: Heart disease is about inflammation and sugar
Dr. Charles noted on the board, as most Zippers-to-be dutifully scribbled his lecture like 10-year-old school children. I just took the whole gestalt in:

OUTDATED VIEW OF CORONARY ARTERY DISEASE	1. Arteries as rigid as stove pipes
	2. Excess fat clogs the arteries
	3. A low-fat diet is prescribed
UPDATED VIEW OF CORONARY ARTERY DISEASE	1. Arteries are dynamic pipes
	2. Inflammation is the central player[4]
	3. Sugar and insulin are key players

"Let's get this part right. I shall write this down on the board and you will commit it to memory.

"What are the roles of cholesterol in the human body?" He wrote as he spoke: "Here are the **roles of cholesterol:**

1. **The liver uses cholesterol in synthesizing bile acids.**
2. **Cholesterol works to repair cell membranes and produces hormones like estrogen and testosterone.**
3. **Cholesterol helps in the growth of cell membranes.**

"So, if cholesterol is so essential to life, where does the complex process of arteriosclerosis actually begin? The precise response is at the microscopic level of the artery. Now, don't get freaked out by the biochemistry here: it's essential to get to know how to avoid coming back here.

"Generally, cholesterol is carried in packages with transporters called **lipoproteins** (low-density lipoprotein or LDL, high-density lipoprotein or HDL, and very-low-density lipoprotein or VLDL) in the body. Wherever in the body these critical chemicals are needed, the transporters link up with cholesterol and delivery is made.

"So there is a very dynamic process of supply and delivery that has worked extremely well for thousands and thousands of years. Over the past century or so, as we started to consume more and more refined sugar, the normal LDL transporter started being attacked by the two villains of modern life:

- **Free radicals** (from pollution and poor nutrition): which is the oxidation of the LDL. (Think of the action of RUST.)
- **Advanced glycation end-products** (AGEs): which are due to excessive sugar consumption and inactivity, and make the LDL sticky, so it passes less easily through the coronary arteries. (Think of the action of GLUE.)

TIP If LDL becomes oxidized by free radicals or glycated by AGE compounds, it increases LDL's tendency to get stuck in the arterial wall, creating blockage.

"These two processes are collectively known as oxidative stress. This is bad news because, as we see below, oxidative stress causes overall degeneration and deterioration of normal health into heart disease, cancers, and other insidious diseases."

Dr. Charles drew a rough diagram of the cross-section of an artery and added this description of how it gets clogged:

LDL cholesterol ("Carrier lipo-protein")
(transports much-needed cholesterol via the ARTERIES
to the body's cells that need it for normal functioning)

1st critical pathological step ↓

Oxidized LDL cholesterol gets stuck
(due to LDL's high susceptibility to oxidation or glycation)

2nd critical pathological step ↓

The body's immune system responds with
an **inflammatory response** to this injury
(the immune response triggers the "big eaters," aka the macrophages[5],
which ingest the debris of inflammation)

↓

Macrophages get bloated with inflammatory debris
plus **platelets** form a blood clot

↓

The coronary arteries get blocked,
leading to the death of heart muscle downstream
(a **myocardial infarct**)

"It is the *rust* (oxidation by free radicals) and the *glue* (of the AGEs) that provoke the attack on the LDL by the immune system's defenses, and lead first to inflammation in the arterial wall and then to a heart attack. So any strategy that is serious about beating coronary artery disease (CAD) should address the root causes, not just the symptoms. Please take care to remember all this in the future, ladies and gents – the two critical steps in the genesis of heart attacks – because those arteries we are going to unblock with the stent must also be taken care of, otherwise the process leading to CAD will start again.

In sum, anything that will oxidize the LDL (free radicals) and any food that elevates blood sugar (leading to AGEs), starts you on the road to heart disease.

"Voilà! That's the first part of my talk on the ways we unwittingly destroy our core asset: the heart's ability to keep the blood moving along. That's it for this morning. I have scheduled a metabolic walk for all of you, after which I will hold another talk on the second truth I spoke of earlier – the metabolic syndrome. That will be at 3 p.m. this afternoon. See you then."

As I walked back to my room, the term "inflammation" stuck in my head: I wondered, Is this why aspirin (a classic anti-inflammatory drug) is effective in decreasing recurrent heart attacks? I could feel a wave of frustration and confusion build up deep inside of me. Why hadn't Dr. Nekkers told me about inflammation? You know, I was getting really fed up with the whole medical system. Why couldn't they get their message straight? The way that Dr. Charles explained it, it came through clearly and already I could start to formulate my strategy out of this mess.

Not so long ago, right after my first check up 2 years previously (health age 61.8 indeed!), I had been told to swear off any animal fats (especially the ones I grew up on, like butter, cheese, beef, and mutton); even certain oils were forbidden to eat. But through Dr. Charles' lectures, I had learned a different story about fats: that fats actually *suppress appetite* and that *essential fats actually cure many modern ailments*, including heart disease and – perhaps – cancers. I had never heard before about insulin, sugar, free radicals, AGEs or inflammation.

Day Three: afternoon session – second truth

Truth 2: the metabolic syndrome – the role of insulin in disease
In the next section, we moved onto the metabolic syndrome.

By 2.45 p.m., a small line of Zipper Club members-to-be started to gather outside Dr. Charles' office, like groupies waiting for rock concert tickets. There was a definite palpable curiosity among us, coming from an accentuated sense of gratitude. Dr. Charles drew a diagram – "The big picture" – up on the blackboard (Fig. 1.1).

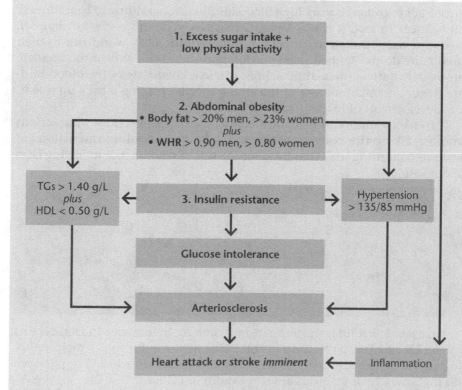

FIGURE 1.1 **The big picture: the metabolic syndrome as a vicious whirlpool**

"OK, folks, here you have the whole game of heart disease!" declared a visibly delighted Dr. Charles. His audience was enraptured, and jotted it all down feverishly.

"The metabolic syndrome is the perfect storm leading to a heart attack, a stroke or diabetes. To understand the metabolic syndrome, we investigate the primary control point of fat accumulation: *insulin*. To become obese, a steady stream of dietary sugars and carbohydrates must develop. These sugars (simple and complex) will be stored by insulin as body fat.

"In detail, within 30 seconds of a rise in your blood sugar level after a carbohydrate[6] (complex or simple sugar) meal or snack, several important physiological events push you towards heart disease. Your pancreas gland is stimulated by blood sugar (glucose) to secrete insulin. The primary effect of insulin is to facilitate the transport and storage of various substances (like sugar and fat) into various organs (such as the liver, muscles, and fatty tissues). Eventually, the fat cells and muscle cells become resistant to insulin, so more is required."

"But Doc," I ventured, "what does insulin have to do with heart disease? Isn't that the diabetes hormone?"

"Yes, but understand that insulin has *everything* to do with physical health. The metabolic syndrome represents a vicious cycle wherein the insulin resistance leads to compensatory high blood insulin levels, leading to heart disease and cancer. In fact, it is way beyond a vicious cycle, it's a *vicious whirlpool*, sweeping many thousands of people in their prime a day worldwide to their premature death. Refined sugar consumption has been shown to stimulate an oxidative stress (premature aging), wherein chemicals in the blood initiate the entire inflammation of the artery, thereby playing a back-up role in the development of heart disease.

"I think it's important that you all have at least a general idea what actions you are asking the body to perform. Take a quick look at the actions of insulin, imprinting into your head for the rest of your life the following facts about insulin":

INSULIN IS A STORAGE HORMONE!
1. It stores excess sugar as fat (triglycerides, or TGs). Blood insulin levels, as the primary regulator of fat storage, are actually proportional to body fat.
2. Insulin provokes the inflammatory process in the arteries, which sets the stage for heart disease, cancer,[7] and autoimmune diseases, such as arthritis.

"In a word, insulin is the ultimate fat generator in humans. In fact, doctors in the US and Europe starting in the 1930s used insulin to get their pathologically underweight or anorectic patients to gain as much as 3 kg per week on high-carbohydrate meals after an insulin injection!"

Truth 3: weight control – fat vs sugar

After a brief time-out from an intense learning session, I made my way back down the hospital corridor to the hospital library for another installment of the Dr. Charles Entertainment Show. "I have been struggling with my weight all my adult life. I have been gaining weight on the low-fat diet and suffering as a result: I am fed up. Or should I say: I feel underfed! Now they say it is sugar that is the villain! What is going on and when will the fad diets stop?"

This was my rather cynical mindset (I know, though, not so good for my heart). It's funny how life teaches us things, if only we took the time and effort to listen. As I was weaving my way through the hospital corridors, past patients not as lucky as myself, this cynical attitude melted away, first to an expansive feeling of gratitude for a second chance at life's game, and then to compassion for the suffering people in the hospital for whom the game was rapidly winding down.

Once settled in, I was determined to use my time here wisely. I raised my hand. "Doc, did you actually say that fat is good for you, that it can prevent or even cure our diseases? That's unbelievable, Doc. Honestly, that flies in the face of everything we have been hearing over the past 20 years. I'd heard that eating carbohydrates, like potatoes, rice, bread, even sugar, was good for you as it contained no cholesterol."

"Sure, Hans. We have come a long way since then. It all has to do with what stimulates your insulin level. Once that insulin is elevated, the metabolic syndrome is near at hand. In fact, let's take the BIG view. Everything you have been hearing on the TV and in magazines – places where propaganda flows freely into passive minds, convincing the viewers that the solutions to their problems are OUTSIDE of them, instead of contained in their heads.

"But, back to my point, listen to YOUR experience and ask yourself if these so-called 'new' ideas fly in the face of your experience? Listen, you have an ancient programming code, called DNA, that is coping with adapting to a series of modern changes that are destroying it. Can any of you name some of these detrimental changes that challenge our DNA every day?"

Hands shot up, and Dr. Charles made a list as we recited the big changes in our world:

1. More sedentary lifestyles.
2. More pollution or air air water.
3. More synthetic chemicals.
4. More deadly wars.
5. More detrimental stress.
6. Less time for contemplation.
7. More toxins in the food chain: fake sugars, preservatives, "mad cow disease," meat and poultry contamination.
8. Fast foods leading to slowed digestion and to early death.

Dr. Charles cut off the rest for fear that the topic would become depressing. "Listen, folks, one of the *really* important changes is the increased consumption of refined sugar, which acts like a poison to our ancient system. Take a step back: over the past 7 million years, what percent of our DNA[8] –

our programming code – has changed? Just 1%, give or take, which means our DNA is still expecting the 'respect' it had millions of years ago, when we were primitive hunters, running about, eating natural unprocessed foods.

"What is critical to understand is that your body is, from a long-term evolutionary point of view, a mere replicator for your DNA. If DNA doesn't get what it wants, it autodestructs the organism (that's YOU!) to protect the gene pool, the species, from fatal mutations. In a word, if you love your genes, take care of them.

"Look at the actual action of refined sugar on this exquisite system:

1. increased TGs;
2. decreased "good" HDL;
3. rapid absorption, leading to a vicious cycle of sugar-craving;
4. stimulation of adrenaline by up to 400%, leading to blood pressure elevations.

"This helps to explain the meteoric rise in heart diseases, cancers, immune issues, uncontrolled infections with super-bugs ... the list goes on and on, with no end to the medical impasse in sight, unless we get back to that DNA issue. And what does DNA need to function properly? Here's the list of essential ingredients:

1. Energy sources: all energy comes from the sun, which creates via photosynthesis.
2. Fresh fruit and vegetables.
3. Ten essential amino acids: arginine (required for the young, but not for adults), histidine, isoleucine, leucine, lysine, methionine, phenylalanine, threonine, tryptophan, and valine.
4. Two EFAs in a 3:1 proportion:
   – linoleic acid (LA: omega-6) – its level must be three times that of alpha-linolenic acid (ALA) to be perfect, such as hempseed oil and walnuts;
   – ALA (omega-3).
5. Fresh water.
6. Fresh air.
7. UV light.
8. Antioxidant supplements from time to time, such as vitamin C and red wine.

> TIP For optimal performance and disease avoidance, the LA (omega-6) should be in a 3:1 ratio with LNA (omega-3). Only **hempseed oil** fits the bill.

"That's all it needs to perform the miracle of life. It certainly does *NOT* need sugar, as the body converts all of its energy sources to glucose and then to ATP (the body's universal energy currency). We don't need to take any sugar at all. Refined sugar actually destroys the system.

"Remember here, folks, that by 'essential' we mean that we cannot make them with our own bodies. We must get them in our nutrition. But my point is that we see nothing about refined sugar on this list of essential ingredients to keep the body in high performance. So why are we eating pastries, cakes, cookies, muffins, ketchup, syrupy desserts, pancakes, white rice, white bread, white flour, and overly refined breakfast cereals? These all vestiges of a bad decision in the 19th century to refine the foods, instead of leaving Nature's gift alone, in its natural state.

"Take the EFAs. Here is a look at the various oils and their proportions of EFAs (Table 1.1). Remember to find those that have the physiologically perfect proportion of 3:1 between LA and ALA. One can clearly see that hempseed oil wins hands down as the perfectly balanced oil for human physiology and is a prime candidate for keeping dreaded inflammation under control."

TABLE 1.1 *Oils and their essential fatty acid contents*

	HEMPSEED	FLAXSEED	WALNUT	CANOLA	SOYBEAN	OLIVE	SUNFLOWER
Total fat %	35	35	60	30	17.7	20	47.3
Linoleic acid (LA ; 18:2ω6, or omega-6) % of total fat	60	14	51	30	50	8	65
Alpha-linolenic acid (ALA; 18:3ω3, or omega-3) % of total fat	20	58	5	7	7	0	0
LA-to-ALA ratio	3	0.24	10.2	4.3	7.1	NA	NA
Oleic acid (18:1, omega-9) % of total fat	12	19	28	54	26	76	23
Saturated fatty acids% of total fat	8	9	16	7	5	16	12

Important note: A properly balanced diet should consist of roughly one omega-3 fatty acid to three omega-6 fatty acids. The standard American diet (SAD) tends to have *up to 30 times too much* omega-6, particularly in relation to omega-3 fatty acids, due, in part, to the widespread use of cooking oils, including sunflower, safflower, corn, cottonseed, and soybean oils. This imbalance contributes to long-term diseases such as heart disease, cancer, arthritis, and even depression. Omega-3 fats are abundant in Japanese and Mediterranean diets, and contribute to low heart disease rates in those cultures.

The EFAs are exceptional allies in the fight against heart disease and disease in general. Look at how human beings need EFAs to create health. Moreover, the human body converts omega-3 fats to what are known as fish oils (EPA and DHA) (Fig. 1.2), which we need for optimal human physiology.

Results of randomized controlled trials have consistently shown that a diet with a high intake of omega-3 fatty acid (flaxseed and hempseed oil) has the following *proven* effects:

1. TGs were reduced in both women and men.
2. C-reactive protein (CRP: an inflammatory marker) was also reduced.
3. Increased insulin sensitivity, thus avoiding the metabolic syndrome and diabetes.

TIP EPA and DHA are generated in our bodies from ALA. One needn't eat oily fish to make them.

4. Decreased risk of myocardial infarction (heart attack) and sudden cardiac death in individuals with coronary heart disease.

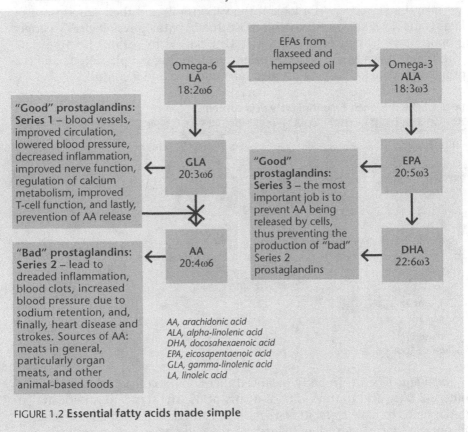

FIGURE 1.2 **Essential fatty acids made simple**

Day Four: pre-op

While waiting for my heart procedure, I sat there quietly meditating on the movement of my breath as Dr. Charles had taught me: just calmly watching my thoughts go by like leaves on a woodland creek. As thoughts of my fears at the operation crept in, I simply came back to my breath and could feel the corners of my mouth curling upwards. I was strangely at peace before the biggest challenge of my life and it felt really good. It had all come down to this moment. It seemed so perfect: lots of fear and some tools to deal with it.

My mind, which would usually be racing, buying into negative thoughts in a most uncontrolled way, stayed clear and calm. I reminisced about the readings I had done here while "captive in the classroom," the Ebenezer Scrooges, the King Lears, the Dr. Fausts, all themes throughout history of redemption and how they were used or missed. I would arrange what was left of my life better than the first time.

Day Four: the stent operation

"Good afternoon, sir. Are you ready?" asked one of the orderlies, as he wheeled in the stretcher.

"Oh, is this for me? Well, yes; just make sure that we are going to the operating block and not to the basement," I said with a wink of the eye. Keep your humour and rise above the storm, I thought. As I lay there on the gurney, the nurse from the operating room informed me that she was giving me a mild sedative through my intravenous port that would make me a little sleepy. The orderlies help me slide over onto the gurney, pulled up the sheet over my chest, slipped on the cap, and inserted the oxygen prongs into my nose. And we were off.

I was wheeled into Room 12, a room completely dedicated to stent placement surgery, where everyone was wearing surgical masks. What a team full of energy, arranging and counting the silver instruments, tinkling like wind chimes. As they slid me over onto the operating table, the last two sensations were my extreme thirst and someone squeezing my hand. As I looked up for one last time, I saw deep blue eyes winking above a mask saying to me: "See you in a few hours. Have a good sleep." It was Dr. Charles. I knew that somehow I wasn't alone. I smiled inwardly.

Day Five: post-op

When I finally awoke, before I unglued my eyes, I felt depressed that I would not be seeing Elke's face by my bedside that morning. I already sensed the brightness of the morning sun coming through the CCU curtains. It was much brighter than usual. Now the beeping was even louder and more rapid. The telephone at the nurses station rang ... *someone* pick it up before it wakes up the whole CCU ... the beeping, the phone. I was alive!

I felt like the stories of death-row prisoners waiting for death, when, at the last possible moment the phone rings: a reprieve from the governor. I was trembling nervously as I dialled the numbers. *Please, let this be real*, I prayed. The waiting was eternal and then, finally, someone picked up the phone on the other end. It was Elke's voice. Her "Hello?" was the sweetest music I had ever heard.

"Hello, Elke, dear? This is Hans!!" I hollered. "How are you, dear?"

"Why, I'm just fine. How are *you*? How did the procedure go? Are you all right?" she asked groggily.

"Just wonderful. The medical team here are stupendous. It's really *greeeat* to hear your voice after all this time! What did you do today?" I wanted to just hear her voice.

"Nothing at all, dear," she replied.

I continued, "Listen, I am coming home early. I'm going to wrap up things at the office tomorrow and catch the red-eye flight tomorrow night. Buy yourself a pretty dress because we're going out on the town to dine together when I get home! I have some things I want to discuss over champagne with you. Go and run right now. Love and kisses. Bye!"

"Goodbye, dear," she said hesitantly. At her end of the phone, she felt she hadn't recalled that level of tenderness or energy in my voice since my earlier days as a graduate student. What must be going on?, she wondered. That night, Elke did not sleep very well.

I slammed down the phone and caught my breath, sitting on the edge of my bed. "Wow! I cannot believe this!" I said aloud to myself.

During my day of recovery, I walked through the cardiology wards as they rolled them in and rolled them out. I spent the last few hours before my discharge chatting with and saying my goodbyes to the friends I was fortunate to have crossed paths with. Once discharged, I made my way back to the hotel room for a real good night's sleep before the long trip home.

Day Six: discharge and back at the hotel

The next morning, I was happy to have got dressed quickly, feeling very fortunate to be tying my own tie and fastening my own cufflinks. Just a quick stopover at the office, then to the airport ....

As I left my room, I noticed what a beautiful day it was, that the colours somehow seemed brighter. When a chambermaid caught me smelling the flowers in the lobby, I gently whispered a "Good morning," looking for the smile and glimmer in her eye. I planned to stop at the hotel bookshop to buy the morning paper, or perhaps buy a book of poetry instead, which I could pour over gleefully while having my fruit salad in the hotel restaurant.

As I took in the sweet nectars through my eyes and mouth, I couldn't help but notice just how much things had changed. But really it was me who had been changed. I didn't want to become just another tragic statistic. I was at last going to take charge.

As I stepped out of the hotel, the familiar doorman asked, "Taxi to your office as usual, sir?"

"No, thank you," I said, smiling. "I think I'll walk today, beautiful day and all." Waving high to the puzzled doorman in my wake, I leapt off the sidewalk, my first step in a thousand-mile journey of discovery. Happy to be alive, I bounded down the bustling city street, disappearing into my new thoughts and into the Hong Kong crowds.

HANS' 7-POINT HAP FOR A HEALTHY HEART

There are seven aspects to Hans' *totally natural* HAP:

1. Control insulin levels using glycemic index (GI).
2. Do BURST walking (see below).
3. Snack intelligently between meals.
4. Shrink the stomach.
5. Control dangerous inflammation.

6. Take flaxseed oil supplements to lower body fat.
7. Eat plenty of clean protein.

Control insulin levels using GI[9] as a guide

The logic here is straightforward:

- One of the best predictors of heart disease is a high blood insulin level, as indicated by a high TGs:HDL ratio.
- High blood insulin levels are a *direct* consequence of eating refined sugars.
- The GI is a physiologically based system that ranks various sugars according to their effects on insulin level: the higher the GI of each food, the more insulin will be stimulated.
- Therefore, the most effective and direct way to avoid heart disease, diabetes and some cancers is to NOT consume high-GI foods.

A 2006 research project at Harvard University of Public Health[10] looked into what aspects of our nutrition put us at risk for heart attacks (the cause of 20% of deaths in the US and 17% of deaths in Europe). The investigators, evaluating data on 82,000 women collected over 20 years, found that if vegetable sources of fat and protein (EFAs in lentils and beans) replaced animal sources (pork and beef) *and* a low-sugar diet was consumed, there was a drop of 30% in heart disease. That is, the authors found a direct association between GI and coronary heart disease.

GI is, therefore, an indicator of the ability of the carbohydrate to raise blood glucose levels, and is positively related to risk of coronary heart disease. The reason for this is because low-GI foods are associated with increased HDL-cholesterol and reduced risk of type 2 diabetes, while high dietary GI is associated with a lower concentration of plasma HDL-cholesterol.[11]

So, in the future, use the GI as a guide to help make intelligent decisions that will improve the quality of your life and overall energy level and vitality.

All this explains many of our complaints in modern society: chronic fatigue, irritability, sleeplessness, overweight, and headaches. GI offers information about how foods affect blood sugar and insulin. The lower a food's GI, the less it affects blood sugar and insulin levels. There is good evidence for links between high blood glucose and gall stones and even some types of cancer.

Practically speaking, *develop a healthy fear of sugar:* never eat sweets before or during long trips or business meetings as they will rob you of the stamina necessary to stay alert. Lower-GI foods prolong physical endurance and stamina. Moreover, if you are serious about getting control of your health (your core asset), avoid convenient, yet highly addictive, high-GI foods (see Appendix I for a GI listing of common foods).

How does the body choose the energy it uses?
1. Activity lasting just 1–2 minutes: the body uses very limited stores of ATP, the universal energy currency made from carbohydrates, fats, and proteins.

2. Bursts of activity of 3–15 minutes: the body uses carbohydrates.
3. Duration of activity > 15 minutes: fats come "on line" to be added to carbohydrates for energy.

NB Understand two critical aspects of your DNA:
1. It chooses the fuel as a function of intensity, and
2. It programs the body to replace afterwards what it has used during activity.

Understand here two critical aspects of your DNA: first, it chooses the fuel as a function of intensity (Fig. 1.3), and second it programs the body to replace *after-wards* what it has used.

At *rest* (including hibernation) or during *moderate* activity (e.g. jogging), the body consumes about 60% of the calories from fat, 35% carbohydrates, and the rest from protein. When the body is doing exercise at moderate levels, the DNA tells it to make more fat to *replace* what has been used during the moderate activity. This is especially true if we eat sugary high-GI drinks and foods afterwards. Joggers and other endurance exercisers traditionally have a *very* hard time keeping fat off (especially if they stop exercising), as they ask the body to make more fat every time they jog. It's a powerful DNA signal that we can control every time we choose an exercise.

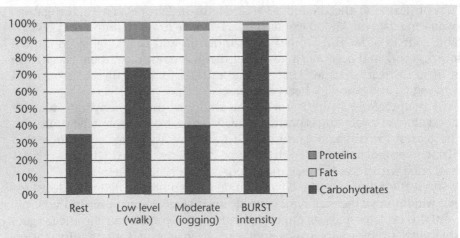

FIGURE 1.3 **The respective contribution of proteins, fats, and carbohydrates to energy metabolism at rest and during various exercise intensities**

During *high-intensity* exercises (and to a lesser extent during walking), the DNA sends a signal to burn 95% carbohydrates, which the body replaces by using body fat. The result is that body fat use is maximal with BURST exercises and nearly as high while walking after meals.

TIP Key ideas
■ BURST exercises are better adapted to our hunter origins.
■ Carbohydrate stores used during BURST are replaced by body fat.

Do BURST walking between meals every day[12]

BURST stands for Build Up Rapid Stamina Training. The first key idea here is to remember your source code: DNA programs your adaptive responses as it did 7 million years ago. As there has only been a 1% mutation in the past 7 million years, it is still programming you to be a hunter with *bursts* of energy, punctuated by short periods of *rest* to recover. Whether you were chasing *after a meal* or being chased *as a meal*, that is the daily rhythm that your DNA programmed the body's adaptive responses.

BURST walking for Optimal Health: Here is how the human being has used energy for millennia. If you respect your hunter's DNA design specifications, you can just watch the body fat (and related issues) disappear. Here's how it should be done:

- **Walk** at a 1 left/right cycle/second rate (a city gait) for a short while (3 minutes at baseline walking rate, to get the joints warmed up).
- **BURST** by then speeding up to *double* that rate (2 left/right cycles/second) for 1 minute (this is the hunting part). You may get out of slightly out of breath – even better if you are 'winded', as this will expand your lung capacity.
- **Rest** by going back to the baseline walking rate for 2–3 minutes (and catch your breath).
- **BURST** again – speed up again to double the baseline rate (2 left/right cycles/second) for 1 minute.
- **Rest** by going back to the baseline walking rate for 2–3 minutes (and catch your breath again).
- Then do a final set for a total of **three sets** of BURST and rest. (By now, the hunter would either have caught the prey or become too tired!) Now walk back to the office or home at your baseline rate, cooling down and breathing deeply (except maybe in polluted cities).

The "post-BURST burn": The second key idea is that BURST walking generates the greatest "post-BURST burn." It is *after* the exercise (often for hours and days later) that the *really* interesting metabolic changes start to happen. The body burns fat in order to replace the carbohydrate stores (glycogen) for the next BURST walk. That is, since during the BURST walking you never actually attain the necessary duration for burning fat (> 15 minutes), the body stores carbohydrates in muscle tissue (as glycogen) instead of adipose tissue as fat. BURST walking burns these carbohydrates, and AFTERWARDS, the body burns much more body fat to replace the body stores of carbohydrate.[13]

Key to progress: Quantify to improve
Body fat is an *extremely* dynamic tissue, ready to be used with the right exercise. The total body weight is composed of two compartments: the lean compartment (muscle, bone, and water) and the fat compartment (Fig. 1.4).

To accurately and definitively control weight and energy, you must measure you body fat. To do so, you will need two pieces of measuring equipment:

- a tape measure in centimetres;
- a pedometer with a pulse (heart rate) monitor.

First, measure your body fat with the tape measure for the formulae provided below.

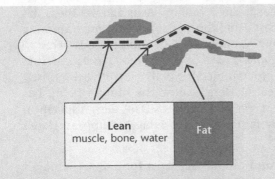

FIGURE 1.4 **Body weight compartments**

Men need to measure the following (Fig. 1.5):

1. Right (or left if left-handed) forearm (RF), 5 cm distal to the elbow) ____ cm
2. Waist (W) at level of the belly button (don't suck the belly in)   ____ cm
3. Hips (H) at the widest point (heels together)   ____ cm

Now, gents, plug the numbers into the following formula:

$$[(W / 2.54) - 3] + [(H / 2.54) + 1] - [(RF / 2.54) \times 3 - 19] = \boxed{} \ \% \text{ body fat}$$

Women need to measure the following sites (Fig. 1.6):

1. Waist (W) at the level of the belly button (don't suck the belly in) ____ cm
2. Hips (H) at the widest point (heels together)   ____ cm
3. Right upper thigh (RUT), just under the buttocks   ____ cm
4. Right calf (RC), at the widest point   ____ cm

Now, ladies, plug the numbers to this equation:

$$[(W / 2.54) + 6] + [(RUT / 2.54) + 4] - [(RC / 2.54) \times 1.5 - 21] = \boxed{} \ \% \text{ body fat}$$

Use a pedometer with a pulse (heart rate) monitor[14,] to monitor your progress by measuring distance and steps walked daily or weekly. With the pedometer, you can start to accelerate your loss of body fat.

Snack between meals

The key here is to increase and maintain an elevated metabolic rate (the amount of energy expended in a given period of time) throughout the day, into the evening. This sort of "gentle grazing" steadily increases the metabolic rate, as all meals do. The best snacks to increase metabolic rate are:

1. nuts (especially almonds and walnuts);
2. fruits (especially grapes, apples, citrus fruits, and kiwis);

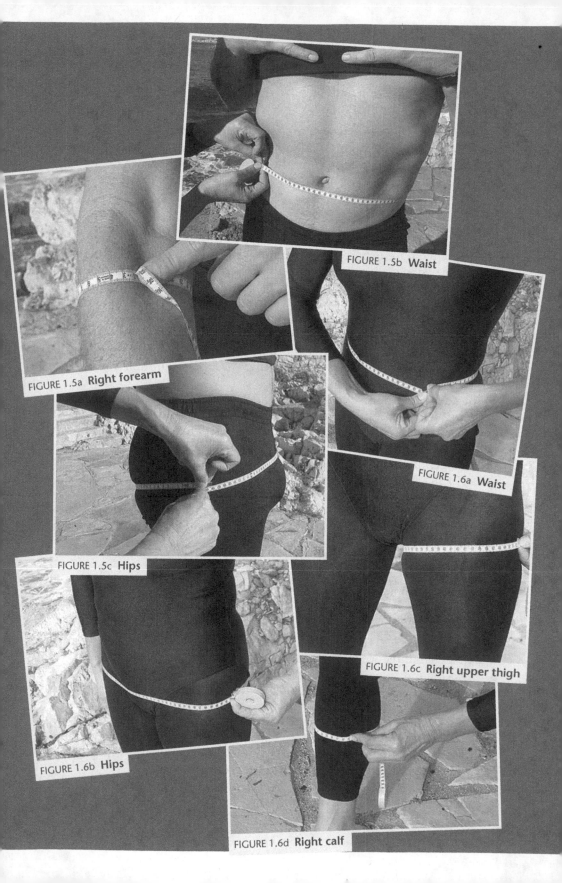

FIGURE 1.5b Waist

FIGURE 1.5a Right forearm

FIGURE 1.6a Waist

FIGURE 1.5c Hips

FIGURE 1.6c Right upper thigh

FIGURE 1.6b Hips

FIGURE 1.6d Right calf

3. water, and plenty of it (still or bubbly);
4. tea (black or green) without *any* sweeteners.

Research has shown that we can easily burn 70% of our daily calories if these are eaten before 2 p.m. It doesn't really mean that you consume fewer calories. So it's smart to consume these calories much earlier in the day, when the metabolic rate is higher.

Shrink the stomach

The principle here is pure mechanical physics. The stomach, as the most distensible (stretchable) part of the digestive system, stretches to accommodate the food bolus. The average resting internal volume of the stomach is about a liter; however, it can shrink, when empty, to a size of 50 cm^3 (a small cup) from an astounding 6 L after a massive meal. As the stomach contracts, it empties its food contents downstream into the intestines and shrinks back to its normal size. Once the brain senses "fullness," it sends a message: "Stop eating. You have enough calories to survive." So far, no problem.

But due to compulsive overeating, usually due to a anxiety-driven hand-to-mouth reflex, the stomach stretches and stretches and stretches, until it no longer resembles its original size. In the hyperstretched state, the stomach cannot send messages of "being full/stop eating" until it fills. In fact, modern surgical techniques have devised a way to actually cut out the extra stomach space, in an attempt to recalibrate the satiety threshold. The result is that the stomach is so big that it never can signal satiety.

So shrink the stomach back to normal size by replacing one evening meal with a large bowl of natural yoghurt, without sugar, and drinking water between meals.

Decrease the smoldering inflammation

Try the following:

- *Green or black tea.* Have 2–4 cups per day. This provides catechins – antioxidants that reduce inflammation.
- *Phytochemicals (polyphenols).* These inflammation-dampening compounds are found in colorful fruits like blueberries, blackberries, strawberries, and raspberries, which also contain flavonoids called anthocyanins that protect against oxidative damage.
- *Quercetin.* This anti-inflammatory compound and natural histamine inhibitor is the most powerful kind of flavonoid. Excellent sources include red grapes, red and yellow onions, garlic, broccoli, and apples.
- *EFAs.* These provide significant benefit to patients with chronic inflammatory diseases, according to a report in the *Journal of the American College of*

Nutrition. The most potent omega-3s are found in hempseed oil, flaxseed oil, dark greens, walnuts, salmon (preferably wild), tuna, mackerel, anchovies, sardines, and herring.

■ *Olive oil*. This is another type of oil that will reduce inflammation. In fact, olive oil has been shown to reduce the risk of cardiovascular disease.

■ *Useful spices*. These include turmeric, curry powder, ginger and garlic, red hot chili peppers, basil, cinnamon, rosemary, and thyme. Turmeric and ginger are powerful, natural anti-inflammatory agents. Turmeric, an Indian spice that gives curry its orange–yellow color, contains curcumin, one of the most powerful anti-inflammatory compounds in nature,

■ *Avoid foods high in sugar*. These have also been associated with dangerous inflammation. Eliminate high-sugar foods such as pastries, sugar drinks, presweetened cereals, and candy.

■ *Avoid junk food*. French fries increase inflammation.

■ *Avoid tooth decay*. Poor oral hygiene leads to bacterial overgrowth in the mouth, leading to generalized inflammation. Studies have found that heart disease is twice as likely in people with periodontal (gum) disease. Finding the potential biological reason in laboratory tests, colleagues removed dental plaque and injected it into rabbits. It was shown that the bacteria caused blood clots, and it only took minutes for these to form.

Flaxseed oil to aid the DNA fat burn

Dr. Udo Erasmus, a world-renowned expert in all aspects of oils, states that flaxseed oil actually "turns on" the part of our DNA that controls body fat burning. Combine this with the metabolic walk after meals for a one–two punch on body fat.

Eat plenty of protein

High-quality protein (salmon, herring, tuna, wild game, poultry, eggs, nuts, and lentils) is the key to optimal nutrition. Good protein intake ensures that enough amino acids are available to promote muscle growth. As genetic hunters, we recognize the signal of plenty of protein in the body – "the hunt is good" – and this promotes the burning of carbohydrates and fat for energy.

HAP summary

1. Switch to low-GI foods.
2. BURST walk for a total of 15 minutes a day.
3. Buy a pedometer and do 5,000 steps a day on weekdays and 10,000 steps a day on weekend days.
4. Shrink the stomach: have water and snacks between meals.
5. Decrease dangerous inflammation with appropriate foods.
6. Take flaxseeds and hempseeds and their oil, and snack on walnuts.

CASE DISCUSSION: LEADING YOURSELF AGAINST ALL ODDS

Once back home after the stent placement, I settled into my work routine, and my energy and productivity were phenomenal, like never before. This also improved my moods as I had time to balance work and home. My excess body fat disappeared, and my blood pressure fell with it. My sugar cravings disappeared. Several months later, pleased with all the progress, I decided to pay a visit to an old friend. I made an appointment with Dr. Nekkers for a follow-up of my medical exam many months previously. It was a very good idea.

"Well, Hans, nice to see you," he started. "It's been too long. You look *really* good. Have you changed somehow?"

"I sure have," I responded with a smile, "from the inside outwards." As he measured my pressure and body fat, and examined my blood results, his bushy brows, instead of adopting the usual frown, were perking up. He would glance at me above his glasses, smiling knowingly. His findings were:

History: 48-year-old male, senior manager, family history for heart disease and diabetes, here today for a routine check-up after many months. Active. Upbeat. High vitality. No medications at all!

Physical exam: Trim vibrant male.
- Blood pressure = 120/75 mmHg (last time it was around 165/105!).
- Resting heart rate = 56 beats/minute (last time it was about 80).
- Body fat = 20% (at the last check it was 35%).
- Laboratory work: all optimal!

"I don't believe this," I heard the doc mutter. I was delighted beyond description.

Overall assessment:
- Health risk level: low.
- Health age: 39.6 years of age!

Plan: (amazing case: totally resolved metabolic syndrome!)
- **Elevated blood pressure**: normalised with lifestyle.
- **TGs:HDL ratio:** < 1, optimal!
- **Excess weight**: robust.
- **Follow-up**: no need for clinic return, except for routine screenings for prostate exam and colonoscopy in 24 months.

Dr. Nekkers was at a loss for words. "I really don't know what to say. Your transformation almost defies science. Look at my flow chart: these figures are amazing! What happened to you?" he finally stammered, as he pushed the report to me.

Hans' third health and fitness report

	NORMAL/ IDEAL RANGE	MY FIRST CHECK-UP WITH DR. NEKKERS	MY LAB RESULTS (JUST BEFORE THE HEART ATTACK IN HONG KONG)	ONE YEAR LATER ON MY HAP
		1st and 2nd chances: still "asleep" ↓	↓	3rd chance: Alive and in control ↓
Actual age (years)		44	46	48
Health age (years)	Actual age (or less)	61.8	59.5	39.6
Blood pressure (mmHg)	< 135/85	165/105	155/95	120/75
Resting heart rate (beats/minute)	< 60	80	84	56
Weight (kg)		98	104	95
Body fat %	< 20% men, < 23% women	35%	37%	20%
Body fat weight (kg)		34.3	38.5	19
Lean weight (kg)		63.7	65.5	76
Waist-to-hip ratio	< 0.90 men, < 0.80 women	1.10	1.30	0.88
Total cholesterol (g/L)	< 2	2.90	2.15	1.90
LDL cholesterol (g/L)	< 1.30	1.85	1.70	1.13
Triglycerides (g/L)	< 1.40	3.50	2.40	0.60
HDL cholesterol (g/L)	> 0.50	0.35	0.39	0.65
TGs:HDL ratio	< 1	10	6	0.92
Fasting blood sugar (glucose) (g/L)	0.70–1.10	1.25	1.1	0.85
Homocysteine[1] level (micromoles/L)	7.0–10	96.6	50.7	4.0
High-sensitivity C-reactive protein (HS-CRP[2]) (mg/L)	Less than 1 mg/L	Not done	15.2	0.4

"Well, Doc, in fact, it's ALL about science. But first of all, armed with courage, I woke up from a nightmare. The first thing I've learned is that, on the physical level, I alone am responsible for the care of my body and mind, and that no one, not even the best doctor (and doctors and nurses like I had were the best), can take as good a care of my body as I can. I've also stopped torturing my body. My foolproof method to controlling my weight is doing BURST walking, but being sure not to lose more than 1% of my body fat per week. Having wholeheartedly adopted that simple strategy, I have never been bothered by excess body fat or related issues since.

"Lastly, I composed this health strategy, called a Health Action Plan, that I actually enjoy doing because not only can I feel the benefits, but I can also see them on paper. That's science at its best. Here's my maintenance HAP, fully updated. Check it out."

My updated HAP for the new millenium

1. Permanently avoid all "whites": white bread, white rice, white flour, white sugar. Turn the insulin "off" to avoid its negative effects.
2. BURST walking: every day for (at least) 15 minutes.
3. Pedometer: 10,000 steps a day on weekend days and 5,000 on weekdays to keep the metabolism roaring and the body fat percent low.
4. EFAs (omega-3/-6 oils):
   - flaxseed oil: 2–3 g/day;
   - hempseed oil: in soups, on salads daily: 1 tablespoon/day.
5. Supplements for health and longevity: Co-Enzyme-Q10 (75–100 mg/day); vitamin C (2 g/day); B complex vitamins and folate to control the homocysteine level (see Appendix I).
6. Natural anti-inflammatory substances: 6–12/week organic eggs, tea, no sugar.

✳ How strange that the shoe was then on the other foot: the patient healing himself for the physician!

As Dr. Nekkers checked my HAP, I could see him slightly squirming in his seat. "Hmm, perhaps I should try some of these things myself," he said ruefully. "I have been putting on a few kilos over the years, and my knees are complaining every time I play tennis. Until we spoke today, I was actually going to start medications. Anyway, thanks, Hans and take care of yourself … "

"Not to worry, Doc, and when you've got your shape back, give me a call for a tennis match!"

CLOSING WORDS FROM A LEADER

Finally, about myself, I always knew that I was, deep down at my core, a warrior. A year ago, I went to Hong Kong with a bad attitude on life and came home with a new faith in myself. This is my story of my "awakening," of how I got a second chance to "get it right," that balance between heart and head, work and play, participation and observation. This is a story of how I transformed my personal and professional life from one where there were a lot of impossible "shoulds" to a multitude of feasible "coulds." And this is really just the beginning. By the way, Elke and myself are doing great and have just renewed our marriage vows.

Despite what I had heard and read over the years, I have something even more valuable than all these sponsored research studies: my *own* experience, my research. And that experience has taught me seven Basic Truths about how I can care for my heart in particular, and my body in general.

My basic truth 1

Many modern managers do *not* have the courage to make the personal changes *before* they need to in order to become a real leader of themselves. Instead of finding solutions, they deny the *whole* problem. I should know. My old management philosophy of "If it ain't broken, don't fix it" works *neither* in business *nor* in health management. My new "lead yourself first" philosophy that works excellent in both business and health is "Fix it before it breaks." I have a *great* work-out in the BURST walking to sculpt my body (and mind), and I am keeping it simple, fun and effective in keeping me (and Elke) young.

My basic truth 2

CAD is the leading cause of death in the US, according to the Center for Disease Control and Prevention. Nearly 700,000 people each year die of heart disease in the US alone (30% of all US deaths). Our present understanding of CAD, obesity and diabetes needs a serious and immediate update worldwide to include this central fact:

> It is elevated insulin in the blood, and the dietary sugars that cause it, NOT FAT or CHOLESTEROL, that is the real cause of heart disease, diabetes, and other diseases of modern life, including cancer and Alzheimer's disease.

My basic truth 3

Inflammation plays a giant role in not just heart disease but most diseases, including cancer. High-sensitivity C-reactive protein (HS-CRP) is one of the primary blood markers, made in the liver, for inflammation, and is used to prevent atherosclerosis and heart attacks. This explains, in part, the preventative effects of acetylsalicylic acid (aspirin) on second heart attacks. In an attempt to control dangerous inflammation, I have started taking natural foods with anti-inflammatory properties, such as eggs. I also started taking vitamin B_3 (niacin). But be aware: if the CRP is measured close to an acute infection (sore throat, urinary tract infections and so on) it may be falsely elevated.

My basic truth 4

Especially given the pollution in major cities worldwide, the body's defenses need help, in the form of supplements. Two well-established critical findings are these:

1. *Vitamin C (ascorbic acid).* The metabolic syndrome, with high blood insulin and body fat levels, involves a simultaneous problem of greater requirements for vitamin C and reduced absorption of vitamin C.
2. *B complex vitamins and folate.* Researchers in the 1930s established an

increased need for the B family of vitamins with increased sugar intake in order to keep dangerous homocysteine low.

My basic truth 5

Low-fat, high-carbohydrate diets lead to an overfat civilization. Dietary sugars (especially table sugar – sucrose – and omnipresent high-fructose corn syrup in sweet drinks), and NOT FAT, actively plays a role in the pathological inflammation that leads to heart attacks, through their effect on the membrane of the artery lining. In this context, dietary fat (particularly essential fatty acids) is actually more beneficial and vitally necessary to the health. Scientific observations confirm this worldwide:

- Over the past decade, the consumption of fat in the US went from 42% to 32%, while obesity (defined as > 30% above ideal weight) went from 20% to over 60%.
- Finland has three times the rate of heart disease of France, even though the fat intake in those two countries is very comparable.
- Among Indians (on largely vegetarian diets) living in Britain, there is a very high incidence of heart disease, despite diets that are low in saturated fat and relatively low levels of blood cholesterol. The same holds true for the Indians in the Republic of South Africa (who have one of the highest rates of coronary disease in the world).
- In Israel and Japan, an increased consumption of saturated fats has been followed by a *fall* in coronary deaths since the end of World War II.

My basic truth 6

EFAs such as flaxseed oil and hempseed oil play a crucial role in controlling the inflammation that accompanies *not just* heart disease, but cancers and diabetes as well. Trying to fight these diseases without the EFAs is like going into battle without a sword!

My basic truth 7

Quantify to improve. That's the the *key* rule to follow in order to progress. My initial obesity was an issue of abdominal fat, *not* absolute weight, that is, my body fat – although not weight directly because my *absolute weight in kilograms has no impact whatsoever on my health*. Initially, at 98 kg, it was the excessive body fat that was putting undue strain on my heart. Now, fully reconfigured at 95 kg, it's my lean mass (bone and muscle) making up that weight that helps my heart.

I no longer make visits to Dr. Nekkers as I have a very good idea of what to follow and how often. There will be six parameters along the way to heart fitness that will signal your progress:

1. Blood pressure < 135/85 mmHg.
2. Resting heart rate < 60 beats/minute.

3. Body fat = < 15–20% (men) or < 23% (women).
4. Waist-to-hip ratio < 0.90 (men) or < 0.80 (women).
5. TGs:HDL ratio < 1.
6. Homocysteine 7–10 micromoles/L.
7. HS-CRP less than 1 mg/L.

LEADERS' TOP FAQS ON THE HEART, OBESITY AND METABOLIC SYNDROME

What is the real definition of obesity?

The crisis of obesity is worldwide in scope – health experts call it "globesity" – with more than 1 billion adults overweight and at least 300 million of them clinically obese. Three measurements of obesity are generally used:

Body fat percent
Here the fat compartment of total body weight, which is fat (as opposed to the lean compartment – water, muscles, and bones), is calculated using either callipers or a tape measure: very reliable. Body fat ideals are < 20% for men and < 23% for women (see earlier for the formulae).

Waist-to-hip ratio
Thickness of fat around the waist is thought to correspond closely with its presence around the major organs of the body. A big waistline in your 40s could almost triple the threat of dementia in old age, according to US research. Researchers working for Kaiser Permanente, one of the biggest healthcare providers in the US, looked at 6,583 people aged between 40 and 45, measuring their abdominal fat. They then followed all of these people into their 70s to see who became ill and who managed to stay in relatively good health.

They found the 20% of people with the largest waistlines had a 270% greater risk of dementia than those with the smallest waists. Obesity is a known risk factor for Alzheimer's disease, but scientists found that even those of normal weight were more at risk if they had a large waist. This finding is not that surprising as a large abdominal girth is associated with high blood pressure and diabetes – major risk factors for dementia. By simply measuring the waist and dividing this figure by the hip measurement, you can calculate the waist-to-hip ratio: ideals are < 0.90 for men and < 0.80 for women.

Body mass index (BMI)
The BMI is equal to a person's weight in kilograms divided by their height in metres squared (kg/m²). The BMI, although widely cited and used, is *not* a worthwhile test as it considers the weight as one block unit: muscles, bones, and fat, all mixed together. Moreover, recent studies in the US reveal that even those reckoned to be normal weight using BMI calculations had approximately a 90% increased risk of dementia if they had a large rather than a small waist. A former MBA student of ours, an Olympian bobsledder weighing 91 kg (200 lbs) was

1.83 m (6 feet) tall had a BMI of 27.2, a BMI that makes the athlete fall into the overweight category, while he had a body like Michelangelo's David!

MEASURE OF OBESITY	STANDARDS	COMMENTS
Weight (kg)	N/A	Absolute weight measures nothing precisely
Body mass index (BMI) (kg/m²)	Men: 19–26 Women: 20–25	BMI is a simplistic formula based on height and weight that is often inaccurate
Body fat	Men: 15–20% Women: 20–23%	Requires only a tape measure
Waist-to-hip ratio	Men: < 0.90 Women: < 0.80	An excellent marker of subclinical atherosclerosis (heart disease)
Weight-to-waist ratio	Curve **up** or **flat**	Requires only a tape measure

In sum, the National Obesity Forum noted that waist size was a far better way to predict future illness than BMI. Remember: "What is good for your heart is also good for your brain."

What role does stress play in obesity?

A recent study by the American Psychological Association showed that the majority of Americans (80%) believed they experienced longstanding extreme stress. Unfortunately, many respond by employing Freud's infamous "hand-to-mouth" reflex: smoking, drinking, and nervous eating, with obvious results – high blood pressure, tension headaches or migraines, heart disease, diabetes, cancer, and premature aging. No diet, however well marketed, can address this epidemic until we learn how to relax (see Chapter 5).

Do artificial sweetners make you fat?

In a study recently published by Purdue University psychologists in *Behavioral Neuroscience*, rats given saccharin-sweetened yoghurt actually ate more and gained more weight than rats given regularly sugared yoghurt. As the researchers explained in their paper: "The data clearly indicate that consuming a food sweetened with no-calorie saccharin can lead to greater body-weight gain and adiposity than would consuming the same food sweetened with a higher-calorie sugar." More and more studies are showing that people who consume more articially sweetened diet drinks are at higher risk of obesity and the metabolic syndrome. The authors suggest that other artificial sweeteners, such as aspartame, sucralose, and acesulfame K, probably have a similar effect to saccharin and perhaps much worse.

Does fruit help control weight?

Anthocyanins found in grape skins, blueberries, blackberries, purple corn, and other foods, which give them their blue, purple, and reddish colors, may help prevent obesity, according to a recent study. The researchers fed mice a high-fat diet for 8 weeks; the mice also given drinking water with purified anthocyanins (an antioxidant) from blueberries and strawberries gained less weight and had lower body fat levels than a control group.

I recently had some liver function tests that were all elevated, to my surprise, though I don't drink much. But I do have a terrible sweet tooth and I have 27% body fat. What do I do?

You are right to be concerned about the liver function tests, as the liver is a tireless workhorse of the body, responsible for the critical functions of:

- filtering and cleansing the blood;
- synthesizing bile, a substance that helps digest fat;
- attaching fats to lipoproteins (cholesterol metaboism);
- storing sugar as fat, helping the body transport and save energy;
- synthesizing important proteins, like albumin and those involved in blood clotting;
- detoxifying many medications, such as barbiturates, sedatives, and amphetamines;
- storing iron, copper, vitamins A and D, and several of the B vitamins;
- recycling red blood cells.

According to the Mayo Clinic, non-alcoholic fatty liver disease is a pathological condition involving the liver in people who drink little or no alcohol. It starts with an accumulation of fat within the liver that usually causes no liver damage, followed by damaging inflammation. This can progress either to cirrhosis, which can produce progressive, irreversible liver scarring, or to liver cancer. Non-alcoholic fatty liver disease affects mostly middle-aged people who are obese, with or without diabetes, and have elevated cholesterol and TG levels. Its true prevalence is unknown, some estimates suggest it may affect as many as one-third of American adults.

While alcohol is *definitely* responsible for a *minority* of liver diseases, it is actually excessive body fat that kills the liver more efficiently and insidiously. The combination of obesity and alcohol is catastrophic to the liver. For example, if you have excess body fat, the liver is four times more likely to develop liver damage than in a normal-weight individual.[15] Adding alcohol to the mix (> 3 glasses/day of alcohol) gives six times the chance of liver disease. And overweight people drinking two or more glasses a day have a 3.4-fold increased risk of this.

So, unless you drink excessively (> 4 glasses a day), it all comes down to your weight. When you lose body fat, not only will you reduce your risks of heart disease, stroke, diabetes, and cancer, but you will reduce your risk of liver disease as well.

Is a big breakfast important for weight control?

A big breakfast (loading up on protein and carbohydrates at breakfast) is the key to slimming for several key reasons:

- It is more balanced and more healthful because people eat more fruit.
- It satisfies the cravings for sweets, carbohydrates and starches, and fast food.
- It may help obese patients with the metabolic syndrome stick to a low-calorie, low-carbohydrate diet the rest of the day,
- It was associated with fivefold greater weight loss than was achieved on a low-carbohydrate, low-calorie diet alone, reported Daniela Jakubowicz, MD, from the Hospital de Clinicas (Caracas, Venezuela), at the Endocrine Society meeting in San Francisco in 2008.
- It speeds metabolism and gives a greater sense of psychological satiety.

The reason for this is that, early in the morning, the body is primed with hormones like adrenaline and cortisol. The key to keeping trim is to eat well in the morning and then watch the carbohydrates and calories during the rest of the day.

It seems that many people, including children and young adults, are on the way to developing heart problems. Is it the soft drinks or what?

This is a very complex issue. Let's start with sugary drinks. There is nothing "soft" about soft drinks! In fact, this is the other "drinking" problem our culture has. Remember the connection between the metabolic syndrome and heart disease; look at the diet first. In a 2007 study, published in the American Heart Association journal *Circulation*, investigators found that people who drank just one or more soft drinks per day, compared to those who drank none, had several disturbing increased risks for heart disease, via metabolic syndrome:

- 25% had higher TGs;
- 32% had *low* HDL ("good") cholesterol levels;
- 30% had increases in waist circumference;
- a 31% greater a risk for developing new-onset obesity;
- a 60% increase in risk for developing the metabolic syndrome.

But there are other factors at play as well. In another study, scientists gathered dietary information on more than 9,500 men and women aged 45 to 64 and tracked their health for 9 years. Overall, a Western dietary pattern – high intakes of refined grains, fried foods, and red meat – was associated with an

18% increased risk for the metabolic syndrome, while a "prudent" diet domi-nated by fruits, vegetables, fish, and poultry correlated with neither an increased nor a decreased risk. But the one-third who ate the most fried food increased their risk by 25% compared to the one-third who ate the least, and, surprisingly, the risk of developing metabolic syndrome was 34% higher among those who drank one can of diet soda a day compared to those who drank none. In general, children are getting not enough of the good meas-ures of hygiene, such as physical activity, proper sleep (to increase their energy, as children usually eat more when they're tired) and natural foods (with fiber and vitamin C – fruits and nuts) and far too much of the bad stuff (sedentary TV/video time, high-GI foods, and sugar drinks).

What about regular fasting – is this good for the health?

A recent study in Utah has now identified the habit of monthly fasting to be the biggest contributor to the robust cardiovascular health most Mormons enjoy. Mormons customarily fast on the first Sunday of every month. They also avoid the use of tea, coffee, tobacco and alcohol. They do go to church, observe a day of rest each week, and routinely donate time or money to charitable causes. Each of these practices was analyzed, and the most benefi-cial of all for heart health was found to be the abstinence from food 1 day per month.

Mormons who fast once a month are 40% less likely to be diagnosed with heart disease than people who do not fast regularly. The presence of heart disease was determined by X-ray scans revealing arterial blockage of 70% or more.

Back in the 1920s when Otto Warburg, a German Nobel laureate and biochemist, proved that cancer cells, during a fast, can switch from *fermenta-tion*, which is significantly less efficient than *respiration*, to generate energy. That is, tumor cells using fermentation will burn upwards of 3000% more blood sugar than normal cells using respiration. This is why humans who are taking chemotherapy for an existent cancer survive longer when fasting, and rats on a low-calorie diets live twice as long as normal rats. Periodic fasting is a safe and reliable way to slow the aging process and prevent disease. Other animal studies show that mice that eat a regular diet while fasting for 1 day once a week live longer than mice that are not fasted.

When you fast, you burn fat for energy. Not only do you lose the extra weight, but you get rid of all the toxins that your body stores in the extra fat. Fasting also helps your body make human growth hormone, along with other anti-aging hormones. This helps you to better use protein to repair cells, tissues, and organs.

Some pointers on fasting:

- Start with a simple 24-hour fruit fast. Don't eat anything but fruits (like grapefruit, kiwis or dried plums) and drink plenty of clean water for a day.

■ The next day when you break your fast, start slowly. Small amounts of fresh vegetables and soups are the best idea.

What is the best way to delay the aging process?

Perhaps the oldest anti-aging technique on record is eating less: caloric deprivation or caloric restriction (aka fasting). There is now good scientific evidence in animal and human studies demonstrating that caloric restriction slows aging by a number of simultaneous mechanisms:

■ It causes numerous hormonal changes in your bloodstream. We now know there is a genetic pathway activated by caloric restriction, which protects you from the damage that causes aging.

■ It slows the shortening of the telomere, which is the master genetic control for your biological clock.

> **TIP** Dr. Sigmund Freud once noted that to be a balanced human being, we need three things:
> ■ friends and love;
> ■ work;
> ■ play.
> Don't let modern life get in your way.

For example, multiple studies show that mice on caloric restriction diets live up to 60% longer (and behave like younger mice in every way) than mice on a normal diet. In human terms, that's like living an extra 50 years! It also lowers the risk of many diseases of aging, including cancer, heart disease, diabetes, osteoporosis, and Alzheimer's disease.

I am aware how fast food, large portions, and sedentary lifestyles all make us obese, but is it possible my medications might also be making me fat?

Doctors are infamous for *not* adequately informing their clientele of the side effects of the medication they prescribe, particularly with regard to the effect on their weight.[16] Two examples include:

■ lithium (a mood swing stabilizer): after 10 years on lithium, two-thirds of patients have gained 10 kg;

■ olanzapine (a antipsychotic): the company's data showed that one-third of patients who had taken the drug for a year gained at least 10 kg, and half of these gained at least 30 kg.

How are women doing in the obesity epidemic?

Not too well. According to a report by the American Stroke Association, growing obesity among middle-aged women has led to an increase in incidence of stroke for women between the ages 35 and 54. According to US researchers, obese middle-aged women are at a very high risk of stroke. Abdominal obesity, as indicated by a waist-to-hip ratio > 0.80, is a known predictor of higher stroke rates in middle-aged women. Specifically, the researchers also found that these same women, if they were obese, saw their stroke rate increase from 47% to 59%.

The psychology of weight loss

Interestingly, the psychology of weight loss is rarely discussed by "experts" because many of them do not understand what various people are going through. Anyone who has been or is overfat knows better. People, according to Freud and others, have a primordial "hand-to-mouth reflex" when they become anxious or stressed. During anxious moments, some put food in the mouths, other chew their nails, others smoke, and still others drink alcohol or sugary drinks.

The body is a template for out mindset. We've never known more about health, yet our waist lines keep growing. Obese people have never had so many good health reasons to control their weight – but have never had more excuses and time wasted.

The mental focus is all wrong here. Being overfat is not a discrete disease: it is a symptom of deep-seated anxiety. It's that simple. The horse (the body) follows the rider (the mind). Clearly, nobody in our "quick-fix," instant-gratification culture wants to hear this truth, especially when there are a myriad of fake solutions out there that offer short cuts to nowhere. No one seems to want to hear that the problem – and the solution – lies within, between our ears, and *not* outside us. Without a fundamental shift in thinking, anyone on a weight loss program will fail, no matter how much torture we endure. In sum, success comes with *both* the right attitude, *and* the right program.

Are there any health benefits to having a nap?

In a study published in the *Archives of Internal Medicine* in 2007, researchers at Harvard University School of Public Health tracked more than 23,000 Greek adults (mostly men) for 6 years to gauge the effect of afternoon naps. The result was that regular nappers (a minimum of 30 minutes three or more times a week) were 37% *less* likely to die of heart disease, probably due to the easing of blood pressure and overall stress during the day.

I have heard that pets are good for your health: true or false?

The finding that a cat at home could cut your heart attack risk by almost a third comes from a 10-year study of more than 4,300 Americans, aged 30–75, which suggests that the stress relief pets provide humans is heart-healthy. Using the main outcome as death from all causes, including stroke and heart events, the researchers found that, over a 10-year follow-up period, cat owners showed a 30% lower risk of death from heart attack compared to non-pet owners.

The same appears true for dogs or any companion. There are good physical and mental rewards for owning and taking care of any pet, as pets are a good positive influence: they are relaxing, friendly, and affectionate. Unlike human, they don't argue. Owning a pet is both a deep pleasure and a calming influence for people in this troubled world.

Why don't the French get as fat as Americans, considering all the baguettes, wine, and fatty foods they eat?

In general, the French use internal cues or signals to govern their food consumption. That is, they stop eating when they no longer feel hungry, and they also walk a lot more than their American counterparts. Americans, on the other hand, have a tendency to use external cues (their plate being clean, they have run out of their beverage or the TV show they're watching is over) to stop eating.

What risk factors should I be aware of for my heart?

The four *real* risk factors we *absolutely* must pay attention to for the heart, brain, and overall health are:

1. an excessive intake of refined sugar[17]/alcohol leading to (see also Chapter 2):
   – a centrifugal distribution of body fat (high WHR);
   – a TGs:HDL ratio that ideally should be < 1;
   – diabetes (or the metabolic syndrome);
2. physical inactivity: move it or lose it (see Chapter 3);
3. poor-quality air, including, but not restricted to:
   – tobacco smoke: passive or active;
   – polluted air: free radicals are increased in activity and quantity by bumping into toxic metals in the body. Thus, toxic metals are a cause of free radicals. Several hundred years ago we did *not* have the burden of toxic metals in our bodies that we now do, and we also did not have such an exposure to free radicals. If you remove the toxic metals from the body, you greatly reduce the activity and the number of free radicals. It is also clear that environmental agents initiate free radical problems. The toxicity of lead, pesticides, cadmium, ionizing radiation, alcohol, and cigarette smoke may all be due to their free radical initiating ability;
4. elevated blood pressure (> 135/85 mmHg) *and* its various causes:
   – depression or loss of zest for life;
   – uncompensated stress (see Chapter 5);
   – anger or hostility-prone behaviour;
   – inflammation: as indicated by high HS-CRP levels;
   – homocysteine blood levels: doctors in Norway studied men with heart disease over a 6-year period and found that those with high levels of homocysteine suffered the highest number of heart attacks. The higher their levels, the lower their chances of surviving.[18] The most effective way to normalize the homocysteine is with a B vitamin/folate supplement.

What does the word "risk" actually signify?

Understand what "risk" actually means and how it is used. If the chance of a disease occurring to you is decreased from 3 per 10,000 to 1 per 10,000, that is a "relative risk" reduction of 66%, which sounds a lot. But in reality, the "absolute risk" has gone down from 0.03% to 0.01%. Put another way, your chance of survival has increased from 99.97% to 99.99% which is really very small and not at all sensational or significant.

How does the US, where hundreds of BILLIONS of dollars are spent every year on health care, compare to the other developed countries?

France, Japan, and Australia rated best and the US worst in new rankings focusing on preventable deaths due to treatable conditions in 19 leading industrialized nations, research showed in 2003. Moreover, other countries are reducing these preventable deaths more rapidly, yet spending far less. If the US healthcare system performed as well as those of those top three countries, there would be 101,000 fewer deaths in the US per year.

Researchers at the London School of Hygiene and Tropical Medicine tracked deaths that they deemed could have been prevented by access to timely and effective health care, and ranked nations on how they did. They called such deaths an important way to gauge the performance of a country's healthcare system. The large number of Americans who have *no* type of health insurance – about 50 million people in a country of about 300 million, according to US government estimates – is a key factor in the poor showing of the US compared to other industrialized nations in the study.

In establishing their rankings, the researchers considered deaths before age 75 from numerous causes, including heart disease, stroke, certain cancers, diabetes, certain bacterial infections, and complications of common surgical procedures. Such deaths accounted for 23% of overall deaths in men and 32% of deaths in women, the researchers said.

France did best – with 64.8 deaths per 100,000 people deemed preventable by timely and effective health care, in the study period of 2002 and 2003. Japan had 71.2 and Australia had 71.3 such deaths per 100,000 people, and the US 109.7. After the top three, Spain was fourth best, followed in order by Italy, Canada, Norway, The Netherlands, Sweden, Greece, Austria, Germany, Finland, New Zealand, Denmark, Great Britain, Ireland, and Portugal, with the US last. The researchers compared these rankings to rankings for the same 19 countries covering the period of 1997 and 1998. France and Japan also were first and second in those rankings, while the US was 15th, meaning it had fallen four places in the latest rankings.

What is the latest on eggs, vis-à-vis heart disease?

Some health experts say with enthusiasm that "Eggs are back," but in fact eggs never left, nor *should* they have. In a recent 2008 study at UConn (USA), researchers found some very reassuring benefits to consumption of three chicken eggs a day:

1. There are increases in blood HDL.
2. Antioxidants in egg yolks (lutein and xeazanthin) exert a strong positive anti-inflammatory effect, as expressed by blood HS-CRP. According to the

journal *Nutrition and Medicine* in 2008, both are highly beneficial in avoiding heart attacks.

On the obesity front, eggs also did very well. A study published in the *International Journal of Obesity* shows that eating two eggs for breakfast, as part of a reduced-calorie diet, helps overweight adults lose more weight and feel more energetic than those who eat a bagel breakfast of equal calories. This study confirms previous research, published in the *Journal of the American College of Nutrition*, which showed that people who ate eggs for breakfast felt more satisfied and ate fewer calories at the following meal. Compared to the subjects who ate a bagel breakfast, men and women who consumed two eggs for breakfast as part of a reduced-calorie diet:

- lost 65% more weight;
- exhibited a 61% greater reduction in BMI;
- reported higher energy levels than their dieting counterparts who consumed a bagel breakfast.

The egg and bagel breakfasts provided the same number of calories and had identical weights (energy density), which is an important control factor in satiety and weight loss studies.

The researchers also found that blood lipids were not impacted during the 2-month study. They found that blood levels of HDL and LDL cholesterol, as well as TGs, did not vary compared to baseline cholesterol blood levels in subjects who ate either the bagel or egg breakfasts. These findings add to more than 30 years of research that conclude that healthy adults can enjoy eggs while decreasing their risk of heart disease.

Thickened blood: how did it happen, and how can I thin the blood?

According to recent studies, thickened blood could increase the risks of strokes and heart attacks if blood clotting factors (especially von Willebrand factor, factor VIIIc, and fibrinogen) are activated. Obesity (excessive body fat), smoking, high blood pressure, high TGs, and diabetes all "thicken" the blood, while exercise, stress management, smoking cessation, and a proper intake of the fat family all "thin" it.

What are AGEs?

AGEs (advanced glycation end-products) are obtained by haphazardly attaching a sugar to a protein (such as hemoglobin or collagen). Once formed, these AGEs will bind to other AGEs and other proteins, in a pathological process called protein cross-linking. As the AGEs build up, they cause overall degradation of the involved tissue, an accelerated aging process, for example:

- cataracts;
- collagen stiffening;

- nervous symptoms;
- in the case of the coronary arteries, gumming up of the normal LDL to clog up the arteries. LDL is particularly sensitive to this glycation. AGE cross-linking is the stiffening process that leads to heart disease (arteriosclerosis). The more LDLs present in the context of high free radicals (oxidizing effect) or sugar (glycated effect), the more these problematic LDLs clog the critical arteries.

What is the relationship between different alcohols and the metabolic syndrome?

The relationship between alcohol and health is complex. In a 2008 study at the Karolinska Institute in Sweden, with more than 4,000 men and women over 60 years of age, researchers found that the metabolic syndrome was far less common among wine drinkers than those drinking spirits and beer (who were more often smokers and also reported a higher intake of sausage and fried potatoes) or even non-drinkers.

Is there any connection between drinking in excess and increased risk for the metabolic syndrome?

Those who drink in excess of the US dietary guidelines (i.e., men who usually drink more than two drinks per day or women who usually drink more than one drink per day), or those who binge drink, are at increased risk for the metabolic syndrome, according to a new study accepted for publication in The Endocrine Society's *Journal of Clinical Endocrinology and Metabolism*. Most people who consume alcohol by binging late at night increase their risk of the metabolic syndrome and related conditions.

Is the metabolic syndrome tied to diet soda?

There is a definite correlation between drinking *diet* soda and the metabolic syndrome. Researchers studied dietary information on more than 9,500 men and women aged 45–64 and tracked their health for 9 years. In general, the risk of developing the metabolic syndrome was 34% higher among those who drank one can of diet soda a day compared to those who drank none.

NOTES AND REFERENCES

1. Homocysteine is an independent risk factor for premature arteriosclerosis of the heart, brain, and leg vessels:
   - Guba SC et al. Hyperhomocysteinemia: an emerging and important risk factor for thromboembolic and cardiovascular disease. *Am J Clin Pathol* 1996; **105**: 709.
   - Welch GN et al. Homocysteine and atherothrombosis. *NEJM* 1998; **338**: 1042.
   - An excellent study from Boston University and Tufts University strongly implicates

how a high blood level of homocysteine in persons age 65 and older is a very significant risk factor for Alzheimer's disease and other dementias. They enrolled 1,092 men and women average age 76 years (range 65–94), measured blood homocysteine levels, and then followed the subjects for 8 years, during which period 111 of the subjects developed dementia, 80% of which was diagnosed as Alzheimer's disease. As people grow older, homocysteine levels increase, so the investigators divided the group into 5-year age categories. They then, in each age group, divided the participants into quartiles from lowest to highest blood homocysteine levels. Those in the highest 25% (the highest quartile) of homocysteine level had a doubled risk of developing Alzheimer's compared to those with homocysteine levels in the lowest 25% (the lowest quartile). Anyone with a blood homocysteine level considered elevated also had a doubled risk of developing Alzheimer's. Seshadri S et al. Plasma homocysteine as a risk factor for dementia and Alzheimer's disease. *N Engl J Med* 2002; **346**: 476–83.

2. Three important studies have elucidated the link between HS-CRP and heart disease:
   - The *British Journal of Urology* published a study that proved the importance of CRP. Researchers tested almost 400 people for CRP levels. They found that once the CRP level reached double the norm, the person was 150% more likely to suffer a heart attack. Mendall M et al. C-reactive protein and its relation to cardiovascular risk factor. *Br J Urol* 1996; **312**: 1061–5.
   - Recent data suggest that hypertension is *in part an inflammatory disorder*. In a study of over 15,000 healthy American women, it was found that HS-CRP and blood pressure were independent predictors of heart attack events, and that HS-CRP added prognostic information at all levels of blood pressure in the prediction of first incident heart attack events. Blake GJ, Rifai N, Buring JE, Ridker PM. Blood pressure, C-reactive protein, and risk of future cardiovascular events. *Circulation* 2003; **108**: 2993.
   - HS-CRP levels were also found to predict incident hypertension in a large study of initially normotensive women, even in subjects having low baseline blood pressure levels. Sesso HD et al. C-reactive protein and the risk of developing hypertension. *JAMA* 2003; **290**: 2945–51.

3. There are potential dangers from the use of prescription drugs. The watchdog group Safe Medication Practices reported that 4,825 deaths and nearly 21,000 injuries occurred in the first 3 months of 2008. The drugs heparin and varenicline were cited as the most dangerous. Earlier reports stating that varenicline could lead to lapses in alertness or motor control led the US Federal Aviation Administration in May 2008 to ban use of the drug by airline pilots and traffic controllers. The Department of Transportation has even limited its use by truck drivers, and the Department of Defense has prohibited its use by aircraft and missile crews. Varenicline accounted for more reports of serious injury than the 10 bestselling prescription drugs combined.

4. Inflammation is a process triggered by infection or wound healing, but also by sugar consumption. Repeated provocation of the inflammatory cascade contributes to a whole spectrum of diseases, including heart disease, cancer, and autoimmune diseases. Blood markers of this inflammation include HS-CRP – which will be elevated – and adiponectin, which will note inflammation by being depressed. Although no one knows exactly how these conditions are connected to cardiovascular disease, it is possible they all spring from the same source – inflammation. Inflammation is an essential part of the

body's defenses. In people with rheumatoid arthritis and lupus, however, inflammation turns against the body and damages joints and other tissues. In heart disease, inflammation kicks off artery-clogging atherosclerosis, keeps it smoldering, and influences the formation of clots, the ultimate cause of heart attacks and many strokes.

5. A marker of macrophage activity found in plasma, FcγRIIIaMo, is significantly increased in patients with CAD but not in those with angina or normal coronary arteries, which is powerful evidence that these immune cells, the macrophages, play a central role in the development of a heart attack. The level increased with age and was associated with obesity, high blood pressure, high LDL, and a high TGs:HDL cholesterol ratio. As risk factors for heart attack increased, so did levels of this substance. FcγRIIIaMo also correlated with the thickness of the carotid artery. This suggests that macrophages are activated during the beginning stages and could be used as a marker of incipient heart attack. Masuda M et al. Soluble FcγRIIIa$^{M\varphi}$ levels in plasma correlate with carotid maximum intima–media thickness (IMT) in subjects undergoing an annual medical checkup. *Mol Med 2008;* **14**: 436–42.

6. Dandona P et al. Metabolic syndrome: a comprehensive perspective based on interactions between obesity, diabetes and inflammation. *Circulation* 2005; **111**: 1448–54.

7. Insulin: a causative factor in cancer? The following studies demonstrate the cancer-causing nature of insulin and insulin-like growth factor:
   - Prostate cancer: *Science* 1998; **279**: 563–6.
   - Breast cancer: *Lancet* 1998; 351: 1393–6.
   - Colon cancer: *Cancer: Causes and Control* 1995; 6: 164–79.

8. DNA, or deoxyribonucleic acid, is our "source code," responsible for coding for the production of proteins (enzymes or catalysts) via the messenger unit RNA.

9. Foster-Powell K, Holt SHA, Brand-Miller JC. International table of glycemic index and glycemic load values: 2002. *Am J Clin Nutr* 2002; **76**: 5–56.

10. Halton TL et al. Low-carbohydrate-diet score and the risk of coronary heart disease in women. *N Engl J Med* 2006; **355**: 1991–2002.

11. Frost G et al. Glycaemic index as a determinant of serum HDL-cholesterol concentration. *Lancet* 1999; **353**: 1045–8.

12. High-intensity exercise, like BURST, can also help you live longer. Another Harvard study compared vigorous and light exercise. Those who performed exercise that was more vigorous had a lower risk of death than those who performed less vigorous exercise. Lee I et al. Exercise intensity and longevity in men. The Harvard Alumni Health Study. *JAMA* 1995; **273**: 1179–84.

13. In a 1994 study, researchers at Laval University in Canada studied two groups: one group did endurance exercise (cycling for 45 minutes without stopping) and another group did short-burst cycling (cycling for 15–90 seconds) punctuated by short rest periods. The results were that the endurance group burned 20% more absolute calories, while the BURST cycling group lost almost 1000% more fat. Tremblay A et al. Impact of energy intensity on body fatness and skeletal muscle metabolism. *Metabolism* 1994; **43**: 814–18.

14. This meta-analysis clearly shows that pedometers are an effective tool in increasing physical activity and improving health, especially if a weekly walking log is kept. As it turns out, that's a surprisingly effective way to persuade people to move more, according to a new report in the *Journal of the American Medical Association*. In a review of over

20 studies, researchers at Stanford University found that people who used pedometers to monitor their daily activity walked about 2,000 more steps every day, or about one extra mile, compared to those who were not counting steps. People who used pedometers also showed statistically meaningful drops in body fat and blood pressure.

15. Zoler ML. Obesity is the cause of most U.S. liver damage: Risk of disease fourfold higher in obese. *Family Practice News*, July 1, 2004.

16. In the year 2004, 32.6 million Americans purchased outpatient prescriptions for anti-depressants, stimulants, antipsychotics, and tranquillizers, up from 21 million in 1997. Overall, around 50 million Americans – one in six of the population – currently take at least one psychotropic drug. Rising obesity in teenagers and even young children over the past 10–15 years coincides with a fivefold increase in prescriptions of antipsychotic drugs in those age groups.

17. The *Lancet* published a startling study that proved the ill effects of refined sugar. The study showed that someone eating 110 g of sugar was five times more likely to have a heart attack than someone who ate 60 g of sugar daily. The average American eats 140 g of sugar daily. Yudkin J et al. Sugar consumption and myocardial infarction. *Lancet* 1972; 296–7.

18. Nygard O et al. Plasma homocysteine levels and mortality in patients with coronary artery disease. *N Engl J Med* 1997; **337**: 230–6.

Nutrition for health, energy, and longevity

Let your food be your medicine and your medicine be your food.

Hippocrates, father of modern medicine, circa 400 BC

The information in this chapter will enhance your health, vitality, and longevity. The case presented here is a popular constellation of symptoms in modern life:

1 Digestive/eating disorders: bulimia, irritable bowel disease, heartburn (gastroesophageal reflux disease), and constipation/hemorrhoids
2 Controlling the acid–base balance in the blood
3 Preventative chemotherapy: to decrease the oxidative stress leading to cancer and upgrade the immune system
4 Hair falling out (alopecia) and skin ailments
5 Chronic "migraine" headaches
6 Chronic fatigue: lung filter blocked by smoking/pollution

Abbreviations and acronyms that you will need to read this chapter smoothly include:

EFA	Essential fatty acid
GI	Glycemic index
HAP	Health Action Plan
HDL	High-density lipoprotein
HFCS	High-fructose corn sugar
LDL	Low-density lipoprotein
MSG	Monosodium glutamate
TGs	Triglycerides

INTRODUCTION

My name is Isabelle. I am presently the 41-year-old director of design at a leading lingerie and bathing suit division of a French company based in Paris.

PROFESSIONAL BACKGROUND

Although it seems obvious, I would like to say that, for a woman to climb the corporate ladder, it takes extra drive and talent. Perhaps this is true because macho attitudes in France are so prevalent, but I can also tell that these archaic tendencies are present in all societies, even the US and UK. But France is special in this regard as the condescending sexist attitudes are mixed into the romantic stereotypes that make France so attractive to foreigners. It is not (always) romantic, and I can tell you by experience, it is *very* difficult. But I have survived this terrain partly because I am a fighter *and* a winner.

After finishing a psychology degree at university, I myself felt depressed, as many of the case studies of mental illness and instability that I studied were taken, it seemed, directly from my family. We were a textbook of pathology, and I was determined to not allow myself to become that way. So I dropped psychology and started a course in style design at a Paris institute.

PERSONAL LIFE

I grew up the eldest in a family of three children in rural France, with a younger brother and sister. There were constant arguments between my parents: it was endless and unrestrained, as though they actually *needed* to fight. Moreover, while I was growing up, it seemed to me that there was really nothing I could do to please my mother. I felt that I was the problem causing all this tension. She never had a kind word of encouragement for me or my sister. Worse yet, when she would make an off-the-cuff statement on my physique or my clothes or whatever, Father would chime in and add to the distress. We could never do anything right. Was she preparing us for something, I used to think privately, like they do in the military training?

To my surprise, my parents finally divorced when I was 16 and the youngest was just 10. The result in me was a mixture of pain and relief, pain (that is, crying-myself-to-sleep pain) because, despite the fighting and pettiness, I loved my parents being together so that I would not have to be another kid from a "broken home." I had a fairy-tale view of marriage, star-crossed lovers, "happily ever after," and all that. There was relief, however, because a child needs a minimum of harmony (even if it is fake). This thirst for harmony definitely played a key role in the choice of partners I was to make several years later: my prince was out there somewhere, waiting for me.

I met Stan, an American investment banker, at a reception at a Paris fashion show, and after a brief and tumultuous trans-Atlantic romance, we got married. As I grew to know Stan more intimately, I realized that he was the *exact* opposite of my father: above all, he was kind, quiet, and smiled a lot, without major manipulations. His love for me, while not fiery, was something I needed to depend on, and I let him know that I needed that reliability.

Months past and I found myself very attracted to the peace and harmony that Stan had brought to my life, especially the fact that he, as an American investment banker, granted a measure of independence that I had never known. I was not impeded to advance my career in any way, nor was he "power-playing" me, as my parents used to do with emotional blackmail. In a word, I felt, early on, that Stan let me "do my life," including smoking the occasional cigarette.

At Stan's request, we moved to New York, where we were to live for 5 years, with our two children, Sophie and Geoff.

NUTRITION

This fell into two phases:

- *Before the US*: The basic French approach: a small breakfast, a hot lunch, a sit-down harmonious dinner, no fast foods, no snacks, and no TV.
- *While in the US*: Basically the whole family was overfed yet malnourished. That is to say, there were massive portions (enough for three French people!), nutrition high in sugary snacks, "diet" or "lite" drinks, loads of chips, fries, cakes, muffins, and cupcakes, and few vegetables, salads, and fruit.

PHYSICAL ACTIVITY

I used to go sailing, played weekend tennis, and went for walks.

Most important leadership quality	Fairness
My idea of great leaders	• Nelson Mandela • Geronimo • Mahatma Gandhi

My most inspiring quotation

It's better to lead from behind and put others in front, especially when you celebrate victory, when nice things occur. You take the front line when there is danger. Then people will appreciate your leadership.

Nelson Mandela

MY WAKE-UP CALL

My wake-up call came gradually as I began to recognize the effects on my body of the standard American diet of refined foods, diet sodas, and super-sized portions, combined with city living. I had rapid weight gain, could not be "regular" without laxatives, and suffered chronic yeast infections, food reflux, heartburn, and hair loss. I could feel myself getting more and more tired (even upon awakening) and even slipping occasionally into depression.

My reflex notion was to consult a psychologist to get some help with the depression, figuring that, as in every other case, I was going to get the old response from Stan to my ailments: "Isabelle, it's all in your head!"

However, to my surprise, the psychologist asked me to first see an internist for the fatigue and a nutritionist for the rest, and then to return if the depressive symptoms persisted. He seemed to believe that they were all related. I could see then that this was going to be a bit more complicated than taking a magic pill.

Isabelle's health and fitness report

	NORMAL/IDEAL RANGE	MY FIRST CHECK-UP
Actual age (years)		39
Health age (years)	Actual age or less	51.6
Blood pressure (mmHg)	< 135/85	110/72
Resting heart rate (beats/minute)	< 60	88
Weight (kg)		65
Body fat %	15–23%	28%
Body fat weight (kg)		18.2
Lean weight (kg)		46.8
Waist-to-hip ratio	< 0.80	0.95
Hematology (blood cells)		
Erythrocytes (red blood cells) (/mm³)	4,500,000–5,500,000	3,900,000
Hemoglobin (gram %)	12.9–17.5	11.2
Hematocrit (% blood occupied by red cells)	40–50%	38%
Mean corpuscular volume (μm³)	80–95	76
Platelets (clot-formers) (/mm³)	150,000–400,000	350,000
Leukocyte family (white blood cells) (/mm³)	4,000–10,000	14,000
Neutrophils (/mm³)	2,000–7,500	6,700
Eosinophils (/mm³)	< 800	950
Lymphocytes (/mm³)	1,500–4,000	4,500
Monocytes (/mm³)	< 1000	900
Liver function tests		
SGOT (aka AST) (U/L)	9–38	58
SGPT (aka ALT) (U/L)	0–41	62
GGT (U/L)	0-61	75

U/L, units per litre.

Prompted by the symptoms of fatigue, constipation, and severe anemia, my internist scheduled a colonoscopy, which revealed many polyps.

"Polyps? What are those?" I queried my internist.

"They are precancerous signs that your digestive system is battling a noxious stimulus, like bad foods or the chemical preservatives in them. The body reacts first by inflammation, then regeneration. Your digestive system is really working hard to get energy from your food. That's one clear reason why you are always tired.

"Now, I have removed the polyps, and they are all benign. We shall repeat this in a year's time to check again. In the meantime, I want you see a dear friend of mine who actually helped my patients and even my family a lot: Dr. Jacky Sagesse. She is a nutritionist, but a *real* one, who practices what she preaches, with outstanding results. I am sure that you will be quite impressed when you meet her."

MY DAY WITH THE NUTRITIONIST: MEETING THE MIRACLE OF DNA

Fearing the worse and figuring I had much to lose if I did nothing, I made the appointment for the next week. As I sat waiting for the doctor, I noticed a sign above the diplomas:

> The doctors of the future will give no medicine but instead will interest his patients in the care of the human frame, in diet, and in the cause and prevention of disease.
>
> **Thomas Edison**

The nutritionist was a woman I had estimated in her late 50s or early 60s, vibrant and smiling, with beautiful teeth, skin, and hair, and a spirited gait. After a brief but polite introduction to Dr. Jacqueline Sagesse (with a PhD in human nutrition), she spent several minutes performing a physical exam and, once finished, leaned over her desk and said to me, "Isabelle, I have a little practice that I use every time I have new patient. Before I meet them in person, I review *all* the pertinent clinical data – the X-rays, laboratory blood tests, and so on – *without looking at the age of the patient*. Once I had reviewed your data, I was certain either you were in your 60s or you had been poisoned or both. What do you think my age is? Well, Isabelle, I am 72 years old."

I reflected, "I should have seen this coming when I moved to the US, but I became so distracted by the fast pace of life and the lack of free time. Until we moved to the States, I had been eating like my French family had been for decades, even longer: fresh food without preservatives, home-cooked meals, and meals were sacred (above all, no TV interrupting the meals). I was just starting to realize the price I had paid for my success. After all, the oldest living human ever, Jeanne Calment, a Frenchwoman, lived to be 122 years of age!

In response to my query about how she was going to treat me, Dr. Sagesse replied to me, smiling: "Isabelle, when I look at your laboratory report, two items leap off the page at me:

1. The first is that you are severely anemic. Your red blood cells are down, as are your hematocrit and hemoglobin. That is due to the polyps that were removed from your intestines. Those figures will improve with iron supplements and vitamin C.

2. The second is that you, or rather your liver, as indicated by your liver function tests, is *really* struggling to purify and detoxify your blood and body.

"So, I am not going to simply treat you. I am going to *cure* you, by using the most ancient medicine in the world: FOOD. I shall let your nutrition cure your ailments, one by one. But on this score, we must work together, if we are to be effective in solving these problems.

"To accomplish that, I practice what is known in medicine as objective-oriented medicine, which basically means I listen to your list of complaints, cluster them under one umbrella, so to speak, and then develop a Health Action Plan, or HAP, that we shall discuss together now. In combination with the HAP you will implement, I offer nutritional workshops every Wednesday evening, to discuss the topics at hand.

"Then, to gauge how effective your HAP has been, I shall see you every 6 months, each time refining the HAP until you are cured. This approach is really the future of medicine.

"You see, Isabelle, we are born with an incredible DNA software program to maintain our homeostasis. It is quite a miracle to behold! To complete its many jobs, it needs your help to:

- be careful not to dump too many toxins into the system;
- give the program adequate clean fuel, water, and oxygen. Since you have done neither, the DNA program has now gone awry. Let's start by removing the poisons and cleaning the filter."

That was just fine with me, as I had been feeling for about the past 3 years quite old and tired, certainly compared to the nutritionist. She continued slowly and deliberately: she was not at all in a hurry. "Let's get started. I have classified your HAP into two stages, because your disease, Isabelle, like *all* other diseases, is caused by either outright poisoning or multiple nutritional deficiencies.

I remember being dumbstruck by her comments of appearing older than my age or "poisoned" (I *did* feel poisoned). Finally, someone was putting their finger directly on the primary problem. The term employed to describe my state – "poisoned" – stayed with me, as that was how I had felt almost all the time for the past several years: always tired (even upon awakening), dealing with chronic constipation, memory and concentration problems, frequent infections, muscle pain, hair falling out, severe headaches, and so on. I pressed Dr. Sagesse to elaborate.

She continued, "When I said earlier that you seemed poisoned, both on a physical examination and laboratory blood studies, I was implicating not just the foods you have been eating, but everything you have been digesting, including medications for your digestive ailments, diet soft drinks, and candy. And you are certainly not alone. We, as a society, have fouled our own nest."

She handed me a 2005 report from the US Centers for Disease Control describing the largest ever investigation into human exposure to industrial chemicals by anyone, anywhere. The latest instalment searched for 148 toxic compounds (out of the over 80,000 possible industrial chemicals in use today) in the urine and blood of 2,400 people aged 6 and older.

I was astonished and alarmed by the reality that adults, children, pregnant women, and the babies they carry have dozens of toxic chemicals in their bodies and brains.[1] The facts as the government agency laid out started to explain why I felt the way I did:

- The discovery of compounds by the name of *pyrethroids* (present in virtually every household pesticide), which are toxic to the nervous system and seriously affect hormones.
- The discovery in urine and blood of *phthalates*, found in nail polish, most fragrances, most beauty products, and soft plastics. In one recent study of human babies, some of these compounds have been shown to detrimentally change male reproductive organs.
- In the Centers for Disease Control research study, one in 18 women of childbearing age had *mercury* levels exceeding those considered safe to the developing fetus. It has been well established that mercury exposure during pregnancy can lower IQ, affecting especially memory and vocabulary.
- And most recently, we have heard about the health dangers posed by *bisphenol A* (BPA), a chemical found in hard, clear plastics and most cans containing foods or beverages. A landmark study of more than 1,400 people aged 18–74, published in the *Journal of the American Medical Association,* found that those with the largest amount of BPA in their urine had nearly three times the risk of heart disease and more than twice the risk of diabetes as those who had the lowest levels. Babies also cannot metabolize the chemical as quickly as adults, so it accumulates in their bodies.

"That's not all, Isabelle. It goes on and on. We have invented chemicals for our modern comfort that end up in our blood and brains and those of our progeny. It's catching up with us," said Dr. Sagesse. "Exposure to these industrial chemicals during pregnancy or at an early age can permanently damage our brains, and only a handful – lead, methylmercury, arsenic, toluene, and polychlorinated biphenyls – are controlled. There are hundreds more chemicals that just don't belong in our system.

"The problem is that the toxicity is well recognized but the toxins may not produce symptoms or disease for years or longer. My point is that we must protect and educate ourselves and our children because we live in a culture that makes dangerous products, like toys for example. The extent of our culture's moral obligation to our children is to simply attach a silly warning label saying that the products is made from chemicals known to cause cancer and birth defects. The same attitude pervades into nutrition.

"Moreover, whenever you start to improve your health, there will always be someone there to turn a profit. That is certainly true in the case of nutrition. What I am going to do is to start with the toxins that the body itself has generated during the normal metabolic processes (such as ammonia produced during the breakdown of protein), and then start to eliminate the industrial chemicals that enter the body through our digestive or respiratory tracts, which have been deposited in your blood and fatty tissue – such as household toxins, pesticides, food additives, medications, pollution, cigarette smoke, and heavy metals."

"**Stage 1: Short term** takes care of your internal poisoning. This lasts 6–8 weeks and has two parts:

1. First and foremost developing what I call a "happy gut," which amounts to re-training the digestive system, through a gentle clean-out to get you back to just 'regular.'
2. At the same time, developing a Supernutrition for the whole family's vitality and long life: for high energy and longevity.

"**Stage 2: Long term** takes care of the other cause of your ailments – nutritional deficiencies – and lasts the rest of your life. There will be bimonthly nutrition workshops over the next several months on the following general topics:

- Workshop 1: *Understanding the acidity of the blood.* Here we discuss how the acid level (the pH) of the blood determines overall health.
- Workshop 2: *Developing a preventative chemotherapy.* The main objective here is, using supplements, to avoid chronic degenerative diseases (such as cancer, arthritis, and heart disease), as well as to bolster the immune system and increase energy levels. There will be lessons to learn that you can take home and apply with your children because they too are becoming sick with these chronic diseases, once thought to be the diseases of old age.

Stage 1

A happy gut, at last!
As Dr. Sagesse started discussing the HAP, she passed me a list of the ailments that constituted her objective-oriented approach to medicine.

- Constipation and piles
- Acid reflux (heartburn)
- Chronic fatigue
- Chronic yeast infections
- Irritable bowel syndrome
- Memory issues
- Alopecia (hair falling out)
- Anemia (low red blood count).

She started calmly. "Isabelle, here is a list of ailments that have been bothering you and they are all, directly or indirectly, due to the foods you have been eating. In nutritional circles, your choices of foods are collectively known as the standard American diet, or SAD[2] for short.

"That is, when you consume essentially only red meat, highly processed foods with little nutritional value – you know, the white flour (in the breads, muffins, and cupcakes), the white sugar (in fast foods, colas, and table sugar), aspartame, margarine, monosodium glutamate (MSG), the antibiotics, pesticides, refined syrups and sugars – all these act like poisons to your system and account for your ailment list. So, to heal the system, simply get rid of them, if you can. Something like aspartame[3] is contained in over 5,000 products including sugary 'lite' drinks and infant medication. Moreover, your diet over the past several years has potentially set you up for cancer, as we have seen already with your colonic polyps, but also *all* sorts of other cancers that are related to your diet."

Dr. Sagesse spoke with such conviction, yet I couldn't believe what I was hearing. In fact, I had grown completely resigned to being tired all the time, taking medications like laxatives, antacids and antispasmotics for the rest of my life. Now I had a second chance to get it right, to push the reset button on my life.

"Doctor, I have had some of these ailments since I was a child. I have always, for example, had trouble with constipation. Are you saying that I won't have to take medications just to go to the toilet. Seems too good to be true!"

"Of course, Isabelle, you can be cured of all these ailments, but I need you to meet me half way and start with me the healing process."

"Given the fact that you are still alive, just missing a brush with colon cancer, I believe that it is in your best interest (that's a 'first') to start in stages. Therefore, for the next month or so, I have a simple strategy to get you back into the fighting shape you deserve. But please don't ask me for a draconian diet: there are plenty of those out there already. In this world, we have enough 'Dos' and 'Don'ts' and enough restrictions of every type. Where is the pleasure in nourishing the body and mind?

"Here is the HAP to maintain optimal health and performance, with pleasure and enjoyment as the keystones of your HAP. Otherwise, you will drop it. I shall schedule an appointment with you for next month to see what progress we have made; in the interim, feel free to call any time."

As Dr. Sagesse passed me the list of her recommendations for Superfoods and supplements (see Appendix I), I felt a sense of excitement, as no one, in the US or Europe, had taken the time with me to discuss a "cure" to my myriad of complaints, especially using the collective term "we" in discussing the whole process of "cure."

Short-term HAP for a happy gut
Sauna or hamman every other day
As the skin is the body's largest organ and a natural purifier, many of your toxins leave via the sweat. For just 15 minutes in a sauna of 40 °C (120 °F), drink 1 L of fresh water. Do not exceed recommended times or your dehydration will only worsen, and do *not* drink alcohol for at least an hour afterwards. We can recommend a home-based mini-sauna adaptable for any shower by Hoesch Design, which is the size of a small printer and is quite cost beneficial.

The big clean-out

Start with a fruit fast (at home) to clean out the intestines of all the residual toxins. Take just juices (use your juicer for the real effect) and fresh and dried fruits, which are full of antioxidants (especially prunes, raisins, blueberries, cranberries, and strawberries) *all* day during a weekend day.

How does this help? Quite simply, the benefit comes from the combination of antioxidants (from the fruits) *plus* the "bottle-brush" effect of the high-fiber fruits *plus* the calorie restriction, which results in the suppression or elimination of disease-causing free radicals and inflammation.

Continue with four servings of fruit and vegetables *per day*. This will help to get more vitamin C[4] (ascorbic acid/calcium ascorbate) into your system.

Fat intake: essential fatty acids (EFAs)

These are found naturally in salmon, trout, mackerel, sardines, and Chinese water snake oil (EPA/DHA), or can be taken in supplements: one tablespoon per day of hempseed oil with soups or salads. AND NO MARGARINE!

Liquid intake

Have fresh water and only green or black teas and a glass of wine per day. No coffee.

Protein intake

Six servings a day of *any* combination of these:

- Yoghurt:[5] without sugar, home-made.
- Eggs: organic, one or two a day.
- Legumes: kidney beans, lentils, chick peas (humus is excellent), and tofu.

No sugar, caffeine, cigarettes, fast food or distilled spirits

Then, come off all forms of aspartame, meaning anything "diet" or "light," and MSG.[6]

Developing a Supernutrition for the whole family's vitality and long life

As I sat waiting for Dr. Sagesse, I gazed around her office. I noticed a small sign behind her desk, just above a photo of three smiling children. It read:

> There can be no keener revelation of a society's soul than the way in which it treats its children.
>
> **Nelson Mandela**

"Those are my grandchildren: my pride and joy. Isabelle, I am sure that as a mother, perhaps someday a grandmother, you are concerned about *your* children. You must be wondering if Geoff and Sophie have the same ailments that you have struggled with. After all, they are living in the same house. You may want to know:

- Are they getting what they need for proper development?
- Are they getting poisoned as well?

- Are they as set up for heart disease, cancer, and diabetes?
- Do they have the foods for high energy levels and longevity?
- Are their brains getting what they need to function optimally?

I replied enthusiastically, "Well, Dr. Sagesse, I am delighted that you even asked about them. Sophie had it in her head to be a top model for a while, which meant a flat tummy, of course. To achieve this feat, she used heavy-duty chemical laxatives to clean out. She got her flat tummy but at what a price: constant belly pain, irregularity in her bowel movements (she often uses the toilet only once every week or so!).

"As for Geoff, he drinks coffee like water and has digestive issues as well, like belly pain, appendicitis, and constipation. They seemed to have inherited my intestines. Moreover, both of them lack the energy they need to get through the day. So they consume loads and loads of caffeine snacks, sugar drinks (some 'diet') and power drinks. They are on the same path to developing the same problems that I have, and I am at my wit's end with them. Frankly, I have not been a good example for them."

Dr. Sagesse was very helpful and encouraging. "They are as hypnotised as much as the rest of our culture. Eating is as much a fashion statement as clothes were for us. For now, have them avoid *anything* with:

1. sucrose (table sugar);
2. high-fructose[7] corn syrup (a common fattening sugar, found especially in soft drinks, power drinks, and commercial juices);
3. caffeine;
4. aspartame: the fake sugar.

"Just stock up on those foods that we call Superfoods (see Appendix I) and start slowly with them. Don't traumatize Geoff and Sophie into your nutritional world. They will reject it. Just do your HAP, just discussed, and they will see your improvement and get into it themselves. When it comes to children, whether you are talking about nutrition, exercise, mind control or whatever, always lead by example. Get over the delusion that your children actually listen to you. They don't really listen, they just pay lip service, and that's probably appropriate, as they have to learn to decide for themselves using all sources of information. Children will follow their parents almost blindly up to a certain point of maturation and then will follow their parents' advice if, and only if, it is wrapped in respect."

Just prior to departing, Dr. Sagesse passed me a monograph entitled *Tips on Preparing Meals* (see Appendix I), which came as a relief to me as I had an avalanche of queries based on how to implement her suggestions at home for the children.

I was a bit overwhelmed by the whole notion of being poisoned by my foods, and I asked Dr. Sagesse what her plans were for the follow-up visit in 6 weeks' time: "Once we discuss what kind of progress we are making against these ailments and I check the results of the purification in your blood work, then we take it to the second stage with a more advanced HAP."

Just before our appointment ended, I asked Dr. Sagesse, "Do you treat *all* your patients like this, with this degree of compassion and thoroughness?"

"When I look at you," she replied, "I don't see just one person: I see a mother, a wife, a friend, a colleague, all connected to our community through service and mutual respect. The proof that this is indeed the case is what happens when a parent, for example, falls ill. It's not just the individual that is affected, it's the whole networked community that feels the loss, the pain. So, I approach my medical practice with the same attitude: I don't just treat the patients but their family and friends as well."

Stage 2

After 6 weeks, I felt re-energized, in great moods (very light feeling), and "regular" (no constipation), as I had never been before. I had nicer hair and nails, and zero "heartburn." I was ready for stage 2.

Workshop 1: The acid–base balance of the blood
Dr. Sagesse started out her morning session, as she usually does, standing in front of the class. "The human body is involved, as we speak, in literally thousands of biochemical reactions. To perform optimally and avoid degenerative diseases, we use foods and the kidneys to maintain an optimal pH of 7.2, which is slightly alkaline. That is, the range of pH is 0–14; pH 0–7 is called acidic, with neutral set at 7, and between 7 is 14 called alkaline or basic.

"To understand this is absolutely critical to your health and wellbeing. Your body will store excess acid in your fat cells (one reason why so many people have trouble losing body fat). Over time, your body will 'borrow' calcium and alkaline stores from your bones in a desperate attempt to retain the pH balance in your body (which is why some people 'shrink' as they get older).

TIP The pH scale goes from 0 to 14 and is logarithmic, which means that each step is 10 times the previous one. In other words, a pH of 4.5 is 10 times more acid than 5.5, 100 times more acid than 6.5 and 1,000 times more acid than 7.5.

"Unfortunately, several aspects of modern life, including an excessive intake of sugars and animal protein, excessive exercise, and uncompensated stresses create a more *acidic* (low pH) level, and the extra acid is excreted in the urine. You can actually detect your overall acidity level and should do this frequently to see how acidic you are: acid (disease) or slightly alkaline (health).

Testing your urine: time to play doctor!
To do this, you will need to buy pH paper. You can do this online by typing the reference on your search engine: "PH TEST TAPE."

Healthful body pH range = 6.2–7.3

< 5	5.5	6	6.5	7	7.5	8	8.5	> 9
	Acid			Neutral			Alkaline (basic)	

Some of the problems associated with excessive acidity that are alleviated by correcting blood pH include:

- increased free radical formation, leading to degenerative diseases;
- disturbed sleep patterns: fatigue, especially in the middle of the day;
- feelings of profound exhaustion: a "washed up" feeling;
- immune deficiency: frequent infections or colds;
- less "friendly" bacteria in the intestines: bloating and flatulence;
- easily stressed: unprovoked irritability or "edginess;"
- hair/nail disorders;
- severe headaches;
- mouth and stomach ulcers;
- inflamed, sensitive gums, and cracks at the corners of the lips.

"Once you have learned to adjust your body's pH, you will have *none* of the above problems. You will have cured yourself, by yourself and understand why."

As Dr. Sagesse spoke, she took a paper strip and dipped it into a beaker of liquid. "You see, my blood pH is 6.3, which is ideal for the morning, and if I were to test it this evening, after the daytime, it would be in the area of 7.3. I use my foods, both acidic and alkaline, to produce the desired effect on my blood and urine, but also the desired effect on my overall performance. It is very simple, just use this guide to adjust the pH of your urine," she said as she handed out the fact sheet on food pH (Table 2.1).

As I looked it over, she mentioned, "You will notice, Isabelle, that a food's ability to create an acid or alkaline milieu in the body has nothing to do with the food's pH itself. Take citrus fruits, for example, like oranges and limes, which are, by themselves, very acidic. However, the end-products they produce after digestion are alkaline so they are considered alkaline-forming in the body. The converse is true of meat, which will test alkaline before digestion, *but* it leaves acidic residues in the body so, like nearly all animal products, meat is classified as acid-forming."

TABLE 2.1 *Fact sheet on food pH*

ACIDIC FOODS (IDEAL = 20%)	ALKALINE (BASIC) FOODS (IDEAL = 80%)
Vegetable protein	ALL vegetables
Pickled vegetables, pinto beans, navy beans	Vegetable juices, parsley, raw spinach, broccoli, celery, garlic, barley grass, carrots, green beans, lima beans, beets, lettuce, zucchini, carob, squash, asparagus, tomato, rhubarb, fresh corn, mushrooms, onions, cabbage, peas, cauliflower, turnip, beetroot, potato, olives, soybeans, tofu, sweet potato, cooked spinach, kidney beans, sprouted seeds
Dairy	
Parmesan, processed cheese	Soy cheese, soy milk, goat's milk, goat's cheese, buttermilk, whey

ACIDIC FOODS (IDEAL = 20%)	ALKALINE (BASIC) FOODS (IDEAL = 80%)
Artificial sweeteners	Apple cider vinegar
Carbohydrates	
White rice, white bread, pastries, biscuits, pasta	Rye bread, wholegrain bread, oats, brown rice
Fruit	
Canned fruit	Coconut, sour cherries, oranges, cherries, pineapple, peaches, avocados, dates, blackcurrants, grapes, papaya, kiwis, berries, apples, pears, grapefruit, mangoes, strawberries, dried figs, raisins, lemons, watermelon, limes
Drinks	
Wine, soda/pop, tea (black), coffee, beer, distilled liquor	Green tea, herb teas, lemon water
Animal protein	
Fish, turkey, chicken, lamb, liver, oysters, organ meat, beef, pork, veal, shellfish, canned tuna, sardines	
Nuts and seeds	
Peanuts, walnuts	Hazelnuts, almonds
Other	
	Supplements: calcium and magnesium, vitamins A and D, vegetable juices (carrot, celery, and beet) and lemon/honey/ginger drink

Important notes on the fact sheet

- For optimal health and vitality, the alkaline or basic (pH > 7) foods should *dominate* your nutrition: you can do this by eating vegetables at every meal. That will buffer the acidic foods.
- Fruit juices become more acid-producing when processed and especially when sweetened.
- Develop an alkaline reserve to anticipate the effect of modern stresses, particularly if you are attracted to protein, animal or vegetable, dairy or sweets.
- For daily maintenance, weight loss and pH balancing, try sipping the following mixture gently: 2 teaspoons of organic apple cider vinegar in 500 mL of water (warm or cool, sparkling or still).

After a brief break, during which nearly everyone in the workshop had taken a bit of the litmus paper to the rest rooms to test their urinary pH, and as the commotion settled down, Dr. Sagesse wrote up on the blackboard Yeats' sonnet "Why Wine is so Good for the Human Being." Once she finished reciting Yeats' classic poem, she looked up to a sea of raised hands. The questions started flying quickly.

TIP If you are a non-drinker, you can get the same (and better!) benefits as wine by eating dark grapes, especially the grape seeds.

Why is wine unique and great?

Even with the proviso that alcohol (wine is roughly 14% alcohol) in excess leads to disease and death, medical research is replete with studies that enthusiastically support the link between a moderate (and regular) consumption of wine and the prevention of various diseases, most notably:

- *Coronary artery disease.* Scores of well-designed studies have demonstrated time and time again the protective effect of moderate red wine consumption against heart attacks, particularly in countries like France, where there is also a high consumption of animal fats. In the UK, for example, recent studies have demonstrated that moderate red wine drinking could reduce the incidence of coronary artery disease by half! What is the mechanism of this natural magic? Wine decreases stress, makes platelets less sticky (although the effect is short-lived – 24–48 hours – so regular wine is better), increases the protective high-density lipoprotein (HDL; see Chapter 1), and makes the body more insulin sensitive (hence, lower triglycerides [TGs] and higher HDL).

- *Strokes.* Strokes account for a significant health burden worldwide. While two to three glasses per day of red wine reduce the risk of stroke, more than five to six glasses per day would actually increase the risk of cerebral hemorrhage due to the combined effects of increased blood pressure and less sticky blood.

- *Diabetes mellitus.* This disease afflicts more than 125 million people worldwide and can be easily treated with diet and low-grade exercise. Grapes have a much lower glycemic index (see Chapter 1), or GI (66), than the sugar in beer (maltose = 150), and therefore will not cause the insulin surging that could lead to central obesity and, in turn, diabetes.

- *Osteoporosis.* Studies have shown that grape skins contain a natural estrogen-like chemical, called resveratrol, that not only keeps the platelets from forming a clot and reduces inflammation, but may act to make bones more massive and less prone to fractures. Moreover, as estrogen positively affects the HDL cholesterol and keeps artery linings smooth, this may help to explain yet another protective aspect of red wines.

- *Cancer.* The oxidative process that plays such a critical role in cancer development is blocked by the antioxidants (resveratrol) in red wine. In October 2008, an article appeared in the journal of the American Association for Cancer Research to report on a study of 84,170 men aged 45–69. Researchers measured the effects of beer, red wine, white wine, and distilled spririts to gauge the risk on lung cancer. The result was that researchers reported a 60% reduction in lung cancer risk in men who drank two glasses of red wine per day. There was no clear effect of beer, white wine or spirits.

Wine is constant proof that God loves us and loves to see us happy.

Benjamin Franklin

Is alcohol protector or poison?

Since *Homo sapiens* stood erect and developed the consciousness of himself as an isolated being, he has reserved the right to find ways to promote the kind of commonality that originally held together primitive tribal communities. In his search for this transcendence, he has discovered all sorts of substances (and ways to use them) to shift his awareness away from his aloneness. In fact, some ethnopharmacology anthropology researchers make very convincing arguments that the entire history of humankind throughout the ages has really been one of (clumsily at first, then with increasing efficiency and refinement) finding "cultural allies" or products that help to capture that eternal moment of commonality experienced by all of our ancestors while discussing, laughing, and dancing around the campfire and intermittently gazing up at the stars.

If I have a body fat of 28%, a TG level of 2.50 g/L, and an HDL of 0.35 g/L, should I have the occasional glass of red wine or not?
Get body fat into the 15% range by walking after meals for 15 minutes, and avoid all high-GI foods, while taking one glass of red wine slowly in the evenings for a month. Re-check your lab tests (total cholesterol, TGs, and HDL) – you will be pleasantly surprised. Adjust the red wine intake according to the results, not exceeding three glasses per day (more alcohol than that may actually increase the TGs).

Which red wines are best?
The best reds are those that have had the chance to soak in the skin of the grape. The powerful chemicals known as antioxidants reside in the skin, doing their job for the grape of protecting it from its own natural enemies: UV rays and fungi. There is an abundance (up to 100) of antioxidants in red wine (a far more plentiful source than white wine, in which the skin is discarded during the fermentation process), though the levels will vary with the grape and the year. Several rules of thumb hold for the reds. To get the best antioxidant concentrations, keep an eye out for the following:

- *The age of the wine.* Wait for the grape skin to soak in the wine for a year, or preferably 5 years.
- *The kind of grape (the cépage).* The thicker the skin, the more the antioxidant load, hence the better for the health. Go for Merlot grape wines (found in St. Emilion, Pomerol, and Médoc wines), Cabernet Sauvignon (blended with Merlot for Pomerol and Médoc, and Chilean wines), Syrah (found in Côte-Rôtie and Australian Shiraz wines), and Sangiovese (found in Italian Chianti wine).
- *Humidity.* Wines grown in the humid regions, such as Burgundy, have developed natural antioxidant defenses against fungal attacks.
- *Temperature.* Grapes grown where they need more protection from the UV rays (hotter climates such as Chile, Portugal, southern France, Australia, and California) will naturally develop more natural antioxidant defenses that they can pass on to you. In particular, the antioxidant phenols (catechin and quercetin) are thought to have the ability to bind and eliminate (chelate) pro-oxidant metals that would otherwise be clogging your arteries.

> It is well to remember that there are five reasons for drinking:
> the arrival of a friend, one's present or future thirst, the excellence of the
> wine, or any other reason.

In sum, it appears that the best drinking pattern is daily red wine consumption with meals. Red wine used in this way should be part of any therapy against the insidious diseases that plague us.

Workshop 2: Preventative chemotherapy – avoiding cancer with supplements
Dr. Sagesse wrote the workshop title on the blackboard, following by a most provacative subtitle:

Cheap health insurance or expensive urine?

She started, "As more than 70% of human cancers are related to our nutrition,[8] it would be wise to develop a strategy of preventative chemotherapy. This stands to reason, as there are four general 'filters' in the human body that must be maintained and cleansed from time to time:

- the *digestive system*: filters the foods we eat for our body's energy needs;
- the *kidneys*: filter the blood;
- the *brain*: filters our experiences;
- the *lungs*: filter the air, for the body's oxygen needs."

The immune system as a radar system
The problem of premature aging and disease is an uncontrolled oxidative process. The oxidative process has been described by molecular biologists as an integral element of a unifying theory of health. This theory incriminates oxygen-induced compounds known as free radicals as causative agents in seemingly unrelated degenerative diseases such as heart disease, cancers, autoimmune diseases, diabetes, arthritis, and premature aging.

So, what are free radicals? They are a molecular fragment with an unpaired electron. In the human situation, all but 95% of free radical load is taken care of by the natural antioxidants of the body's defenses (assuming, of course, that the immune system – like a radar system – is functioning normally, unaffected by stress, malnutrition or disease states). The remaining 5% of free radicals escape "capture" and damage the cells of the body at the molecular level, eroding the body's natural defenses and increasing our susceptibility to degenerative diseases, such as heart disease, diabetes, and cancers.

Although millions of free radicals are produced as the normal metabolic and chemical processes take place every day, there are two ways in which we can decrease their negative effects:

1. avoiding generating new free radicals (sources of free radicals include UV radiation and pollution – including cigarette smoke and frying, especially deep-frying, foods);

2. taking in our nutrition the critical elements (the antioxidants) that can scavenge those free radicals that escape the body's normal defenses.

Antioxidants benefit the health in a number of different ways:

■ They stabilize the destruction of cells through neutralization of the free radicals that initiate and promote tumor growth.
■ Substantial data from animal and human research models suggest that antioxidants block the process of arteriosclerosis (by blocking the oxidation of low-density lipoprotein [LDL] cholesterol, an important step in plaque build-up in the cells of the arteries, eventually leading to heart attacks and strokes). These powerful allies in health work by blocking this detrimental process of oxidation.
■ Compelling evidence indicates that a diet low in antioxidants (e.g., vitamins C, A, and E, beta-carotene, and selenium) increases the probability of developing cancers such as lung, breast, and prostate. The protective mechanism involves blocking free radicals and polycyclic aromatic hydrocarbons from damaging DNA.

So, to avoid inviting cancer into your life, increase your internal resistance by:

■ getting more active – disease hates moving targets!;
■ optimizing body fat (< 20% for men and < 23% women) – walk away from cancer;
■ sleeping – pay all REM (rapid eye movement sleep) debts this month;
■ mind control – accepting the delivery of only positive thoughts;
■ controlling negativism in your life – laugh heartily every day;
■ getting plenty of sunshine.

Decrease oxidative stress by eliminating external carcinogens:

■ No cigarettes
■ No fried foods
■ No sugars.

Get checked out from time to time:

■ testicles and prostate for men;
■ breast, cervix, and ovaries for women.

And get some help from supplements (see Appendix I).

6 MONTHS LATER AND BEYOND … BUILDING ON YOUR PROGRESS

After 4 weeks on the Supernutrition diet, I was much closer to my former self than in recent memory, and my health figures reflected that:

Isabelle's second health and fitness report

	NORMAL/IDEAL RANGE	1st chance MY 1ST CHECK-UP	2nd chance MY 2ND CHECK-UP
Actual age (years)		39	39
Health age (years)	Actual age or less	51.6	34.7
Blood pressure (mmHg)	< 135/85	110/72	100/65
Resting heart rate (beats/minute)	< 60	88	54
Weight (kg)		65	58
Body fat %	15–23%	28%	23%
Body fat weight (kg)		18.2	13.3
Lean weight (kg)		46.8	44.7
Waist-to-hip ratio	< 0.80	0.95	0.89
Hematology (blood cells)			
Erythrocytes (red blood cells) (/mm³)	4,500,000–5,500,000	3,900,000	4,900,000
Hemoglobin (gram %)	12.9–17.5	11.2	15.8
Hematocrit (% blood occupied by red cells)	40–50%	38%	45%
Mean corpuscular volume (µm³)	80–95	76	90
Platelets (clot-formers) (/mm³)	150,000–400,000	350,000	342,000
Leukocyte family (white blood cells) (/mm³)	4,000–10,000	14,000	5,900
Neutrophils (/mm³)	2,000–7,500	6,700	2,700
Eosinophils (/mm³)	< 800	950	350
Lymphocytes (/mm³)	1,500–4,000	4,500	2,400
Monocytes (/mm³)	< 1000	900	450
Liver function tests			
SGOT (aka AST) (U/L)	9–38	58	15
SGPT (aka ALT) (U/L)	0–41	62	13
GGT (U/L)	0–61	75	23

Looking over my test results, after only several weeks of diet changes and supplements, I could barely contain myself and my relief was immense. I was ready to take all this a step further.

Stage 2 HAP

Updated HAP for the new millenium:

1. Off red meat altogether.
2. Only red wine and organic apple cider[9] as fermented beverages.
3. Something sweet you crave: choose fresh fruit or black chocolate.[10]
4. Fried foods phased out *completely*.
5. Continue with Supernutrition (see Appendix I).
6. Fast[11] once a month.
7. Avoid *permanently* all "toxins": go organic.
8. Continue EFAs (omega-3/-6 oils):
    - Flaxseed oil: 2–3 g/day;
    - Hempseed oil: in soups, and on salads daily: 1 tablespoon per day.
9. Supplements for health and longevity:
    - vitamin C;
    - Co-Enzyme-Q10;
    - blue–green algae (aka spirulina);
    - apple cider vinegar.

> **TIP** The battle for optimal health is happening at the cellular level every second of every day!

CLOSING WORDS FROM A LEADER

Life for any manager in the international arena is challenging, and doubly so for a woman. We are charged with our corporate responsibilities, but also have the time-honored responsibility for *all* aspects of the family as well. Out of necessity and ambition, more and more women are working at top managerial levels, complete with the stresses that go with it. The implications are that, if we take the lead ourselves, the family will follow.

After many years of struggling with my diet and nutrition and a multitude of ailments, I feel that, for once in my life, I have gained control of my body and my life, becoming a true leader. I am very grateful for a multitude of "second chances" that have been accorded me. I could have become just another statistic in the annals of medicine, just another colleague who succumbed to a common group of what Dr. Sagesse called "modern diseases of prosperity."

Like any true leader, I have no intention of forgetting hard-learned lessons. One last word: after having a real brush with colon cancer, I am absolutely convinced that, together with excellent and evolving science and a purified lifestyle (including mental health), we, as a culture, can beat this cancer epidemic.

It is often cited that roughly one in three people in industrialized countries will be diagnosed with cancer, usually at a young age. I found myself on the wrong side of that nasty statistic several years ago. That was not bad luck or bad karma; that was, pure and simple, bad management of my nutrition. In most cancer studies, a full 80% of common cancers (lung, colon, prostate, and breast) are lifestyle related, not genetic. That means that the vast majority of cancers in industrialized countries could be avoided by five simple measures:

1. *Diet and exercise.* 40% of cancers could be avoided by eating more fruit and vegetables, less red meat, less sugar, fewer additives, and less fake food.
2. *Superfoods to protect us.* The stars here are broccoli, onions, garlic, yoghurt, spinach, green tea, and turmeric spice to snuff out cancer cells while they are still vulnerable.
3. *Smoking cessation.* Another 30% or more of cancers, not just lung cancers, can be avoided.
4. *Moderate alcohol.* 12% of cancers can be avoided.
5. *Fewer toxins in our environment.* This would reduce the carcinogenic load even further (see footnote 1):
   – aspartame: a neurotoxic "sweetener;"
   – alkylphenols in cleaning products;
   – phthalates and parabenes in cosmetics and shampoos;
   – bisphenol A: from microwave heating of liquids in plastic containers;
   – pesticides, heavy metals, polychlorinated biphenyls, benzenes, and estrogen-like chemicals in plastics.

Moreover, the adopted children of parents who died of cancer before age 50 had the *same cancer risk as their adoptive parents*, not their *biological* ones. This astounding fact implies that we, as parents, pass on to our progeny cancer-causing lifestyles. Yet less than 10% of research funding goes into determining the causative factors (nutrition, stress, and low activity). Cancer is not some genetic flip of the coin; it is the failure to recognise the role lifestyle plays in combating this scourge.

I have included a complete nutritional guide in Appendix I to assist all future and present leaders. Just remember the key rule to progress:

Quantify to improve

LEADERS' TOP FAQS ON HUMAN NUTRITION FOR ENERGY AND SUCCESS

What causes heartburn (stomach acidity refluxing into the esophagus)?

Consuming mints, chocolate, and alcohol, wearing tight-fitting clothes, and lying down within an hour of your meal.

What are the health benefits of chocolate?[10]

Black chocolate (the best is 70% pure cocoa) has very high amounts of antioxidants known as flavonoids, natural antioxidants found also in fruit, vegetables, tea, and wine. Recent studies have yielded the following delightful results:

- Researchers found that a few pieces of black chocolate every month might make your life both sweeter and longer. The researchers studied the chocolate-consuming habits of more than 7,800 men. Those who ate chocolate one to three times a month lived longest. Those who indulged three or more times a week died earlier. Those who ate no chocolate at all died the earliest – up to a year earlier.

- Chocolate has four times more flavonoids than black tea and a glass of red wine. This means that black chocolate can thin your blood, like red wine or aspirin.
- Chocolate's antioxidants have positive effects on cholesterol levels. Those who ate regular chocolate had their HDL levels go up by 11.4%. Black chocolate was even better, producing a rise of 13.7%. LDL oxidation was also reduced (see the role of LDL as "glue" in Chapter 1).
- Chocolate helps you keep your arteries flexible. Chocolate increases the release of nitric oxide, which relaxes the smooth muscles in blood vessels. This allows increased blood flow and has positive effects on blood pressure and libido.
- High-fat/low-sugar content black chocolate has higher proportions of cocoa and more heart-healthy flavonoids.
- Conversely, chocolate with a high sugar/full-fat milk chocolate or white chocolate content can adversely elevate insulin and blood sugar levels, and body fat. It effectively negates the benefits from flavonoids.

I have heard that fructose, the natural sugar in fruit, is actually harmful to the health. Is this true?

Fructose, as it appears in fruit, is fine because you are getting fiber and water in the deal, both very important in maintaining optimal intestinal health. The problems arise when it becomes highly concentrated and ubiquitous, such as high-fructose corn syrup (HFCS). HFCS is one of *the* sweeteners for food manufacturers because it is cheaper, sweeter, and easier to blend into beverages than other sugars. It is the primary ingredient in all non-diet drinks marketed as "healthy" alternatives, as well as in most health bars.

Here is what the recent research concludes:

- *HFCS is directly linked to abdominal obesity*, according to a study in the *American Journal of Clinical Nutrition*. The researchers report that body weights in America rose *slowly* for most of the 20th century until the late 1980s. At that time, the rate of obesity and related health problems *surged*.[12]
- *HFCS also spikes blood TGs, increasing risk of heart disease*. The United States Department of Agriculture has implicated HFCS in heart abnormalities. Rats normally live for about 2 years. However, when fed a high-fructose diet, they died after 5 weeks. Researchers abruptly stopped one of the few human studies of high-fructose diets when four of the 24 subjects developed heart abnormalities.[13]
- *HFCS alters the hormones involved in appetite regulation*. The hormone leptin lets you know that you have eaten enough. A study in the June 2004 issue of the *Journal of Clinical Endocrinology and Metabolism* found that a drink with fructose equivalent to that in two cans of sugary soda caused low levels

of leptin. This in turn causes high levels of ghrelin, a hormone that stimulates eating. The net result is that your hormones tell you to keep eating.[14]

- *HFCS diets cause diabetes.* Fructose reduces stores of chromium, essential for normal insulin function. HFCS can also damage the liver. Your liver is the only part of your body that can metabolize fructose. Animals fed large amounts of HFCS develop fatty livers, cirrhosis, and alcoholic-like liver damage.[15]

What are some of the benefits of tea: green and black?

Green tea contains an antioxidant called EGCG (epigallocatechin-3-gallate), which protects the brain from premature aging, even more effectively than resveratrol and vitamin E. Numerous studies have found drinking black tea to be associated with a lower incidence of heart disease and cancer. Moreover, EGCG attacks cancer cells, particularly in the prostate, bladder, esophagus, lung, stomach, large intestine, and skin.[16] The positive data from the studies just keep pouring in:

- One such study, linking tea with less ovarian cancer, followed more than 61,000 Swedish middle-aged and older women for about 15 years. Those who drank at least two daily cups of tea had the lowest rates of this cancer, but even one cup a day decreased a woman's risk by 25%. The lowered risk appeared even after adjustments were made for factors influencing ovarian cancer risk, like a woman's weight, age, past pregnancies, and consumption of calories, fruits, vegetables, and alcohol.
- An earlier study in China compared women with ovarian cancer to a group of healthy women. Daily tea drinkers were 60% less likely to develop this type of cancer, and those who had drunk tea for more than 30 years had a more than 75% lower risk. Black or oolong tea seemed as protective as green tea, but since this study took place in China, more than 90% of the tea drinkers chose green tea.
- In one Chinese study, women with ovarian cancer who drank at least a cup of green tea daily were more than twice as likely to survive as non-tea drinkers.

What is the impact of meat-eating on the ecology?

The winner of the Stockholm Water Prize 2008, Dr. John Allan of King's College, London, said flat out that meat was bad for the environment. "Non-vegetarians consume 5 cubic meters of water per day. Your bath is a tiny puddle compared to that. It is the water for food that is the big problem. Be rational and eat less meat."

Nothing will benefit human health and increase the chances for survival of life on Earth as much as the evolution to a vegetarian diet.

Albert Einstein

What are some of the health benefits of saunas?

Increasing numbers of medical clinics use supervised sauna bathing for detoxifying the body of toxic chemicals. Here is list of direct quotes from referenced benefits:

- "The principle is summed up as follows: The body's fat must be warmed to increase its solubility; the warmed fat must be transported to the sweat glands which excrete fat; the process must continue long enough for appreciable 'fat sweat' to occur; the temperature must be low enough that the person does not lose significant amounts of water or electrolytes; the sweat must be vigorously washed off. Using this method, doctors have been able to measure toxic compounds released in the sweat of their patients. These chemicals are often toxic to the immune system, nervous system, endocrine system, and liver. 'Sweating it out' reduces chemical stress on the body and generally leads to improved health."[17]

- "Fourteen firemen exposed to polychlorinated byphenyls (PCB's) and their by-products generated in a transformer fire and explosion had neurophysiological and neuropsychological tests six months after the fire. They were restudied six weeks later after undergoing two to three weeks of an experimental detoxification program consisting of medically supervised diet, exercise, and sauna. Retesting following the detoxification program showed significantly improved scores on three memory tests, block design, and identifying figures."[18]

- "Concentrations of zinc, copper, iron, nickel, cadmium, lead, manganese, sodium, and chloride were determined after collections utilizing a total body washdown technique (sweating in sauna). The concentrations of nickel and cadmium in sweat were higher than those reported for urine, and similar for lead. The loss of non-essential or toxic trace metals in sweat could be of toxicologic and therapeutic importance."[19]

- "A recent study on 200 participants of sauna therapy revealed blood chemistry changes consistent with the detoxification process. Lab analysis included elevated liver enzymes, as well as decreased glucose, cholesterol, and triglyceride levels. Patients often experience general health improvements upon completion, such as increased mental clarity, restored energy levels, fewer allergies, improved sleeping patterns, and lowered blood pressure. Released toxins are then eliminated from the body by perspiration and through the intestinal tract."[20]

- "Despite best efforts, large human populations are at times exposed to toxic chemicals. When these chemicals are lipid soluble and do not metabolize easily, they accumulate in the body and may present a health risk for the individuals' entire life. Reduction of chemical body burdens is one goal of treatment for the chemically exposed. Other goals include remission of reversible physiological and behavioral effects associated with chemical exposure. We present the results of treatment in a controlled study of electrical workers with HCB and other chlorinated chemical body burdens. In addition, we summarize other research on body-burden reduction using the Hubbard method of sauna therapy. Previous work showed that persistent body burdens could be significantly reduced. Adipose tissue concentrations of hexachlorbenzene (HCB), four other pesticides, and ten polychlorinated biphenyl congeners were significantly reduced by enhanced mobilization and excretion through the method of daily treatment for 3 weeks, consisting of heat stress (sauna therapy), niacin administration, and polyunsaturated oil, with other components to provide protection from mobilized chemicals.

"All 16 target chemicals were found at quantifiable levels in adipose tissue of all participants. At post-treatment, all 16 chemicals were found at lower concentrations in the adipose tissue of the treatment group, but 11 were higher in the control group.

"HCB body burdens were reduced by 30% at post-treatment and 28% at 3 month post-treatment. Enhanced excretion appeared to keep pace with mobilization. Reductions in chemical body burdens after this treatment method had been confirmed earlier for chlorinated pesticides and polyhalogenated biphenyls. In 1983, large reductions were reported in patients exposed to pesticides and polychlorinated biphenyls and a continued reduction over a 9-month period in the absence of any other treatment."[21]

We enjoy the occasional fried dishes (fish and chips). What are the best oils to do this in?

The excessively high heat that comes with frying is one way to introduce billions of dangerous free radicals into the body, particularly for the refined healthful oils (EFAs and polyunsaturated oils). In fact, saturated fats (like butter), although less healthful in general, are more stable against high temperatures, which brings us back to the French paradox once again. Alternatively, do as the traditional Chinese do and start by adding a bit of water into the pan or with the vegetables before adding the oil, which should be the more stable monounsaturated sort (olive) or tropical oils – coconut, palm, or cocoa butter – peanut or sesame.

I have had in the gas in the gut for ages. What should I do?

You're not alone, as this is a very common problem. Gas in the gut will definitely not kill you, unless you work in a submarine, but it will make your life miserable ... and it's really very easy to take care of.

Think of the causes. Remember that the air you breathe right now has a fairly standard composition: about 70% nitrogen, 20% oxygen, and 10% carbon dioxide and hydrogen. Gas in the gut comes either from swallowed ambient air (60% of cases) or from production in the gut (40%). If you swallow air, because you bolt your food or chew gum, the oxygen is reabsorbed but the nitrogen is expelled as flatus. The key in that case is to slow down your eating.

Interestingly, the combination of the acid from the stomach (hydrochloric acid) and bicarbonate from the small intestine and pancreas is one of the sources of intestinal gas (carbon dioxide). During a meal, 75 milliequivalents of acid from the stomach may react with 75 milliequivalents of bicarbonate from the pancreas generating 1875 cm^3 of carbon dioxide into the small intestine. While most of the gas diffuses back into the blood, some remains to add to the intestine's gas load to be expelled later on.

More commonly and more abundantly, gas comes from fermentation by bacteria in the large intestine (colon) of unabsorbed foods (like the hulls of beans or milk sugar lactose) to hydrogen and methane, both of which are combustible. In that case, watch injudicious mixtures of foods, particularly proteins and starches, and soak the beans.

What about a vegetarian diet?

According to the Worldwatch Institute, to produce a pound of feedlot steak costs the world 2 kg of grains, about 10,000 L of water, 4 L of gasoline, and 15 kg of eroded topsoil. To make more grazing land for cattle, the tropical rain forest, a vital source of oxygen and a treasure trove of natural medicines for man, is destroyed at the rate of 4% per year. High temperature and long cooking hours will "kill" the vitamins and enzymes in the food as well.

There were some studies in the 1990s that linked meat with cancer, particularly colon (large intestine) cancer. Are there any updates on this?

Colorectal is one of the most common cancers in developed countries. More than 940,000 cases are diagnosed each year, and about 492,000 people die from the illness, according to the International Agency for Cancer Research in Lyon, France. The DNA damage may be repaired naturally in the body, and fiber in the diet may help the process. A diet rich in fat, animal protein, and refined carbohydrates along with a lack of exercise are risk factors for the illness. Most cases are in people over 60 years old (about 70% of colorectal cancers could be prevented by changes in diet and nutrition) compared to about 5% of colon cancers that are inherited.

Studies shows why meat may increase cancer risk:

- By studying cells from volunteers eating different diets, reseachers discovered that red meat raises levels of compounds in the large bowel that can alter DNA and increase the likelihood of cancer.
- The chance of developing colorectal cancer was 33% higher in people who regularly ate more than two portions of red or processed meat a day compared to those who ate less than one portion a week.

■ In one study, published in the journal *Cancer Research*, the scientists studied cells from the lining of the colon from people who consumed red meat, vegetarian, high red meat or high-fiber diets for 15 days. They found that red meat consumption was linked to increased levels of substances called *N*-nitroso compounds, which are formed in the large bowel. The compounds may stick to DNA, making it more likely to undergo mutations that increase the odds of cancer.

Findings could lead to improved self-detection for the early stages of disease: watch for rectal bleeding as an early symptom.

What is the "final word" on fats: good or bad?

Fat is neutral as a macronutrient, but most modern trans-fats, found in cakes, biscuits, margarine, processed meals, and junk food, are nutritional dead ends! Moreover, these "modern fats" are hurting your heart by thickening the blood and increasing levels of oxidized LDL[22] (see Chapter 1). On the other hand, liquid fats like EFAs (like omega-3, in hempseed and flaxseed) can save your life. In a large-scale clinical trial organized by the Italian National Association of Hospital Cardiologists, it was demonstrated that adding just 1 g of omega-3 fatty acid daily to other lifestyle recommendations could lower the risk of death after a heart attack by 20%. Eat unprocessed vegetable fats like avocados, nuts, and virgin olive oil. Avoid corn oil, all hydrogenated oils, and margarine.

How does broccoli work to help boost the immune system and prevent disease?

In a the study (published in the *Journal of Allergy and Clinical Immunology*), researchers at UCLA have found a chemical in broccoli (and other cruciferous vegetables) that holds the key to protecting the body's immunity, which is in decline as we age. Sulforaphane, a chemical in broccoli, brussel sprouts, cabbage, cauliflower, bok choy, kale, collards, broccoli sprouts, Chinese broccoli, broccoli raab, kohlrabi, mustard, turnip, radish, rocket, and watercress switches on a set of antioxidant genes and enzymes in specific immune cells, which then cancel the deleterious effects of free radicals that can damage cells and lead to disease.

Free radicals are byproducts of normal metabolic processes, and these molecules can cause oxidative tissue damage, leading to disease, for example triggering the inflammation process that causes clogged arteries. Oxidative damage to body tissues and organs is thought to be one of the major causes of premature aging. Moreover, a dynamic equilibrium exists in the body between pro-oxidant and antioxidant forces that could determine the outcome of many disease processes that are associated with aging, including cardiovascular disease, degenerative joint diseases, and diabetes, as well as the decline in efficiency of the immune system's ability to protect against infectious agents.

What is so special about apple cider vinegar?

How many drinks can make this claim? Put two to three tablespoons of organic apple cider vinegar into a large glass, and add a spoon of honey and lemon juice. This supplies the body with over 90% of the minerals needed on a daily basis.

Why is red wine so unique?

In a study by the Institut National pour la Santé et la Recherche Médicale (INSERM) in Bordeaux, designed to see whether beer protects the heart from heart attacks, researchers found that those middle-aged men who drank two to five glasses of wine a day had a 29–33% lower death rate over abstainers. Beer drinkers had no such reduction in death rates, although both wine and beer drinkers had lower rates of heart disease and stroke. Moreover, human-kind has been using wines and fermented beverages for centuries to mark a date or celebrate a stage of life: a birth, a death, a major accomplishment or just a friendship. Unfortunately, as a culture, we ran out of ideas to celebrate and now, using alcohol, we simply medicate ourselves against the stresses and angst of modern life, getting back to basics on the celebration of life.

Alcohol seems to effect social contexts, including sex, often and usually for the negative. Why is this?

Alcohol has two conflicting effects: decreasing awareness of social cues and signals while imparting an exaggerated sense of verbal facility and sense of self-importance.

As a Chinese manager living in Hong Kong, I have been struck by the differences in alcohol tolerance (the facial redness) between my Western colleagues and myself. Why is this?

This flushing reaction that happens to Asians (Japanese and Chinese) and non-Asians (American Indians) is due to the higher levels of acetaldehyde (a toxin) and a lack of a special enzyme (aldehyde dehydrogenase). However, in a Swedish study, there emerged a syndrome known as "alcohol allergy," which included a constellation of asthma, skin swelling, nausea, and faint-ing present in up to 4.5% of all subjects.

What about women, menopause, and alcohol?[23]

Women who drink alcohol at a reasonable rate could be putting off their menopause, according to a 2-year study of more than a thousand women aged 45–49. Of the women who drank no alcohol, 25% had reached the menopause, while only 6% of the women who drank one drink or more per day had reached it. The mechanism may be the estrogen-boosting influences of alcohol.

Is it best not to drink at all?

While heavy drinking (more than six drinks a day) causes blood pressure to rise, up to three drinks a day is associated with reduced coronary heart disease. Studies have shown the relative risk of dying (mostly from coronary disease) to be 38% higher among non-drinkers compared to responsible drinkers.

How long have we been drinking wine as a species?

The consumption of the juice of the fermented grape probably happened by chance some 8,000 years ago in Mesopotamia (present-day Iraq) and moved eastward at a rate commensurate with its ease of production and improving taste. Wine-growing technology arrived about 4,000 years ago in Greece, where it was exported to southern Italy by 1000 BC, hitting the Roman Empire (which had effective ways of storing wine in wooden barrels and glass bottles) just in time for distribution to the full extent of the empire: to Spain, Portugal, France, and even Britain.

After the fall of the Roman Empire, fearing that the secret of wine would be lost during the Dark Ages in Europe, the Church (as a vast land owner) became intensely involved in wine cultivation, both as a product and as a way to know God (at least for the priests who imbibed during the Mass and the altar boys who did so afterwards). In fact, wine's sweep throughout Europe was greatly accelerated by the Christian monasteries that perceived a vested interest in cultivating wine. It was that same precious nectar that might some day be converted into the blood of Christ during the Mass, in the same way that Christ himself had transformed the water into wine at a Canaan wedding many centuries earlier.

Centuries later, in a moment in 1926 of particular lucidity, the Catholic Church in the US announced its opposition to compulsory Prohibition, saying that Prohibition was contrary to the Bible and that wine had benefits "ranging from the supreme honor paid wine with bread, as the matter of the holy Eucharist, to its general work of moistening and enlivening the rough fare of laborers."

The folklore of wine has continued to the present day, fueled not only by the improved taste, but also by reports that wines, particularly red wines, have mystical health powers. It is most particularly in France where we can see the confounding magic at work in the form of the French paradox. Do the vaulted claims about wine's life-giving properties and beneficial effects on health and longevity have any basis at all in scientific fact? The answer is simple: yes.

Humankind has been in a gyrating tryst with alcohol per se since 6000 BC. Only recently have we begun to really understand that something we enjoy as part of a ritual of celebration also has wonderfully beneficial effects on health and longevity. The issue of alcohol's impact on health and culture has been hotly debated in scientific research forums around the world, as neither scientist nor layperson can ignore the central paradox inherent in alcohol use. That is, while alcohol can produce a natural euphoria and promote health, it also has the dubious status as the substance that has had the most profoundly detrimental effects on humankind throughout history. The earliest civilizations in Mesopotamia, China, and Egypt stumbled eagerly upon fermented honey (mead), grains, sap, and fruits, probably after watching the effect of these on birds, squirrels, bears, and elephants.

What are some of the downsides of alcohol?

You scarely need more than picking up the morning paper or walking down the street of any city worldwide to see the ravages of excessive dependence on alcohol. We would all be well advised to keep an eye on the Dark Side of booze. Listed below are some of the detrimental effects of alcohol:

- Alcohol is metabolized at a rate of roughly one unit or drink (half-pint of beer, a glass of wine or a shot of spirits) per hour, so after six drinks at 10 p.m., the blood alcohol level and stuporous effects of the alcohol would be approaching nil by 4 a.m. As this happens, we experience a rebound hyperexcitation, accompanied by increased adrenaline levels in the blood, insomnia, higher blood pressure, rapid heart rate, sweating, headaches, and nightmares.
- Alcohol is responsible, at least in part, for such scourges as slavery, domestic violence, accidents, poor sexual performance, low self-confidence, depression, and suicides. It would be irresponsible to claim otherwise.
- Alcohol causes marked water and mineral losses.
- Alcohol can worsen borderline blood pressure problems.
- Alcohol is calorifically dense: 7.2 calories/g. When alcohol is consumed on an empty stomach, 25% passes directly through the unprotected stomach lining.
- Alcohol is a brain depressant, which when used in excess to control stress, can destabilize positive attitudes and relationships.
- Alcohol can increase TGs.

    ... So enjoy it in moderation.

What is a hangover (gueule de bois)?

Hangovers are caused by a constellation of metabolic problems including dehydration, low blood sugar, and a build-up of metabolic poisons. There are two metabolic pathways for alcohol (ethanol), which could account for the symptoms of a hangover.

The most commonly accepted pathway is:

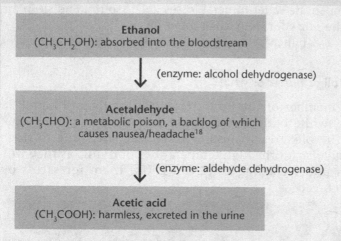

Ethanol
(CH_3CH_2OH): absorbed into the bloodstream

↓ (enzyme: alcohol dehydrogenase)

Acetaldehyde
(CH_3CHO): a metabolic poison, a backlog of which causes nausea/headache[18]

↓ (enzyme: aldehyde dehydrogenase)

Acetic acid
(CH_3COOH): harmless, excreted in the urine

Another pathway, less commonly implicated in symptoms is:

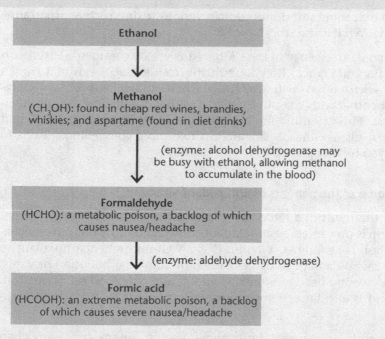

Ethanol

↓

Methanol
(CH_3OH): found in cheap red wines, brandies, whiskies; and aspartame (found in diet drinks)

↓ (enzyme: alcohol dehydrogenase may be busy with ethanol, allowing methanol to accumulate in the blood)

Formaldehyde
($HCHO$): a metabolic poison, a backlog of which causes nausea/headache

↓ (enzyme: aldehyde dehydrogenase)

Formic acid
($HCOOH$): an extreme metabolic poison, a backlog of which causes severe nausea/headache

How should I avoid a hangover?

Compensate – avoid dehydration:

- Avoid drinking on an empty stomach, so start with fruit juice or olives.
- During drinking evenings, alternate alcohol with fruit juices.

- Before sleep, compensate water/mineral losses, take aspirin, and sleep on your right side, the side your stomach empties on.
- Watch the old "1–2–3–punch": the chips–fatty-snacks–alcohol–coffee cycle.

Should I cook with oil or butter or what?

Oils, which are a member of the unsaturated fat family, are liquid at room temperature, while butters and cheese are members of the saturated fat family. The oils are, because of their reactivity (due to their unsaturation), *unsuitable* for the high temperatures of frying, as they will form free radicals under cooking conditions. Use them for salads or dipping your grain bread.

> If you still fry, do so sparingly and rapidly, such as stir frying with palm oil or butter.

I had heard that some soft drinks contain various toxins, such as aspartame and benzene. What is the story?

The Food Standards Agency in the UK tested over 200 commercial drinks on sale in Britain and France. They found dangerously high levels of a known carcinogen – benzene – which was formed when sodium benzoate, a preservative, and ascorbic acid (vitamin C), used together, formed the deadly chemical benzene. This scientific finding plus the super-high GI of HFCS that leads to heart disease and obesity are just two more compelling reasons to encourage you to start juicing your own drinks.

What are some of the benefits of antioxidant vitamin C?

Strokes are the result of a build-up of fatty deposits in the brain's arteries. This build-up is prevented by antioxidants, throughout the body. Its mechanism of action is as follows. Vitamin C is a well-researched antioxidant to help repair micro-damage to tissues caused by smoking, pollution or stress, and helps in wound healing, iron absorption, and red blood cell formation. Ascorbic acid is also an extremely powerful antioxidant. It is found naturally in:

- *fruit*: raw or dried – oranges, cantaloupes, apples, lemons, limes, strawberries, watermelons, and kiwis;
- *vegetables with the highest amounts of natural antioxidants*: especially broccoli, tomatoes, bell peppers, spinach, cabbage, cucumbers, avocados, onions, and garlic.

NOTES AND REFERENCES

1. In a 2005 review published in the *Lancet* medical journal, Dr. Philippe Grandjean of Harvard School of Public Health and Dr. Philip Landrigan of Mount Sinai School of Medicine indentified over 200 industrial chemicals proven to be toxic to the brain.

2. The typical standard American diet of today would consist of the following annual consumption rates: 65 kg potatoes, 75 kg sugar, and 100 kg of white flour!

3. For a complete view of this toxic additive, type "aspartame + Blaylock" on Google and see the testimony of a reputed neurosurgeon, Dr. Russell Blaylock. You will *never* eat "lite" or "diet" again.

4. The higher the vitamin C blood level, the lower the rate of all-cause mortality from heart disease, cancers, strokes, and autoimmune diseases.

5. Yoghurt is simple to make at home, and cultures that live to great ages do so daily. Get a pot of organic yoghurt from the organic aisle of your market and a liter of organic full-fat milk. Gently heat the milk, but DO NOT bring it to the boil. Having turned off the heat, mix the yoghurt into the milk using a ladle to aerate the mix – drawing up a ladle-full and spilling the mix back into the bowl from a height of say 30 cm. Repeat this 15–20 times. Cover the mixture with a clean cotton cloth and a plate. Let it sit in a warm dark pantry or closet. In the morning, it will be ready to eat with dried fruits, seeds, and nuts for a perfect breakfast.

6. People who use MSG as a flavor enhancer in their food are more likely than people who do not use it to be overweight or obese even though they have the same amount of physical activity and total calorie intake. Researchers at the University of North Carolina at Chapel Hill School of Public Health published the first study to show a link between MSG use and obesity in humans. In this study, more than 750 Chinese men and women, aged between 40 and 59, in three rural villages in north and south China were monitored. The majority of study participants prepared their meals at home without commercially processed foods. About 82% of the participants used MSG in their food. Those users were divided into three groups based on the amount of MSG they used. The third who used the most MSG were nearly three times more likely to be overweight than non-users. The researchers found that prevalence of overweight was significantly higher in MSG users than in non-users.

7. HFCS is typically 55% fructose and 45% glucose. One of the reasons people on low-carbohydrate diets may lose weight is that they reduce their intake of HFCS, a type of sugar that can be made into body fat with surprising speed, according to a study appearing in a 2008 issue of the *Journal of Nutrition*. For the study, six healthy individuals performed three different tests in which they had to consume a fruit drink formulation. In one test, the breakfast drink was 100% glucose, similar to the liquid doctors give patients to test for diabetes – the oral glucose tolerance test. In the second test, they drank half glucose and half fructose, and in the third, they drank 25% glucose and 75% fructose. The tests were random and blinded, and the subjects ate a regular lunch about 4 hours later. The researchers found that the process by which sugars are turned into body fat (lipogenesis) increased significantly when as little as half the glucose was replaced with fructose. After fructose consumption, the liver increased the storage of lunch fats that might have been used for other purposes. The bottom line is that people trying to lose body fat should *not* remove fruit from their lives (as it provides

clean energy, fiber, and water), but definitely should be eliminating sugar drinks and any other processed foods containing HFCS.

8. In 1900, approximately 1 in 20 American women could expect to get breast cancer. That figure is now 1 in 8.

9. The extraordinary benefits of apple cider vinegar include the following:
   - The malic acid and acetic acid present help to combat fungal and bacterial infections and relieve painful joints. The malic acid dissolves the deposits of uric acid, which form around the joints, and slowly pushes the uric acid deposits out of the body.
   - Apple cider vinegar contains fermented fruit acid, which is loaded with pectin and minerals like potassium, chlorine, magnesium, sodium, and calcium.
   - Calcium, an important constituent of apple cider vinegar, is important for the bones and for combating osteoporosis.
   - The small amounts of beta-carotene it contains actually counter effectively the damage made by free radicals.

10. There are several good references on the health benefits of chocolate:
   - Landers SJ. Sweet relief. *Health Sci* 2004.
   - Taubert D et al. Chocolate and blood pressure in elderly individuals with isolated systolic hypertension. *J Am Med Assoc* 2003; **290**: 1029.
   - Serafini M et al. Plasma antioxidants from chocolate. *Nature* 2003; **424**: 1013.
   - Mursu J et al. Dark chocolate consumption increases HDL cholesterol concentration. *Free Radic Biol Med* 2004; **37**: 1351.
   - Lee I-M, Paffenbarger RS, Jr. Life is sweet: candy consumption and longevity. *BMJ* 1998; **317**: 1683–4.

11. During fasting, drinking only water, for one, two or three units of 24 hours, our deposited fat starts to supply between 80% and 90% of our energy needs, while protein (converted to glucose by the liver) makes up the rest.

12. Bray GA, Nielsen SJ, Popkin BM. Consumption of high-fructose corn syrup in beverages may play a role in the epidemic of obesity. *Am J Clin Nutr* 2004; **79**: 537–43.

13. Teff KL et al. The dangers of corn syrup. http://www.menshealth.com

14. Teff KL et al. Dietary fructose reduces circulating insulin and leptin, attenuates post-prandial suppression of ghrelin, and increases triglycerides in women. *J Clin Endocrinol Metab* 2004; **89**: 2963–72.

15. Hallfrisch J. Metabolic effects of dietary fructose. *FASEB J* 1990; **4**: 2652–60.

16. References for the benefits of green tea abound:
   - Ahmad A. Green tea constituent EGCG and induction of apoptosis and cell cycle arrest of human carcinoma cells. *J Natl Cancer Inst* 1997; **89**: 1881–6. (Note: "apoptosis" means the disintegration of cells into membrane-bound particles.)
   - Gao YT. Reduced risk of esophageal cancer associated with green tea consumption. *J Nat Cancer Inst* 1994; **85**: 855–8.
   - Katiyar SK. Tea and chemoprevention of cancer: Epidemiologic and experimental studies. *Int J Oncol* 1996; **8**: 211–38.

17. Schmidt AM, Schnert KW, Smith LH. *Beyond Antibiotics*. Berkeley, CA: North Atlantic Books, 1993.

18. Kilburn KH, Warsaw RH, Shields MG. Neurobehavioral dysfunction in firemen exposed to PCBs: Possible improvement after detoxification. *Arch Environ Health* 1989; **44**: 254–5.

19. Cohn JR, Emmett EA. The excretion of trace metals in human sweat. *Ann Clin Lab Sci* 1978; **8**: 270–5.

20. Gard ZR, Brown EJ. Literature review and comparison studies of sauna/hyperthermia in detoxification. *The Townsend Letter, The Examiner of Alternative Medicine* 2006; (193): 76–86.

21. Reduction of Human Body Burdens of HCBs and PCBs. Presentation by David W. Schnare, MD (US Environmental Protection Agency, Washington, DC) and P.C. Robinson (Foundation for Advancements in Science and Education, Los Angeles, CA) presented at "Hexachlorbenzene: Proceedings of an International Symposium," Lyon, France, 1985.

22. Mensink RP, Katan MB. The effect of dietary trans fatty acids on HDL and LDL cholesterol levels in healthy subjects. *N Engl J Med* 1990; **323**: 439–45.

23. Could the active component of red wine, resveratrol, actually help in preventing breast cancer? It appears so. In a new study published in *Molecular Cell* in late 2008, investigators from the National Institutes of Health investigated methods by which mutations in tumor suppressor genes such as *BRCA-1* led to breast cancer. The researchers found that resveratrol, a key component of red wine, grape skins, and grape seeds, warded off the cancers by via several mechanisms:

    - resveratrol strongly inhibits the growth of *BRCA-1* mutant tumors in both cultured cells and animal models;
    - resveratrol enhances the activities of SIRT1, thus reducing the expression of the cancer booster, survivin.

    "Resveratrol may serve as an excellent compound for targeted therapy for BRCA1 associated breast cancers," stated study author Dr. Chu-Xia Deng.

Using the advice contained in this chapter, Fadi could take care of the following health objectives:

1. To develop an effective fitness program that:
   - is automotivating, to help meet the demands of work
   - allows us always to enjoy a high-energy state, even after a long day
2. To use the heart's pulse as a way to increase the efficiency of the heart
3. To develop a healthy, pain-free back
4. To have an health age (internal health) in the 40s for the rest of our lives
5. To prevent prostate disease
6. To avoid the painful gout crises

Abbreviations and acronyms that you will need to read this chapter smoothly include:

BURST	Build Up Rapid Stamina Training
CO	Cardiac output
EC	Exhalation count
HAP	Health Action Plan
HDL	High-density lipoprotein
HR	Heart rate
LDL	Low-density lipoprotein
PSA	Prostate-specific antigen
RHR	Resting heart rate
SV	Stroke volume
TGs	Triglycerides
WHR	Waist-to-hip ratio
WWR	Weight-to-waist ratio

INTRODUCTION

Hello, my name is Fadi. I am the 42-year-old director of a marketing division in a family shipping business based in Beirut, Lebanon.

PERSONAL LIFE

I come from a large extended family. In fact, the business that I (and my brothers) manage is very successful and was started in Saudi Arabia by my grandfather. Part of the family's success stems from our confidence and a real taste for challenge. I have always been a very extroverted, risk-taking optimist, ready to exchange ideas with anyone. After all, I am *Lebanese*!

My wife, Djamila, and I were childhood sweethearts; our parents approved, and soon enough we were blessed with four children, Kamal, Fatima, Khadijta, and Mohammed.

My first son, Kamal, was very bright but *incredibly* lazy, at least by my standards. My impression, based on discussion with colleagues in the West or Asia, was that this generation of children is different than we were ... by far. While growing up in Lebanon, we *read* (every Lebanese child has had the entire works of Khalil Gibran read to them) and we *played* outside (usually football, but also tennis and running); computer games did not exist, nor did the Internet. This generation are perhaps more cerebral in the abstract sense, but to me, it seems, they are content to have a good time with their mates.

To my chagrin, Kamal had fallen into the video game fever of the 1990s and could be found in his room at any time, either playing Dungeons and Dragons or buying such trash online. That Kamal's grades suffered bothered me, but not as much as the fact that he could not stop playing video games or playing on the computer, with the result that he started gaining weight *rapidly*. I noticed that he was leaving his T-shirt on when he swam. When I asked him, he started in with all this noise about the sun's harmful UV rays, and then he turned a cold shoulder. I desisted in my efforts to confront him ... for then.

PROFESSIONAL LIFE

My role in the family business was clearly a priority for me, as I have been fortunate enough to have inherited the business. But with these privileges come a multitude of responsibilities (to clients and to the family), and a great deal of pride and even competition among the male members of the family. Everyone wants to shine in the eyes of my parents. Our greatest collective nightmare is failing these family responsibilities, "dropping the ball," as we say. This means long hours and sometimes tense moments when things do not go according to plan.

> **TIP** Doing as little as a 15-minute walk every day and a 4-minute work-out every morning can dramatically transform your health and stamina, while decreasing your risk of premature death by more than 30%.

HEALTH PROFILE

Up to a certain age (I would say about 35), I felt *great* and that's what counted. Sure, like those around me, I had lots of "prosperity tissue" around my waist. As the business grew, I found less and less time for tennis and golf, and started putting on the kilos and getting out of breath even walking up two flights of stairs.

Then there was the *poor sleep* of late, not because I was worried (I stopped that a long time ago), but I think my sleep problem has been due primarily to urinary difficulties, especially in the middle of the night. Combine this with an old cigarette habit (about 25 cigarettes a day for about 15 years), and you have yourself someone who isn't really the best example for small kids, but that's life.

Mentally, I must say that I attribute much of my sanity to my religion, and I find it quite easy to live as a modern manager and live morally within my faith guidelines (alhamdulillah). I am grateful for this gift and can only hope that my children find the same for themselves.

NUTRITION

I have what is euphemistically known as a "sweet tooth," which is to say I am a "dulceholic." Moreover, unlike Europe, we in the Middle East have no pub culture to get together and catch up with news of the family. That happens generally in restaurants, where I spend much of my business life. With my family, our main time to get together is over big (very big) family meals, with lots of delicious foods, some of which are not particularly good for the waistline or heart.

PHYSICAL AND INTELLECTUAL ACTIVITY

This involved occasional jogging, plus the odd game of tennis, and golf (when the back was not acting up).

Most important leadership quality	Commitment to those we lead
My idea of a great leaders	• Mohammed the Prophet • Mahatma Gandhi • Crazy Horse

My most inspiring quotation

You must love those you lead before you can be an effective leader. You can certainly command without that sense of commitment, but you cannot lead without it. And without leadership, command is a hollow experience, a vacuum often filled with mistrust and arrogance.

General Eric Shinseki, Secretary of Veterans' Affairs, Obama Administration

MY FIRST WAKE-UP CALL: A GOUTY CRISIS

My wake-up call came one Saturday while I was attending an alumni reunion at Wharton Business School. I started having these severe deep aches in both hands and my left big toe that were so severe that I had to limp. My old class-mates were dying of laughter at the "old man" until they saw the beads of sweat on my forehead and my anguished look. "Fadi," confided one of my mates, "my wife is a doctor, let her take a look at your foot." I frankly couldn't stand the thought of someone even *touching* my foot, so severe was the pain, but the doctor was very cool and gentle.

"The diagnosis is clear," she said, "acute gouty crisis. For this crisis, you will need some standard medications. But after the crisis calms, as part of a strategy to prevent further attacks, you should increase drastically your water intake (as over 65% of all cases are caused by decreased excretion via the kidneys) and fresh fruit consumption, as they eliminate the uric acid, as well as a couple of vitamins and supplements:

- Vitamin B$_5$ (pantothenic acid), which converts the uric acid into the more harmless compounds urea and ammonia. You can get it from these foods too: egg yolk, broccoli, fish, shellfish, chicken, milk, yoghurt, legumes, mushrooms, avocado, and sweet potatoes.
- Vitamin E, as a lack of this vitamin allows the excessive production of uric acid.
- Apple cider vinegar, as it contains malic acid, which dissolves uric acid deposits that form around the joints, helping relieve joint pains. This dissolved uric acid is gradually eliminated from the body. That's it."

I thought to myself that even if the gouty crisis was something of an embarassment during the reunion, I had earned something important about how to manage it and got a lot closer to some old mates from business school.

MY SECOND WAKE-UP CALL: SCIATICA AND PARALYSIS

My second wake-up call came while I was engaged in one of my infrequent tennis games with my brother in law, Mamoud.

Once again, allowing my ambition to exceed my talent and condition, I started well, running left and right. Then, in a tie-breaker, I ran and slid for a tough shot, twisted, and felt something snap and that was it: I was flat out on the ground, unable to move. And I mean really vicious shooting pain and spasms. Mamoud could see my discomfort and immediately called the ambulance. This was the beginning of my journey.

So here I was at 42, laid up, unable to work, barely able to speak because of the pain, seriously stressed out (but we in Lebanon are used to that!), and waiting for a possible operation to decompress the nerves pinched in my back. I felt totally powerless and, frankly, a little depressed. To add to my good fortune, Dr. Abdel, the surgeon, was making his daily rounds with a rather larger following of other care-givers.

"Salaam alaikum and good day, Sir. I am Dr. Abdel Rahman, the attending physician on the orthopedic service; I oversee and supervise all activities here. Your direct care will be taken care by a visiting surgeon, Dr. Peter MacGregor, from Ireland, who is with us for a year to learn and teach."

After the team moved on, Dr. MacGregor came back into my hospital room and announced that my blood work revealed an additional problem – an enlarged prostate gland (discovered during my admission physical exam) – plus a high prostate-specific antigen (PSA) level, both of which indicated a state of inflammation in the prostate.

Dr. MacGregor, a powerfully built man with a shock of red hair anchored by grey sideburns, spoke gently and with a beautiful brogue, "Sir...," he started, but I had to interrupt, "Please, Doc, call me Fadi; everyone knows me as Fadi and no one as 'Sir'."

"Sir, I mean, Fadi, first please allow me to introduce myself. I have spent the past 25 years doing just what I am doing here in Lebanon, learning what each specific culture has to offer in the care of the human frame and function.

"As for your specific situation, Fadi, something has to be done here. You are looking down the barrel of a loaded gun: heart disease, strokes, diabetes ..." He hesitated. "Just look at these test results of yours."

Fadi's health and fitness report

	NORMAL/IDEAL RANGE	ME (BASELINE)
Actual age (years)		42.4
Health age (years)	Actual age (or less)	61.8
Blood pressure (mmHg)	< 135/85	165/95
Resting heart rate (beats/minute)	< 60	78
Weight (kg)		110
Body fat %	< 20% men, < 23% women	35%
Body fat weight (kg)		38.5
Lean weight (kg)		71.5
Waist-to-hip ratio	< 0.90 men, < 0.80 women	1.20
Weight-to-waist ratio	Up	Down
Fasting blood sugar (glucose) (g/L)	0.70–1.20	1.25
Uric acid (mg/L)	< 8.0	18.5
Cigarettes/day	0	28
Indian squats (number/minute until winded)		4
Jumping jack (number/minute until winded)		6
Press-ups (number/minute until winded)		3
Jump rope (seconds until winded)		5
Exhalation count (seconds)	> 100	12

	NORMAL/IDEAL RANGE	ME (BASELINE)
Early prostate cancer antigen-2 test (EPCA-2) (ng/mL)	< 30	25
Kamal's body fat	15–20%	28%

"I think I get it, Doc. I am in a real mess and I am just 42: bad back, the gout, and an inflamed prostate – three serious health problems for the price of ONE!" I said, making a vain attempt at levity in the face of bad news.

"I am not even certain that you need back surgery now," continued Dr MacGregor. "I am in favour of a 'wait-and-see' approach. No need to rush when it comes to the back. My fervent wish to see you discharged from here with a clean back. Dr. Rahman has, in the 6 months I have been here, never gone against my recommendations."

"Why not?" I asked, slightly disappointed. It wasn't that I actually wanted an operation on my back, but I never wanted that kind of pain again.

"For three very simple reasons:

- First of all, the rule of thumb in surgery is 'You cut only when you need to cut.' Let's make sure that you need it because once we manipulate the back, in this extreme fashion, it is never the same again. For now, your nerves and muscles are cooling down with the rest and anti-inflammatory medications.
- Secondly, your nuclear magnetic resonance scan shows no permanent or irreversible damage of the architecture of your lower back, and your physical exam is improving rapidly.
- Lastly, this operation is not without risks, in terms of the general anesthesia and the actual impact on your lower back and future mobility."

I was astounded to find a surgeon that actually insisted on letting my body heal, instead of cutting.

"So, Fadi, if we err it will be on the side of caution. I hope you understand. Any further questions, Fadi?"

"Yes, Doc, what do you recommend I do here for the next day or so without getting totally bored while we are waiting for my body to heal?"

"Well, you already know about the gout and what to do: loads of water (until the urine runs light yellow) and apple cider vinegar. That will signify that you are clearing the uric acid. Otherwise, we have you on vitamin B_5 acid and vitamin E for the gout, painkillers and anti-inflammatories for the back, and aspirin to keep your blood from getting too thick while you are immobile.

"You are not really in that big of a mess, at least if you take a moment to reflect on the various opportunities being offered here to you. The bottom line is that your lifestyle plus your genetics are literally killing you or, at least, turning you into a handicapped person at a very young age. If you want a reasonably normal lifespan, exercise is non-negotiable.

"Based on what I have learned around the world in places like India, Tibet, the Amazon basin, Mexico, and China, I believe that, once this crisis clears, I could have you back in fighting shape in 4 weeks max!"

"Doctor, with all due respect, I come from a large family, where, once passed 40, we all get heavy, the gout, and, quite often, diabetes. Frankly, I am resigned to falling into the same traps. If you could give me a little motivation to keep my promises to myself to do exercise, stay fit, and drink enough water ...," I replied.

"Right then, Fadi, let's start with your comment of *motivation*. If I could walk you through this orthopedic ward, what you would see would make you cry: children who will never walk again, crippled by birth defects of the spinal cord, teenagers paralyzed by accidents, poor workers who were injured on the job, handicapped for life. This hospital is full of people who had no choice but to be here. You *have* a choice! They don't have the option of letting their health go – you do!"

His eyes flashed. "Don't move [I *couldn't*], I want you to meet my assistant." Just then, the doctor made a hasty retreat and reappeared followed by a small fellow in a wheelchair, arms in a sort of spasm, wheeling *backwards*, propelled just by his legs. He maneuvered his wheelchair with uncanny agility, coming to a spinning stop just next to Dr. MacGregor. It was apparent that Abdul was a victim of cerebral palsy, a condition wherein the baby's brain undergoes birth trauma or infection, but in Abdul's case, the intelligence was intact.

"This is my faithful assistant, Abdul. This young man of 27 has a doctorate in physiology, has run 3 marathons *backwards*, and supports a wife and two children with his research on cerebral palsy." I was dumbstruck as I looked at his twisted body; I could not imagine him running at all, let alone an organized race. How did he do those things? Where did he get the fight, the grit to run a marathon? My mind raced and, with astonishment, I blurted out something that I could not believe.

"Abdul, I shall commit to getting myself fit and free of the diseases that are killing us. Just give me the dates for the next marathon and I am IN! You don't know me, but when I decide something, it's as good as money in the bank! Let's meet later for lunch to discuss your findings and thank you loads for coming by to say 'hello'." And off he went, as quickly and smoothly as he had entered.

"How does he do that?" I stammered.

The doctor explained, "He makes it look so easy, but behind every purposeful movement, anything voluntary takes the concentration of a chess master. Now, *there's* a motivated individual!"

I blurted out, "I want to run a marathon, too!"

"I wouldn't recommend that. New data have shown something we have suspected for a while: that long distance running is *not* for everybody. Only a *very* small percentage of people, if anyone at all, should be doing long distance running and those sorts of endurance exercises.[1] You see, your situation need not be so bad, but you really do need to focus a little bit on *your* health. I think I have just the thing for you."

MY INTRODUCTION TO BURST *(see Chapter 1)*

Dr. MacGregor continued, "I would like to propose a *completely* different, highly efficient way to get back into the fighting shape of a teenager, while feeling great in just 30–45 minutes a week: I call it BURST. BURST stands for Build Up Rapid Stamina Training, because that is what is happening: after a couple of days of BURST, your energy will be bursting!

"It is perfect for someone like you, who is committed to health and stamina, but lacks the time, the facilities, the motivation. The 30–45 minutes per week is a small price to pay to get in top shape, because *you* cannot afford to get sick. There are too many people who are counting and depending on you. I'm not just talking about your immediate family, but your company, and your country! When it comes to BURST, remember the key idea:

> How you feel *before* doing exercise has nothing to do with how you feel *after* the exercise.

"OK, OK, Doc, you are right, when you put it *that* way, it seems so simple and time-efficient. I am ready! Let's go! Just help me overcome the inertia, the internal resistance to exercise. What I need is to develop an exercise program that not only motivates me short term, but continues to grow with my needs. Tell me a little about BURST. What are some of its benefits?"

Dr. MacGregor started, "There are so many, I shall give only the prominent ones here:

- The best single benefit is the time needed for measurable improvement: 30–45 minutes per week! No excuses possible here.
- It can be done anywhere (such as traveling), using any activity, including walking, a jump rope, running up stairs or swimming.
- BURST poses absolutely no problem for the back. Au contraire, it helps to strengthen the abdominal muscles that support the back.
- In a study from the *Archives of Internal Medicine*, men who did high-intensity (BURST) training had lower body fat, blood pressure, and triglyceride (TG) levels, and higher protective high-density lipoprotein (HDL).[2]
- In the Harvard Health Professionals Study, researchers followed up 7,337 men (aged average 66 years) and discovered that the key to exercise was neither endurance nor length. Rather, it was *intensity*. The more intense the exertion, the lower the men's risk of heart disease. Moreover, in the same study, high-intensity exercises (like BURST) provided a 10-fold decrease in heart disease over aerobic training.[3]

"During my travels around the world, Fadi, I have had the good fortune to be able to write some manuscripts on topics of interest to you. Here is a list; just tell the nurse and she will bring them as needed. Some are in straight medical prose, while other manuscripts follow the Question and Answer format. They are *really* interesting to see the queries from all over the world on a vast array of issues.

"For obvious reasons I would start with something to read like the healthy pain-free back manuscript, which the patients here are given to help them avoid coming back. Happy reading, Fadi."

From a huge collection of writings, I chose the following to keep me busy for the next day or so:

1. Juliette's work-outs:
   - yoga for a healthy pain-free back;
   - for back pain relief ... *fast*;
   - for longevity and vitality.
2. High-vitality BURST work-outs: the 4-minute work-out for total fitness.

After 3 days recuperating in the hospital, I arrived home with my intention to get fit, with my son Kamal in tow if possible . My enthusiasm was met with a full range of emotions from disbelief (Djamila) to derision (Kamal). I was undeterred. Now was the time.

JULIETTE'S YOGA PROGRAM FOR A PAIN-FREE BACK

The common folklore is that bad backs are reserved for those who make a living moving pianos. According to the medical journal *Spine,* more than 80% of people in industrialized countries will be debilitated by this problem at some time in their adult lives. In fact, the more sedentary you are, the greater is your risk of developing severe back problems. That makes most of us at high risk for developing back pain that will limit our mobility, both on the tennis court and in our jobs.

Moreover, back pain means a major loss of money to companies due to days off work. In the US alone, back ailments, as the second leading reason for hospitalization (after pregnancy), cost industry *$14 billion per year*, including 93 million lost working days.

Watch your posture. By maintaining the natural S-shaped curve to the back, you not only keep the muscles strong, but also stay mentally focused. That is, your posture will determine in large part your attitude and inner chemistry by sending internal signals that you are either in control (shoulders back, head high) or dejected and beaten (stooped shoulders, head down). This 15–20-minute yoga program will improve your back flexibility and your ability to connect with your right brain (see Chapter 4).

Low back stretch

Lie on your back, with your knees bent and your feet flat on the ground (Fig. 3.1).

- **Inhale,** and bring your *right* knee with your hands toward your chest (Fig. 3.2a).
- **Exhale,** lift your head toward your *right* knee, and hold your breath (Fig. 3.2b).

- **Inhale**, and come back to the starting position.
- **Exhale**, relax and change to the *left* side.
- Now, with BOTH knees ... **Inhale**, bring both knees with your hands toward your chest (Fig. 3.3).
- **Exhale**, lift your head toward your knees, make a nice round ball with your body, and relax with your lungs empty (Fig. 3.4).
- **Inhale**, and come back to the starting position.
- **Exhale**, and breathe softly.

FIGURE 3.1

FIGURE 3.2a

FIGURE 3.2b

FIGURE 3.3

FIGURE 3.4

Half-bridge

Lie on your back, knees bent, feet flat on ground, and arms alongside your body (Fig. 3.5).

- **Inhale**, and lift your hips (Fig. 3.6).
- **Exhale**, and hold the position.
- **Inhale**, and lift your whole back (Fig. 3.7).
- **Exhale**, and bring your spine down disc by disc until you reach your starting position.

FIGURE 3.6

FIGURE 3.5

FIGURE 3.7

FIGURE 3.8

FIGURE 3.9

FIGURE 3.10

Shoulder stand

Lying on your back (Fig. 3.8):

- First, lift your legs as shown, breathe softly and relax (Fig. 3.9). Hold the position as long as it is comfortable while breathing through and come back VERY SLOWLY disc by disc to the starting position. With time you will be able to straighten your legs out and lift up your back into the shoulder stand as shown (Fig. 3.10).

Plough

Lie on your back, with your knees bent, and support your lower back with your hands.

- First, bring your knees onto your forehead, relax, and breath through (Fig. 3.11).
- When you can, gently straighten your legs behind your head while breathing softly, relaxing the facial muscles, neck, and shoulders (Fig. 3.12).
- Come back VERY SLOWLY disc by disc to the starting position. Relax and breathe.

Sit up in position

- To sit up, place your hands flat on the floor under your lower back (Fig. 3.13).
- Push down on your hands to lift up your upper body into a sitting position with great ease (Fig. 3.14).

Cobra and Mountain

Start by supporting yourself on the palms of your hands and the balls of your feet, with your arms and legs at shoulder width, and **exhale** (Fig. 3.15).

- **Inhale**, and raise your buttocks with your arms and legs straight, on your toes, head down (Fig. 3.16).
- **Exhale**, return to the starting position, and repeat this three times while following your breathing.

Frog

Sit on your heels, knees open.

- **Inhale**, and stretch forward with your arms straight (Fig. 3.17).
- **Exhale**, lay your upper body down, still sitting on your heels, and with your head down on the floor, completely relax and breathe through very slowly (Fig. 3.18).

FIGURE 3.11

FIGURE 3.12

FIGURE 3.13

FIGURE 3.14a

FIGURE 3.14b

FIGURE 3.15

FIGURE 3.16

FIGURE 3.17

FIGURE 3.18

Turtle

- Still sitting on your heels, close your legs, bend forward to make a nice round ball with your body, head down and arms relaxed along your sides.
- Breathe softly, relax completely, and let your body heal itself (Fig. 3.19).

> **TIP** With a little care and forethought, you will defy the adage: "Once a back patient, always a back patient."

Now stand up and continue Juliette's yoga routine for another few minutes.

Lateral stretch

Staying in one plane, without leaning forward or back, and with the legs spread as wide as comfortable (Fig. 3.20):

- **Inhale**, arms open on each side.
- **Exhale**, while bending toward your right side (Fig. 3.21).

Mentally mark the spot where your right hand was able to reach down and look up at your straight left arm, hold your breathing, and relax.

- **Inhale**, and return to the center.
- **Exhale**, while bending towards your *left* side (Fig. 3.22).

FIGURE 3.19

FIGURE 3.20

FIGURE 3.21

FIGURE 3.22

Salute to the sun

This is a more advanced group of linked movements to integrate mind and body health nicely in just a few minutes.

- **Place your palms together** (Fig. 3.23).
- **Inhale**, and lift up your arms (Fig. 3.24).
- **Exhale**, and bend forward while bending your knees (Fig. 3.25).
- **Inhale**, and extend your *right* leg behind (Fig. 3.26).
- **Exhale**, and extend your *left* leg behind you to form a board (Fig. 3.27).
- **Bend the knees** and then bring the arms forward (Fig. 3.28).
- **Inhale**, adopting the Cobra postion (Fig. 3.29).
- **Exhale**, and lift your buttocks into a triangle (Fig. 3.30).
- **Inhale**, bring the left foot forward, and look straight ahead (Fig. 3.31).
- **Exhale**, and bring the right foot next to the left foot (Fig. 3.32).
- **Inhale**, and stand up while lifting your arms backward (Fig. 3.33).
- **Exhale**, with the palms together (Fig. 3.34).

Now sit down and continue Juliette's yoga routine for another few minutes.

FIGURE 3.23

FIGURE 3.24

FIGURE 3.25

FIGURE 3.26

FIGURE 3.2

FIGURE 3.28

FIGURE 3.29

FIGURE 3.30

FIGURE 3.31

FIGURE 3.32

FIGURE 3.33

FIGURE 3.34

Gentle self-massage

■ Lie flat on your back and bring your knees with your hands toward your chest. Breathe very slowly while relaxing your facial, neck, shoulders, and low back muscles (Fig. 3.35).
■ Very gently, rock your knees from side to side to massage your lower back while breathing through (Fig. 3.36).

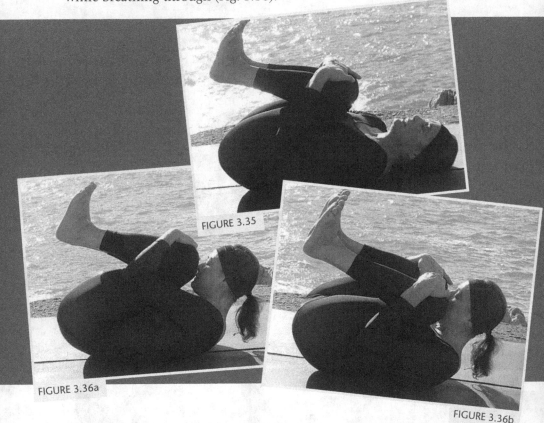

FIGURE 3.35

FIGURE 3.36a

FIGURE 3.36b

Back to wall stretch

■ Sit next to a wall, bringing your buttocks as close as possible to the wall. Then lie down on your back and lift your legs against the wall.
■ First, with the knees bent, make sure that your spine is in full contact with the floor. Relax and breathe smoothly.
■ If you feel no discomfort, straighten your legs onto the wall, breathe, and relax.

JULIETTE'S PROGRAM FOR BACK PAIN RELIEF

There is a whole array of therapeutic modalities (massage, hot water bottles, manipulation, acupuncture, ultrasound, deep heat, traction, shoe inserts, and surgery), none of which is 100% successful. In fact, the best approach is to rest and start with:

- *Arnica montana* for daily twists and stiffness and discomfort. (Don't forget that homeopathy is best on an empty stomach, under the tongue for maximum efficacy.)
- *Aspirin* for more severe tightness and pain. (Remember that aspirin is acetylsalicylic acid and therefore needs to be taken on a full stomach to avoid gastritis.)
- *Hot showers* to run on your injured back (watch the pressure of the water).
- *Rest* as much as possible, avoid driving, and move to a minimum until you have gained relief.
- *If still in pain*, see a doctor or a back professional.

JULIETTE'S LONGEVITY AND VITALITY PROGRAM

Flexibility and balance

Think about the oak tree and the sapling facing very strong winds: the sapling can bend while the oak tree remains rigid and stiff, resisting until it finally breaks. Stiffness and poor balance are true indicators on how old our body is. Many injuries occur as we grow in age because of a lack of balance as we get in and out of our bathtub, walk down a high step or stand on a stool to change a light bulb.

While Juliette's program will help you to regain balance and flexibility, it will also increase your strength and stamina with as little as 15 minutes every other day.

Start by standing.

Deep breathing

With your feet apart at shoulder width, and your eyes closed:

- **Inhale** softly (Fig. 3.37).
- **Exhale** completely while relaxing.
- Repeat this three times.

Big bird

- **Inhale**, grab your *left* foot with your *right* hand. Stand straight and relax, and hold your breath for a few seconds (Fig. 3.38).
- **Exhale**, and bring your left foot down.
- **Inhale**, grab your *right* foot with your *left* hand and stand straight and relax, hold your breath for a few seconds (Fig. 3.39).
- **Exhale**, and bring your right foot down.

Eagle

- **Inhale**, and lift your *right* knee at 90° (Fig. 3.40).
- **Exhale**, and straighten your *right* leg out (Fig. 3.41).

- **Inhale**, and bend your right knee to 90°.
- **Exhale**, return to the starting position, and repeat with the left leg.

"O" breathing

- Stand feet apart at shoulder width, with your eyes closed.
- **Inhale**, softly and deeply.
- **Exhale**, making an "O" with your lips (Fig. 3.42).

FIGURE 3.37

FIGURE 3.38

FIGURE 3.39

FIGURE 3.40

FIGURE 3.41

FIGURE 3.4

Blind balance

- Stand straight (Fig. 3.43).
- Place your right foot in front of your left foot, with your arms down. Control your balance by contracting your buttocks and by pushing your big toes down into the ground. Now close your eyes, breathe softly, and control your balance (Fig. 3.44).
- Rest, and change foot.

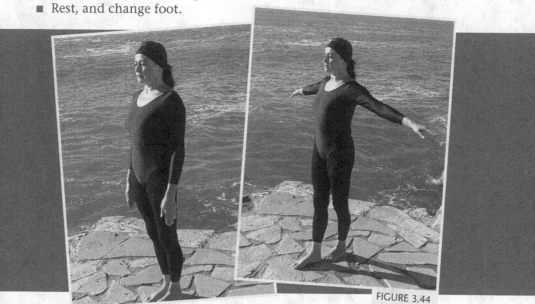

FIGURE 3.44

FIGURE 3.43

Shiva

- **Stand straight**, with your arms opened to the side (Fig. 3.45).
- **Bend** your right knee and place your right foot onto your left inner thigh, breathe, and find your balance (Fig. 3.46).
- **Place** your arms above your head with your palms facing each other (Fig. 3.47).
- **Breathe**, and relax. Slowly come back to the starting position. Rest, and change foot.

Deep breathing with abdominal snap

- Stand with your feet apart, shoulder width, and your eyes closed.
- **Inhale**, and bend forward, resting hands on your knees (Fig. 3.48).
- **Exhale completely** while snapping your belly in and out (Fig. 3.49).
- Repeat three times.

Continue by sitting down.

FIGURE 3.45

FIGURE 3.46

FIGURE 3.47

FIGURE 3.48

FIGURE 3.49

Table

- Sit down, with your back straight, hands flat on the ground BESIDE your HIPS, and your legs outstretched in front of you (Fig. 3.50). (Bend your knees if needed.)
- **Inhale**, lift your hips as you bend your knees, feet flat on ground, gently dropping your head back. Try to make a nice flat table with your body (Fig. 3.51).
- **Exhale**, and return slowly to the starting position.

Vertebral tree

- Still sitting, bend your knees and grab them with your hands (Fig. 3.52).
- **Inhale**, and bring down your spine very slowly, disc after disc (Fig. 35.3), until your back is in full contact with the floor.
- **Exhale** completely.
- **Inhale** slowly and deeply with your chin up.
- **Exhale**, bringing your chin down to your chest

FIGURE 3.50

FIGURE 3.51

FIGURE 3.52

FIGURE 3.53

Abdominal crunch

- With your back flat on the floor, raise your legs slightly bent (to assure full contact of the spine with the ground) (Fig. 3.54).
- **Inhale**, and lift your upper body as high as possible with your arms straight (Fig. 3.55).
- **Exhale**, and come down to the starting position, legs up and bent. Do as many abdominal crunches as possible in 30 seconds (don't forget to breathe as above).

FIGURE 3.54

FIGURE 3.55

Low back self-massage

- While catching up your breath, hold your knees and very gently massage your lower back from side to side and by making little circles with your knees to the right and to the left (Fig. 3.56).

Obliques abs

- **Lie** on your back, with your right leg bent and left leg straight, hands behind your head without pulling your neck.
- **Try** to touch your left elbow with your right knee and then your right elbow with your left knee without stopping for 30 seconds (Figs. 3.57 and 3.58).

Relaxation

This is as important as your work-out: it will allow body and mind to memorize the benefits of the movements you have just performed.

- Lie flat on your back, with your legs straight or bent (Fig. 3.59).
- **Inhale**; let the air travel from your belly to the top of your chest, and relax your neck and shoulder muscles.
- **Exhale** softly and fully. Wait for the next inhalation to come.
- Repeat five times.

Once I had finished these concise manuscripts, I realized that I had been doing (jogging) was, in most instances, *exactly the opposite* of what Dr. MacGregor was recommending.

Time flew by, as I had had such a huge learning experience since I left the university. My back was (almost) back to normal. I had pretty much a complete range of motion about all the major joints.

Prior to being discharged from the hospital (I really needed that rest!), Dr. MacGregor explained to me that, in his eclectic practice, he always starts a

FIGURE 3.56

FIGURE 3.57

FIGURE 3.59

FIGURE 3.58

Health Action Plan (HAP) by doing some follow-up measurements in 6 months' time to gauge progress.

His parting words to me were: "This is the only way to go as a doctor, always checking your therapy, always keeping yourself accountable to the patient, always concerned whether you are being an effective agent of healing. So, Fadi, once your back has calmed down a bit, let's do some measurements in 6 months, and I promise, if you are not better, we shall hold each other accountable."

"Doc, you are ON!"

HIGH-VITALITY BURST FOR DEVELOPING TOTAL FITNESS

There are four sections to the 4-minute BURST:

1. quantify to improve;
2. the necessary equipment;
3. the warm-up;
4. the BURST.

Warning: If you have any of the following findings, consult with your doctor:

TIP Check with your doctor, and even then start slow: go for after-meal walks, limit sugar, stretch … to avoid accidents and to give yourself a fighting chance to develop the patience and skills necessary to continue having fun while setting back the biological clock.

- Blood pressure > 160/100 mmHg
- A TG:HDL ratio > 5
- Smoking > 20 cigarettes a day
- Low-density lipoprotein (LDL) > 1.60 g/L
- Body fat > 30%
- Resting heart rate > 110 beats/minute
- Cardiac chest pain
- Inability to walk 3 km.

Quantify to improve

There will be *three* parameters along the way to fitness that will signal your progress.

Your resting heart rate (RHR)
The reason your heart rate will start to slow as you get more fit (hence, become more efficient) is illustrated in the following relationship between three critical measures:

1. the **cardiac outout (CO)**: the amount in milliliters (mL) put out or pumped by the heart every minute. At rest, the CO is 5000 mL/minute;
2. the **heart rate (HR)**: the number of beats every minute;
3. the **stroke volume (SV)**: the volume (in mL) pumped in every stroke or beat.

The pulse can be checked in the positions shown in Figure 3.60, without pressing on the artery too hard, as this will obliterate the pulse.

Important note: The *SV increases* with BURST, as indicated by a *lower HR*. There are three differnt ways to express how these are related:

$$CO = HR \times SV \quad or \quad HR = CO/SV \quad or \quad SV = CO/HR$$

Let's look at a couple of examples:

- **HR of 72 beats/minute.** With a CO at rest of 5000 mL/minute, the SV is 5000 mL/minute divided by 72 beats/minute = 69 mL/beat.
  Verdict: *very inefficient heart function.*

FIGURE 3.60a

FIGURE 3.60b

- **HR of 50 beats/minute.** With a CO at rest of 5000 mL/minute, the SV is 5000 mL/minute divided by 50 beats/minute = 100 mL/beat. Verdict: *very efficient heart function.*

Your weight-to-waist ratio (WWR)
Use the table below to determine if you have too much fat in the mid-section.

IF YOU ARE THIS WEIGHT (kg) ...	WAIST CIRCUMFERENCE (cm) SHOULD NOT EXCEED:
50	78
55–60	81
65	83
70	Excellent → 86
75	89
80–85	91
90	— OK → 94
95–100	97
105	Problematic 99
110–115	101
120	→ 103
125	106
130	110

To gauge whether or not you are at high risk for health issues, draw a line from your weight to your waist circumference.

- If the line is UP, that's **excellent** news.
- If the line is FLAT, that's less excellent but still **OK**.
- If the line is DOWN, you are in the **risky business** territory.

Your exhalation count (EC)
Get your baseline (starting) rate by counting *aloud*, at a standard 1-second rate: "one-and-two-and-three-and-four-and-five-and" as you exhale. Over time, the EC, a critical reflection of lung capacity (and longevity), will improve, and your health and vitality along with it.

Necessary equipment

You will need to have access to the following equipment/material:
- A stopwatch
- A tape measure
- A caraf of lemon/lime water
- A (solid) chair
- A 2–3-storey stairwell

- A jump rope (weighted)
- A bicycle (optional)
- A treadmill (optional)
- An ocean or pool (optional).

Warm-up routine for *both* fitness levels (180 seconds)

1. *Replace water losses that have occurred during the night's sleep.* Upon awakening, start with a glass of (room temperature) water with a full lemon or lime squeezed into it.
2. *Stand erect and rub your palms together* **vigorously**, as if warming them, for 15 seconds. Rest and drink a glass of lemon/lime water.
3. *Center your mind.* Before actually starting your physical work-out, in preparation for the day's stresses, 1 minute of either deep breathing, pranayama, meditation or mantra[4] will do. Choose according to your liking.
4. *Lateral stretch.* With your bare feet spread as far as they can be comfortably and your arms held out at the sides, palms down, slide your right hand along your right thigh and lower leg until you hit a sticking point where it is difficult to go any further. Breathe deeply and watch the muscles and tendons get more supple. Mentally mark the spot where your right hand was able to reach toward your ankle. Come back up and repeat on left side. *Hydrate*: have another glass of lemon/lime water.
5. *The abdominal snap.* This is a great 30-second morning work-out for toning your abdominal muscles that will also help to keep the intestines regular. Breathing calmly and deeply, stand with knees slightly bent and the feet at the width of the shoulders, with the palms of the hands on the thighs, just above the knees. Slowly expel all the air from your lungs and then suck in your gut as far as possible. While still holding the breath gently, *snap* the gut out and repeat three times for that exhaled breath. This can tone the abdominal muscles while giving a "wake-up call" to otherwise lethargic intestines. *Hydrate*: have another glass of lemon/lime water.

Important note on breathing: When doing *any* physical training, such as BURST (but also strength or resistance training), you should generally exhale on the exertion (or most difficult part of the exercise) and inhale on the recovery (easiest part of the exercise). For example, when doing a crunch, you should exhale when you lift your shoulders off the ground, and inhale when you lower your shoulders down to the ground.

The following work-out allows you to increase strength, endurance, and flexibility without a heavy investment in time. Two variations have been provided and you should select the appropriate one according to whether you are:

1. a stage 1 (*beginner*) athlete: in 30 minutes/week:
   - RHR > 72 beats/minute, *or*
   - Waist-to-hip ratio (WHR) > 1.0, *or*

- WWR line is **flat or downwards,** *or*
- EC < 30 seconds.
2. a stage 2 (*intermediate to advanced*) athlete: 45 minute/week:
   - RHR < 60–72 beats/minute (or less), *or*
   - WHR < 0.99 (or less), *or*
   - WWR line is **flat or upwards,** *or*
   - EC > 30 seconds (or more).

The BURST 4-minute work-out

Make best use of this grid to mark your progress over 1 month. There is no need to measure more often than that.

DATE	MONTH 1	MONTH 2	MONTH 3	MONTH 4
RHR (beats/minute)				
Weight (kg)				
Waist (cm)				
Hips (cm)				
WHR (cm)				
EC (seconds)				

Menu of routines
You can choose from any of the following routines. Focus on *functional strength*. That is, develop the strength to delay fatigue and battle stress, and develop stamina situations. *Repeat each exercise until you are winded, every time.* That's the key to recuperating lost physiological territory in terms of the RHR and the lung's EC. When you approach the point of being "winded," at this point take an *extra bit of air* to fully expand the lungs. Over time, this will start to increase lung volumes, one of the most reliable indicators of longevity.

> **TIP** The beauty of this BURST work-out is that you can (and should) vary the work-out to improve every part of the body.

Sink push-ups
Against the sink or desk, either with the knees bent or straight-legged, flat on the ground or at 45° (Fig. 3.61), perform the maximal number of push-ups (counting aloud) possible in 1 minute (no more!). Rest in the up position only, while breathing out on elevation. *Objective*: Try to achieve the same number as your age.

Swimming laps
In either a pool or the sea, swim freestyle until breathless. Over time, you will be able to go from one lap (50 meters in the sea) to two laps and so on in less and less time. Rest while lying on your back floating, and meditate on your slowing HR and breathing pattern.

FIGURE 3.61a

FIGURE 3.61b

Running in place
Next, for 1 minute while breathing deeply, lift your heels high enough to touch them with your hands, at the same rhythm and bounce as you would run on the beach or in the forest. *Hydrate*: rest and have a glass of lemon/lime water.

Chair dips
Using a chair (or any solid object of comparable height), keep your body straight and lower your buttocks to the ground, without resting them there, forming a right angle (Fig. 3.62). Repeat for a 1-minute count (no more), exhaling every time you come up or strain. *Hydrate*: rest and have a glass of lemon/lime water.

Jump rope
Get a rope made from leather or a coated wire cable (for speed) of 2.85 m in length. Check that the handles have ball bearings to make the swing smooth. For footwear, I prefer very light old running shoes. At the beginning, you may need long jogging pants as the leather rope may inadvertently slap your leg, causing a distraction. Perform for 1 minute or until winded. *Hydrate*: rest and have a glass of lemon/lime water.

Jumping jacks
With bare feet together, hold your arms at your sides, palms down (Fig. 3.63a). When ready, jump up in the air, smoothly spreading your feet just wider than your shoulders, while your arms form a semi-circle, gently touching over your head (Fig. 3.63b). Jump back to the original standing position. As the legs help return blood to the heart, they represent a "second heart." Invest in them. Perform for 1 minute or until winded. *Hydrate*: rest and have a glass of lemon/lime water.

Curl-ups (the "crunch")
Lift your head and shoulders off the ground about 15–20°, while sliding your hands along the floor towards your knees about 10 cm (Fig. 3.64). Perform the maximal number of curl-ups (counting aloud) possible in 1 minute (no

FIGURE 3.62a

FIGURE 3.62b

FIGURE 3.63a

FIGURE 3.63b

FIGURE 3.64a

FIGURE 3.64b

more). This action selectively strengthens the rectus abdominis muscles (those abdominal muscles in front known by body builders as the "six-pack") and provides frontal support to the lower back.

Do this slowly and completely until you feel the muscle "burn," and then do five more. As a variant to the above maneuver, tilt to the left and right side while coming up. This will strengthen the internal and external oblique muscle groups that act as a girdle to the side aspects of the abdomen. Exhale every time you come up or strain. *Use the sliding forward of the hands as an indicator of whether you are doing these correctly. Objective*: Try to achieve the same number as your age.

Stair climb

Everybody has access to a stairwell, either at work or at home. This is a super-convenient way to get several BURST work-outs into the day. Just before lunch, at breaks or before a stressful meeting, scurry up 3–4 floors *and back down*, engaging the legs by climbing *two steps at a time* (the quadriceps and the hamstrings are the body's biggest, strongest, most fat-burning muscle group). This is an *excellent* work-out for the lungs and for the heart. *Hydrate*: rest and have a glass of lemon/lime water.

Indian squats

Stand normally with your back straight and your feet slightly separated to the width of your shoulders, arms raised in front of you. Begin to bend the knees to come down to the squatting position (Fig. 3.65a). Gently squat as far down as you can, while keeping your *heels flat on the floor*, with your arms extended in front of you on the floor. Keeping your back always straight, come up while swinging your arms over your head as you come up (Fig. 3.65b, c). Perform for 1 minute or until winded. *Hydrate:* rest and have a glass of lemon/lime water.

FIGURE 3.65a

FIGURE 3.65b

FIGURE 3.65c

Stationary bike or rowing machine (RM)
Set this on an intermediate resistance setting and respect the timings.
Hydrate: rest and have a glass of lemon/lime water.

BURST for a stage 1 (beginner) athlete

Important note: To build up your heart (SV), lung capacity, and muscle mass more efficiently, choose different muscle groups and durations of repetitions, as suggested below.

Example 1 of a stage 1 BURST

WARM-UP ROUTINE	BURST CU	REST AND HYDRATE	BURST JJ	REST AND HYDRATE	BURST SPU	REST AND HYDRATE	BURST CD	REST AND HYDRATE
60 s	30 s	60 s	15 s	60 s	10 s	60 s	5 s	90 s

S = Seconds CU = Curl-ups JJ = Jumping jacks SPU = Sink push-ups CD = Chair dips

Total time = about 35 minutes/week
or

Example 2 of a stage 1 BURST: bike required

WARM-UP ROUTINE	BURST JJ	REST AND HYDRATE	BURST SB	REST AND HYDRATE	BURST CU	REST AND HYDRATE	BURST RP	REST AND HYDRATE
60 s	30 s	60 s	30 s	60 s	15 s	60 s	15 s	90 s

S = Seconds JJ = Jumping jacks SB = Stationary bike CU = Curl-ups RP = Running in place

Total time = about 40 minutes/week
or

Example 3 of a stage 1 BURST: pool or ocean required

WARM-UP ROUTINE	BURST JR	REST AND HYDRATE	BURST SL	REST AND HYDRATE	BURST IS	REST AND HYDRATE	BURST SC	REST AND HYDRATE
60 s	30 s	60 s	15 s	60 s	10 s	60 s	5 s	90 s

S = Seconds JR = Jump rope SL = Swimming laps IS = Indian squats SC = Stair climb

Total time = about 35 minutes/week
Continue this BURST until your:

1. RHR falls under 72 beats/minute, *and*
2. WHR is between 0.90 and 1.0
3. WWR line is **flat**
4. EC > 30 seconds.

Then proceed to stage 2 (intermediate to advanced) BURST.

> **TIP** These are to be done every morning before going to work, to help you get your blood oxygenated in the morning and build up your endurance in preparation for the day's stresses ahead of you.

TIP For those times when you are "on the road," traveling around the world, front load your day with this "anytime/anywhere" quick, intense, 4-minute BURST work-out

BURST for a stage 2 (intermediate to advanced) athlete

Important note: To build up your heart (SV), lung capacity, and muscle mass more efficiently, choose different muscle groups and durations of repetitions, as suggested below.

Example 1 of a stage 2 BURST

WARM-UP ROUTINE	BURST JJ	REST AND HYDRATE	BURST RP	REST AND HYDRATE	BURST SPU	REST AND HYDRATE	BURST CU	REST AND HYDRATE
60 s	60 s	90 s	50 s	90 s	40 s	90 s	30 s	90 s

JJ = Jumping jacks RP = Running in place SPU = Sink push-ups CU = Curl-ups

Total time = about 60 minutes/week
or

Example 2 of a stage 2 BURST

WARM-UP ROUTINE	BURST CU	REST AND HYDRATE	BURST JJ	REST AND HYDRATE	BURST SPU	REST AND HYDRATE	BURST CD	REST AND HYDRATE
60 s	60 s	90 s	60 s	90 s	30 s	90 s	30 s	90 s

CU = Curl-ups JJ = Jumping jacks SPU = Sink push-ups CD = Chair dips

Total time = about 60 minutes/week
or

Example 3 of a stage 2 SUPER BURST: adapted from the original Japanese study

WARM-UP ROUTINE	BURST SB	REST AND HYDRATE	BURST SB	REST AND HYDRATE	BURST SB	REST AND HYDRATE	BURST SB	REST AND HYDRATE	BURST SB	REST AND HYDRATE
60 s	20 s	60 s	20 s	60 s	20 s	60 s	20 s	60 s	20 s	60 s

SB = Stationary bike

(the ultimate time-saver: < 20 minutes/week)
Continue this work-out until your:

1. RHR falls under 60 beats/minute, *and*
2. WHR is < 0.90 (men) and < 0.80 (women)
3. WWR line is **flat**
4. EC > 90 seconds.

Two months later ... Doc kept his promise and I kept mine.

Both myself and Kamal are now well-trained athletes, capable of just about anything. I feel as though somehow I led my son away from early disease by doing so together. In fact, he's talking about doing the Paris marathon together next April, and Djamila will accompany us – to shop!

Fadi's second health and fitness report

	NORMAL/IDEAL RANGE	Baseline BEFORE the 8 weeks of the 4-minute BURST work-out ↓ ME (BASELINE)	Follow-up AFTER the 8 weeks of the 4-minute BURST work-out ↓ ME (2 MONTHS LATER)
Actual age (years)		42.4	42. 9
Health age (years)	Actual age (or less)	61.8	37. 3
Blood pressure (mmHg)	< 135/85	165/95	130/76
Resting heart rate (beats/minute)	< 60	78	60
Weight (kg)		110	100
Body fat %	< 20% men, < 23% women	35%	21%
Body fat weight (kg)		38.5	21
Lean weight (kg)		71.5	79
Waist-to-hip ratio	< 0.90 men, < 0.80 women	1.20	0.85
Weight-to-waist ratio	Up	Down	Flat
Fasting blood sugar (glucose) (g/L)	0.70–1.10	1.25	0.85
Uric acid (mg/L)	< 8.0	18.5	0.5
Cigarettes/day	0	28	2
Indian squats (number/minute until winded)	> 40/minute	4	24
Jumping jack (number/minute until winded)	> 60/minute	6	60
Push-ups (number/minute until winded)	> 35/minute	3	43
Jump rope (seconds until winded)	> 60 seconds	5	60
Exhalation count (seconds)	> 100	12	95
Early prostate cancer antigen-2 test (EPCA-2) (ng/mL)	< 30	25	0.65
Kamal's body fat	15–20%	28%	19%

CLOSING WORDS FROM A LEADER

When I was young, like many young kids growing up these days, I had a serious weight problem, which I wrote off to my inherent laziness. It got so bad that when I was 14, one of my teachers read my end of year report card in front of all my schoolmates:

> Fadi is lazy and lacks sufficient motivation to accomplish anything in life. He has an above average mind and below average discipline. His future is in doubt.

My school mates laughed riotously, but my father did not find that amusing. "Another disappointing year, Fadi. This won't do."

For nearly all my adult life, I found many reasons, excuses, and pretexts to actually avoid exercise and getting more active: my job responsibilities and the general stresses of modern life. After years of profound neglect leading to low energy and low productivity, I found that it only took a few sessions of focused exercise to get a reasonable semblance of fitness. Until I actually quantified my physical state (heart rate, body fat, WHR, EC, WWR, and so on), I had no idea what was happening under the surface. In fact, I wasn't in an irreparable state of body (Djamila's shopping bags *are* heavy!), only a doubting state of mind.

But after I (fortuitously) met some great people – Dr. MacGregor, and especially Abdul – that all changed. Being totally inspired, I shattered the "glass ceiling" or obstacles to health that I had constructed for myself. In a word, I had been listening to the wrong people, whom I had allowed to severely limit me with their discouragement.

The experience of having trained with Kamal was one of the peak experiences that *any* parent could have. We bonded completely. Arguments desisted. Now, when arguments with him get a little hot, he halts and interjects a little health into it by saying, "Whatever, Dad. Listen, I'm a bit frazzled. Let's go for a BURST work-out. By the way, I choose the music!"

But when I met Abdul, I met a *true* leader, because he taught that no teacher, no parent, just no one has the final world on how much one can achieve, how far your arrow can fly. Only you decide that. The other thing is that we find motivation in many forms, many hidden sources. A true leader finds inspiration and motivation in EVERYTHING. I don't try to create a hard time for myself; I just weave my exercises into my daily routine, especially on days I know will be packed with meetings.

Every time I walk up the four flights of stairs at my office (no longer the Himalayas they used to be), I know that my legs are helping my heart by "milking" the blood returning to my heart (my "venous return") with my leg muscles. I realize now that I cannot wait for any magical holiday or retirement to get fit. The battle for self-mastery plays out every minute of every morning.

> It comes down to one of a leader's highest qualities: self-awareness.

But, despair not, the good news that has been proven to me time after time is that it takes longer to get *out* of shape than to get back *into* a fit shape.

We are never more than a couple of weeks away from top shape. So now, in finishing, I lead myself and life is great! I have changed my view of exercise. It is no longer a dreaded option to avoid; it is a delightful privilege to engage my body (and mind). Now, I exercise at a level appropriate to my level for energy, not exhaustion. I take special delight in all sorts of small exercises to fine-tune and sculpt my body (like the BURST exercises, the longevity maneuvers, and pre-bed stretch: 25 Indian squats).

In my lexicon, what you do with your time and energy is your responsibility, your fun. No one is going to schedule life-saving, life-affirming exercises or any other fun for you. If you have scheduling conflicts or just find yourself wishing for 25 hours in the day, perform a "lifestyle audit": what aspects of your lifestyle, including work, are keeping exercise out? "Bosses," "Children," "Spouses" are all doubtful responses. There is only one guaranteed benefit that motivates best, the biggest payoff – feeling great – especially during these sometimes marathon negotiating meetings, when I seem to be the only one *not* falling asleep!

There's some activity for every taste and size, so do your own thing, whatever gives you pleasure just anticipating it. Just remember the key rule to progress:

Quantify to improve

In my particular case, there will be several health parameters along the way to fitness that act as gauges to my progress:

1. My RHR. This puts me squarely in charge of my fitness, allowing me to determine the effect of a day's work-out on my RHR.
2. My WWR.
3. My uric acid level.

But mostly:

4. How great I feel when I awake, knowing I shall able to enjoy as many aspects of my life for as long as possible!

HAP SUMMARY FOR FADI

1. BURST work-out *every* day.
2. BURST walking for 15 minutes after meals.
3. Juliette's yoga for a pain-free back three times per week.

LEADERS' TOP FAQS ON PHYSICAL FITNESS

I like using my RHR as an indicator of health. Does it have any predictive ability as to mortality?

Yes; in general, the lower the RHR, the more efficient the heart. Moreover, pulse rates give a reliable indication of the amount of work the heart is doing:

- RHR < 60 indicates a highly efficient pump: power to spare.
- RHR 80–94 indicates deteriorating health and imminent coronary artery disease;
- RHR > 94 indicates a 400% increase in mortality over the < 60 RHR group.

What are the essential medical tests that I need to monitor?

Get checked out before you get sick in case you can head off any future problems. See Table 3.1 for relevant tests.

TABLE 3.1 *Essential medical screening procedures*

MEDICAL TEST	IDEAL RANGE	COMMENTS
Medical screening procedures		
Blood pressure screening	< 135/85 mmHg	Home blood pressure machines are widely available and are especially helpful for those trying to monitor the effects of a stressful day
Body fat	< 20% men, < 23% women	Two or three times a year
Colonoscopy	Clear of polyps	According to the American Cancer Society, an estimated 104,950 colon and 40,340 rectal cancer cases occured in 2005, making colorectal cancer the third most common cancer in both men and women
Rectal exam	No occult blood, no prostate nodules	Also checks for prostate and occult blood in the digestive system
Mammogram	Normal for you	The American Cancer Society recommends annual mammograms for women aged 40 and older who are in good health. If there is a family history of breast cancer, the physician may recommend a different schedule
Breast exam	Normal for you	Every month outside of menstruation (see note below)
Pap smear (cervical cancer screen)	Normal for you	Women < 30 years old: every year; women > 30 years with 3 normal Pap tests for 3 consecutive years: every 2 or 3 years

MEDICAL TEST	IDEAL RANGE	COMMENTS
Skin check		Any change in the "ABCDE" of skin cancer: asymmetry, border, color, diameter, elevation
Testicular check	No masses or pain	Testicular cancer is usually diagnosed among young men in their early 20s, but it can occur in the younger age group and indeed up to the age of 50
Eye exam and pressure tests		Test for glaucoma
Laboratory blood tests		
Hematology (blood cells)		
Erythrocytes (red blood cells)	4,500,000–5,500,000 /mm³	Test for anemia
Hemoglobin	12.9–17.5 g%	Test for anemia
Hematocrit (% red cells in blood blood)	40–50%	Test for anemia
Mean corpuscular volume	80–95	< 80 = blood loss, > 95 = vitamin (B_{12}/folate) deficiency
Platelets	150,000–400,000 /mm³	Clot formers
Leukocyte family (white blood cells)	4,000–10,000 /mm³	First-line defense against inflammation or infection: elevation = "invader" present
Neutrophils	2,000–7,500 /mm³	Bacteria-busters
Eosinophils	< 800 /mm³	Allergies
Lymphocytes	1,500–4,000 /mm³	Viruses
Monocytes	< 1, 000 /mm³	Rocky Mountain Spotted Fever, malaria
High-sensitivity C-reactive protein	Less than 1 mg/L	Non-specific inflammation in the body; measure once a year
Homocysteine	7.0–10 micromoles/L	Once a year for cardiac risk
Uric acid	3.0 and 7.0 mg/dL	Men who drink sugary drinks have an 30% increased risk of gout
Lipid profile[5]		
Triglycerides (TGs)	< 1.40 g/L	These are the fats in the blood
High-density lipoprotein (HDL)	> 0.50 g/L	"Cleans" the arteries: higher = better
TGs:HDL	< 1	Excellent indicator of the artery's patency

MEDICAL TEST	IDEAL RANGE	COMMENTS
Low-density lipoprotein (LDL)	< 1.30 g/L	"Clogs" the arteries: lower = better
Fasting blood sugar (glucose)	0.7–1.20 g/L	Everybody should know their fasting blood sugar
Kidney exams		
Creatinine	8.0 – 13.0 mg/dL	Kidney check : if > 13, increase water intake
Liver function tests[6]		Measure enzymes produced by the liver which show up in blood when the liver is injured
SGOT (aka AST)	9–38 U/L	See Reference 6 for elaboration
SGPT (aka ALT)	0–41 U/L	
GGT	0–61 U/L	Sensitive to alcohol
Prostate		
Prostate-specific antigen	< 40 ng/mL	An annual PSA test for men over age 50 is recommended
Early prostate cancer antigen-2 (EPCA2)[7]	30 ng/mL (nanograms per milliliters) or higher indicates a risk for prostate cancer	Unlike PSA, this protein is not found in normal prostate cells, but is found in relatively large amounts in prostate cancer cells

Note: Obesity affects prostate tests. The PSA test used to check for prostate cancer may give abnormally low results in obese men, who have more blood in their bodies, thereby diluting the concentration of the PSA protein. Most obese men had concentrations of PSA 11–21% lower than men of normal weight. Finally, watch your PSA velocity – the measurement of how your PSA levels rise over time. You need at least three PSA measurements to get an accurate PSA velocity. Your PSA measurements should be between 6 months and 2 years apart. A normal PSA velocity is less than 0.75 ng/mL per year. Any higher is an indication of an increased risk for prostate cancer.

The importance of breast exams

The risk of developing breast cancer increases with age, and the incidence of breast cancer is rising with an aging population. A general rule of thumb always applies to cancer, particularly breast cancer: survival is linked directly to early detection. The American Cancer Society reports that, after skin cancer, breast cancer is the most frequently diagnosed cancer among women in the US and the leading cause of cancer death among women aged 40–54. However, with early detection, more than 95% of women with breast cancer survive at least 5 years after diagnosis. There are two steps to breast self-examination:

1. Women, including teenagers, should examine their breasts several days after their menstrual periods — when the breasts are least tender and

nodular. First, hold your arms at your sides and look at your breasts in the mirror to check for changes in size, shape or color, puckering or dimpling of the skin. Check the nipples for any secretion or blood. Repeat with your arms raised over your head.

2. Then, lie down and use the fingers on your right hand to examine your left breast. Use light pressure followed by medium pressure and then firm pressure on each coin-sized area before moving on to the next. Using this method, cover the entire breast, including from collarbone to belly button and armpit to sternum. Repeat on the other side.

What indoor exercise equipment should I buy?

Consider investing in the following equipment, particularly if you live where the weather is cold and wet, and have a family and a little space:

- *Treadmill.* Get one with a real motor (1–2 horsepower is best) as walking briskly up an incline of 10–20° is comparable to jogging. Make sure that the handrails can support you while you are running.
- *Rowing machines.* These exercise not just the upper body; in fact, if properly done, the work done by the extension of the leg can be up to 75% of the total work done. Try the wind-resistance type (more natural) and always keep your back straight by pulling your elbows tight against your body during the pulling phase.
- *Stationary bicycle.* Try the ones with a friction belt or wind as resistance. There are several things to note here: (a) the seated models are easier on the back; (b) use the pedal rat-traps to exercise the muscles both in the front and at the back of the leg; and (c) adjust the seat so that your knees are slightly bent (160°) to prevent undue wear on the knees.
- *Stair-climbers.* These are an expensive choice. Keep your knees over your feet, your back straight and your arms lightly on the handrails for the optimal work-out.
- *Ski simulators.* These give the most intense work-out, using both the upper and lower body. But considerable skill is required, and for non-skiers this may be an obstacle.

As a Muslim, I do not drink alcohol. Are there other ways to get the benefits of wine without drinking?

Everyone knows that a glass of red wine is beneficial to the heart: rates of heart disease among the wine-loving French are 50% lower than in the US. But red wine is not the only (or even the best) way that you can avail yourself of these benefits: grape seeds are even more powerful. They contain anti-oxidants that have been scientifically proven to:

- decrease the size of solid tumors;
- fight infections;
- improve blood sugar and insulin sensitivity;

- slow aging of the brain and increase mental capacity;
- boost HDL and strengthen blood vessels.

The superingredients in grape seeds are something called proanthocyanidins (or PCOs). They go after free radicals, and are 20 times stronger than vitamin E and 50 times stronger than vitamin C.

Years of scientific research back this up:

- Studies from the University of New York show that grapeseed oil raised HDL by 13% and lowered LDL by 7%. TGs went down by 17%.
- Studies show that high levels of linoleic acid (an essential fatty acid) prevent blood from clotting and help prevent heart attacks and strokes. In a Japanese study (published by the American Heart Association), researchers found that linoleic acid lowered the risk of stroke by 34%. They also found that it lowered blood pressure and improved circulation in small blood vessels.

What is the key to long life?

In a study published October 2008 in the *Archives of Internal Medicine*, it was reported that men who exercised, were the right weight, and did not smoke during retirement increased their chances of living for another 25 years – and the chances of reaching 90 were surprisingly dependent on behaviour from age 70 onwards. The researchers gave a list of negative factors and their estimated effect on the odds of a 70-year-old man reaching 90. These included high blood pressure, lack of exercise, smoking, obesity, diabetes, and a sedentary lifestyle.

In this particular study, the researchers used the data from 2,350 men from the Public Health Service study. Those who were included were born on or before December 31, 1915, did not have any serious life-threatening diseases and "had the potential to live to or beyond 90 years during a 25-year follow-up" (i.e. they were around 70 years old at the start of the study).

The main interest of the study was survival to age 90, an age the researchers considered to be of "exceptional longevity" and far greater than the expected lifespan (46–52 years) of men born in the US between 1900 and 1915. Data on the occurrence of major age-related diseases (cancer, heart disease, and stroke) were also collected. A smaller group of the men (686 of them) answered a questionnaire about their physical function and mental health in the 16th year of follow-up.

Exercising in the city: a good or bad idea?

It can be as dangerous to be outdoors behind a city bus – walking or bicycling – as it is to be in front of one. The main problems are:

- ozone, which causes the airways in the lungs to become smaller and more resistant to oxygen exchange;

- particulate matter, which is emitted by the diesel engines;
- carbon monoxide from cigarette smoke and automobile exhaust. This has a tremendous ability to force oxygen out of our circulatory system. Over-exposure may lead to headache, dizziness, confusion, and dangerous increases in body temperature.

To protect yourself, exercise indoors, preferably in an air-conditioned room. If you must go outdoors, the early morning or late evening is best. It will be cooler, the sun is not at its peak, and the ozone levels will be at their lowest.

Is exercise good for fatigue?

According to a 2008 study in *Psychotherapy and Psychosomatics*, sedentary people who regularly complain of fatigue can increase their energy levels by 20% and decrease their fatigue by 65% by engaging in regular, low-intensity exercise.

The volunteers were divided into three groups. The first engaged in 20 minutes of moderate-intensity aerobic exercise three times a week for 6 weeks, the second engaged in low-intensity aerobic exercise for the same time period, and the control group did not exercise. The low- and moderate-intensity groups had a 20% increase in energy levels over the control group.

I am pregnant and have occasional "blue moments" of gentle depression. Should I exercise?

A study in a recent issue of the *Journal of General Internal Medicine* presents data that cite exercise as an effective means for preventing deterioration in physical function and emotional health for pregnant women. Researchers observed significant changes in health during pregnancy, including a decline in the ability to perform daily functions and increased signs of depression, both of which improved during the postpartum period. The American College of Obstetricians and Gynecologists suggests 30 minutes of moderate exercise for pregnant women on most, if not all, days of the week. Statistics show that over 90% of women in the workforce continue to work up to the month before delivery. Of the 60% of women who return to work in the year after delivery, two-thirds return to work within 3 months.

What are the most time-efficient ways to gain real stamina?

There are three key ingredients to achieving high stamina (stamina = capability of sustaining prolonged stressful effort) – attitude, exercise, and nutrition:

- Work not from compulsion (that's workaholism), but from the enthusiasm that comes with being part of the dynamic world economy. Staying excited about life will keep your energy focused.

- Avoid confused and cynical people: they will demoralize and de-energize you.
- Surround yourself with people with a sense of mission and grand design – the fastest way to get energized.
- As the day wears on and you notice your first yawn, take five deep breaths, do 45 (or your age) desk push-ups or BURST Indian squats, and take another five deep breaths. Alternatively, catch a cat nap – drop your head to your chest, smile, and let go in the taxi on the way to the airport or while waiting.
- Drink lots of water and freshly squeezed juice. Replace coffee with kiwi juice with vitamin C crystals. Avoid carbohydrates because they tend to raise blood levels of serotonin, a natural tranquilizer for the brain.

Should I, as a woman, work out with weights?

Weights twice a week can help women prevent "middle-aged spread" and keep their hearts healthy, a 2008 study shows. On average, middle-aged women gain 1 kg of body fat every year from 40 years of age. Over 20 kg can put them in the same risk category as men of the same age, particularly if the body fat is distributed around the waist. After 2 years, the study demonstrated, the women in the weight-training group lost an average of 4% in body fat, while the women in the control group showed no change in body fat. The study also found that weight training reduced intra-abdominal fat, which is associated with heart disease and metabolic disturbances.

Am I exercising too much?

Not if you are free of these cardinal signs of overtraining:

- body fat < 5%;
- soreness, injuries, frequent infections, high pulse (> 68 beats/minute);
- moodiness, depression, fatigue, insomnia, and low appetite.

My friend said we all should do some jogging, but I cannot stand it. Any ideas?

To determine the physical exercise most appropriate for you, do a mental exercise. Imagine your genetic ancestors, many thousands of years ago, sitting around a camp fire. We are all descendants from various tribal forebears and, as such, we all had roles: some of our forebears were group hunters, some were lone hunters, some were gatherers, some were planners, and some were care-givers. Everybody had a role that best suited their personality and body habits. Running is for the ancestral hunters while walking is for everyone, at all ages, regardless of health status.

Why do we do the BURST 4-minute work-outs to the point of being "winded"?

In a Japanese study on the maximum volume of oxygen that could be utilised in 1 minute of exercise – the gold standard of cardiopulmonary fitness (the VO_2 Max) – cyclists were divided into in two groups. One group did endurance, mid-intensity (70% VO_2 Max) cycling for 60 minutes, and the other did bursts (seven sets of 20 seconds with 10-second rest periods in between) of high-intensity cycling (170% VO_2 Max levels). Over a 6-week period, both groups exercised 5 days a week.

The results were that the mid-intensity endurance group had *inferior* performances in both the aerobic (VO_2 Max) and the anaerobic energy supply systems. Therefore, to gain in efficiency of the cardiopulmonary system, it must be expanded by imposing intensive stimuli on it.

	TOTAL TIME OF WORK-OUT PER WEEK (MINUTES)	VO_2MAX INCREASE	ANAEROBIC INCREASE
Mid-intensity endurance group	300	8	0
BURST high-intensity group	< 20	15	30

Am I actually increasing the quantity of my life by being health-conscious?

You are improving not just the quantity, but the quality as well. Researchers studied the medical records of 366,000 people in Chicago to determine the effects of pursuing a "low-risk lifestyle" (blood pressure of 120/80 mmHg or lower, no cigarettes, total cholesterol < 2.0 g/L, and no diabetes or known heart disease). Their health was tracked for 20 years, during which time 38,000 died. The conclusions were that:

- low-risk men aged under 40 had an 89% lower death rate from coronary artery disease over others in their age group, with no deaths from stroke;
- low-risk men aged 40–59 had 64% less strokes than higher-risk men;
- overall low-risk men had a 50% lower death rate from cancer;
- low-risk women had a 17% lower death rate from cancer;
- low-risk men and women aged 40–59 had a 78% lower death rate.

Would you recommend long-distance races such as marathon running?

Yes and no. Yes, because what you learn during the 4 months of disciplined training is fantastic. Every marathoner knows the contemplation and its benefits that come from long runs in the forest, along the sea, and in the fields. No, because it can be hazardous to your health. The Harvard Health Professionals Study supports this. Researchers followed over 7,000 people and found that the key to exercise was not length or endurance, but *intensity*. The more intense the exertion, the lower their risk of heart disease.

How safe are health clubs?

In a series of random surveys of fitness clubs in the US, researchers found that many (28%) failed to screen new members to identify potential risks, 92% failed to conduct emergency drills, and 60% had no written medical emergency response plans available. Recommendations by the American Heart Association include the above measures, together with full certification in cardiopulmoney resuscitation. Gyms could invest in defibrillators as well, since their populations are getting older and older.

Is exercise effective for depression?

The Mental Health Foundation in the UK published the results of a 2008 survey showing that the number of GPs prescribing exercise as a treatment for depression has gone up in the last 3 years. The study found that 22% of GPs now prescribe exercise as one of the three preferred treatments for depression. Three years ago, this figure was only 5%. Over the last 3 years, the Mental Health Foundation has been campaigning for doctors to increase their use of exercise therapy to treat mild to moderate depression.

The new report shows there has been a significant change among GPs in their beliefs about the effectiveness of exercise as a way to treat depression. Over 60% of them now believe that a supervised exercise regime is a "very effective" or "quite effective" way to treat mild to moderate depression. This compares with just over 40% 3 years ago. The GPs said they were also noticing an increase in patients' interest in exercise therapy as way to treat depression.

As an obese female manager (body fat = 35%), what is the *minimum* amount of exercise needed to get back into shape?

According to a new study, just 10–30 minutes of exercise every day can greatly improve the quality of life for older, overweight women. Researchers stated that minimal exercise has the ability to greatly improve the health of obese postmenopausal women.

The study looked at 430 obese women with an average age of 57. The study proved the long-held belief true, that exercise can make older women have more energy and just feel better; even with just 10 minutes of exercise each day, women can see benefits. The study found that women who exercised ended up being much happier, and also having more social skills due to the newfound confidence of feeling fit and being energetic. Women also experienced better daily functions, such as better physical condition, as well as the ability to do things they were able to do when they were younger.

After exercising for 6 months, the women improved almost 7% in physical function and general health, 16.6% in vitality, 11.5% in performing work or other activities, 11.6% in emotional health, and more than 5% in social functioning.

Most of the exercise was divided into three or four sessions a week. When not in organized exercise, these women were fitted with pedometers. Researchers also advised older women to join gyms that had specific sections for women or that were targeted at women.

Is sex safe after a heart attack?

Yes, in fact, love-making should be prescribed for patients with a heart problem in the same way that we prescribe pure nutrition, medications, and exercise. In a study of more than 850 men and women who had survived heart attacks, it was demonstrated the chance of provoking a heart attack with sex was less than 2 in 1,000,000! This is particularly true if sex is supplemented with a regular walking program, as the well-conditioned muscular system is more efficient in extracting oxygen from the blood and delivering it to the heart.

When should I do a work-out?

Any time during the day that suits you. If you cannot work out, eat light and walk.

Is 4 minutes long enough to condition the body?

Our research indicates that, done properly, the BURST 4-minute work-out prepares both the body and the mind for the inherent stresses facing the business community. That's a total investment of less than 30 minutes a week!

Why can't I sleep well after activity?

You are overexcited. Do the work-out in the morning.

Does sex count as exercise?

Optimal sexuality is as good as any motivator (and better than most). Although sexual expression is obviously a complex and highly individualized affair, essentially what is happening is that we are using the body to connect with our partners, to lose our separation: a sort of emotional and physical meltdown.

It helps to have a body that can manage its way through physical intimacy. So exercise can increase your endurance and optimize your body fat so that a pleasurable experience lasts even longer and is more intense. That's because of the effect of regular aerobic exercise on the reproductive and cardiovascular systems: muscles are better toned and conditioned, arteries supplying the sexual organs are open and delivering oxygen and glucose to the penis better, and men have more testosterone in their blood. All these effects are important in maintaining erections. Psychologically, a toned body also provides the necessary confidence and self-esteem to allow you to let the body "do its thing" without a lot of neurotic interference.

What are some tips for the fasting months of Ramadan?

1. Cinnamon tea; water (sodas are dangerous to weight and brain)
2. Iftar: go easy and slow: lots of protein, no sugar
3. Load up on barley, wheat, oats, millet, semolina, beans, lentils, wholemeal flour, unpolished rice
4. To avoid constipation: vegetables (green beans, peas, spinach), fruit with skin, dried fruit (dried apricots, figs, prunes), almonds.

My father, who is a recent widower, is alone and wants to stay active. Any ideas?

Have your father try Tai Chi Chuan (Tai Chi for short) because it improves *balance*, thus reducing the incidence of falls. Almost 40% of ambulatory people over the age of 65 living in a community fall every year. Another 50% of the same age group living in long-term care facilities suffer from at least one fall annually, 10% of these falls in turn resulting in a fracture. These untimely falls and fractures represent the leading cause of death for people over 65, and the number of fall-related deaths continues to increase with every passing year.

How does Tai Chi help?

■ Tai Chi consists of fluid, gentle, graceful, and circular movements that are relaxed and slow in motion, making it appropriate for any age group.

■ Exercises involve dynamic weight transition between different types of posture, exchange between loading and unloading of the two legs, and coordination between lower extremity and upper body movements.

■ Over time, Tai Chi accelerates blood circulation, strengthens and mobilizes joints and muscles, and significantly improves both physical fitness and mental relaxation.

■ Practitioners are generally more alert, flexible, and physically active, all positive factors that could theoretically reduce the risk of falling.

■ In a study involving 256 physically inactive adults, aged 70–92, all subjects could ambulate independently and had no cognitive impairments. Each participant was randomly assigned to either the Tai Chi group or the stretching group (control) for 6 months, with a 50-minute exercise session given three times per week. The functional balance of members of the Tai Chi group improved significantly, whereas the control group showed no such improvement. Only 28 falls were reported during the post-intervention period for the Tai Chi group, compared to 74 falls for the controls.

Can doing exercise help teenagers feel confident?

Unconfident teenagers would feel less awkward if they took more exercise. This 5-year study revealed that teenagers' physical self-worth decreased significantly between the ages of 11 and 16 for females but not for their male counterparts. The study found that this corresponded with a drop in activity levels at this age. It was found that there was a sharp decline in physical activity for girls aged 13–15 but not for their male classmates.

The reasons for these decreases may be due to the increased self-consciousness experienced during adolescence as well as increased academic pressures felt due to the Standard Attainment Tests. This may affect females more because they perceive academic success as more important than excelling in sports. This may result in decreases in physical activity and physical self-worth.

How much exercise do children need? Will being active protect them against diabetes, cancer or heart disease later in life? Will it prevent them from becoming overfat and losing confidence?

The official view is clear: the American Heart Association recommends that children and young adults under the age of 18 should be active for at least 60 minutes each day. Furthermore, the undisputed benefits of exercise, the panels said, are that it can lead to stronger muscles, greater endurance, and bones that are denser and have greater mineral content. In addition, when obese children exercise regularly, their body fat, blood lipids, and blood pressure may fall. But why don't they do it, then?

Is there any link between physical inactivity and the emotional issues that teenagers seem to have more and more?

A Finnish study, published in a late 2008 issue of *Medicine & Science in Sports & Exercise*, involved more than 7,000 boys and girls between the ages of 15 and 16 answering surveys about their activity levels and their emotions. Both boys and girls shared similar issues with social and attention problems when compared to their physically active peers. Boys who reported less than 1 hour of moderate to vigorous physical activity a week had more symptoms of anxiety, depression, and withdrawal, as well as thinking problems. Physically inactive girls had comparable problems but more commonly reported psychosomatic somatic complaints and rule-breaking behaviors. Compounding that with the negative mental and emotional effects brought on by physical inactivity does not. Physical activity could be a highly effective and relatively easy way to help young people ease into adulthood and to develop a healthful, disease-free lifestyle throughout life.

Caffeinated energy drinks: hazardous to your health?

According to the manufacturers, caffeinated energy drinks are aimed at people wanting to combat mental and physical fatigue. A 250 mL (8.3 fl oz) can contains:

1. 21.5 g of *sucrose* (table sugar) and 5.25 g of *glucose*, another simple sugar. Note that sugar-free caffeinated energy drinks have no sucrose or glucose, but have aspartame instead.
2. 50 mg of *inositol* – a type of sugar that is structurally different than glucose. It is a basic part of cell membranes, crucial in brain, nerve, and muscle function. It comes from plants and can be commonly found in many foods. It is presently being studied for potential cancer prevention.
3. 1000 mg of *taurine* (also known as 2-aminoethanesulfonic acid, or sulfonic acid). This is an organic acid and a major ingredient of bile. It is also present in small amounts in the living tissues of humans and most animals.
4. 600 mg of *glucuronolactone*, a naturally occurring chemical compound produced by the human liver during glucose metabolism. This is a crucial component of nearly all our connective tissues. It is commonly found in plant gums. It is added to drinks because it is said to boost energy.
5. 20 mg of *niacin*, a type of vitamin B that increases blood HDL levels.
6. 5 mg of *vitamin B_6* (known as pyridoxine). We need this for the synthesis of the neurotransmitters serotonin and norepinephrine, and for myelin formation around the nerves.
7. 5 mg of *vitamin B_5* (pantothenic acid). It is water-soluble and the body cannot store it. If the body cannot use all of the vitamin it takes in, the excess leaves the body through the urine. It must therefore be replaced every day. As well as being essential for growth, it helps the body break down and use food (metabolism).
8. 0.005 mg of *vitamin B_{12}* (cobalamin). We need it to make red blood cells and DNA; it is also used to keep nerves healthy. It is commonly given to cancer patients, along with folate, to help reduce the side effects of cancer treatment with antimetabolites.
9. 80 mg of *caffeine*. Caffeine is a mild diuretic – a substance that increases the amount of urine you pass – so it makes you shed more water/liquid. It also acts as a psychoactive stimulant drug. In humans, caffeine can restore alertness temporarily. It is commonly found in coffee, tea, soft drinks, and energy drinks. It is the most popular psychoactive substance on earth. A 250 mL can of caffeinated energy drinks has about the same amount of caffeine as one would find in a 250 mL cup of coffee – about double what you would consume if you had a 330 mL can of cola.

In comparison, here are the caffeine concentrations of a 355 mL serving of some commonly consumed beverages:

- Brewed coffee: 200 g
- Instant coffee: 140 mg
- Brewed tea: 80 mg
- Mountain Dew: 54 mg
- Dr. Pepper: 41 mg
- Coca-Cola Classic: 34.5 mg
- Canned or bottled tea: 20 mg.

I have noticed that, during major sporting events, my mates and I can get quite "red in the face," particularly when the action gets hot. Any health hazard here?

The researchers studied patients who had contacted emergency services and had been treated by an emergency doctor at the time of the football World Cup in summer 2006. Taking all seven games, the number of emergencies per day (the rate) was 2.66 times that of the control periods, and this difference was statistically significant (i.e. less likely to have occurred by chance). The rate of male emergencies was 3.26 times the rate of the control period, while the female rate was 1.82 times that of the control period.

Almost half of the people who had emergencies when Germany played already had heart disease, and the rate of emergency for them was four times the rate during the control period. The researchers who carried out the study advised that the effect was so significant that men with known heart problems should be given medication before watching a big match.

Can exercise reduce the risk of Alzheimer's disease?

A 2008 Mayo Clinic study found that regular physical exercise may help protect against mild cognitive impairment, a disorder of the brain involved in thinking abilities. Individuals with mild cognitive impairment can function reasonably well in everyday activities but often have difficulty remembering details of conversations, events, and upcoming appointments. Most (but not all) patients with mild cognitive impairment develop a progressive decline in their thinking abilities over time. Alzheimer's disease is usually the underlying cause.

A team of Mayo Clinic researchers randomly identified 868 individuals 70–89 years old of whom 128 had mild cognitive impairment and 740 were cognitively normal. The team conducted surveys to gather data on the individuals' physical exercise between the ages of 50 and 65, and 1 year prior to the survey. They found that moderate physical exercise 2–5 times per week during age 50–65 was associated with a reduced risk of mild cognitive impairment. However, the individual's exercise habits 1 year prior to the survey did not appear to be associated with a reduced risk. How does it happen? Exercise induces brain chemicals that protect brain cells, *plus* provides a strong social network.

The best ...

- The best time to work out ... early morning: high resolve and motivation, high oxygen
- The best way to get in shape in only 30 seconds ...a chin-up bar (also the cheapest)
- The best way to improve abdominal tone ... the crunch + abdominal snap
- The best hotel work-out ... yoga, jump rope, BURST 4-minute work-out
- The best maneuver for back stiffness ... the Indian squat
- The best maneuver for back pain ... the knees-to-chest maneuver
- The best exercise for preventing back pain ... the abdominal crunch (curl-ups)

NOTES AND REFERENCES

1. Endurance exercises are not the most effective way to get into shape or even live a long life.
2. Williams PT. Relationships of heart disease risk factors to exercise quantity and intensity. *Arch Intern Med* 1998; **158**: 237–45.
3. Lee I et al. Relative intensity of physical activity and risk of coronary heart disease. *Circulation* 2003; **1087**: 2220–6.
4. Mantra, meaning beyond the (left) mind.
5. There have been new developments in cholesterol testing. Traditional cholesterol scores are *not* very good indicators of early cardiovascular disease. Many people with high cholesterol never develop heart problems, and at least half of the people who have heart attacks have *normal* cholesterol levels.

    A better test has finally arrived though may not be available near you just yet: the VAP (Vertical Auto Profile) cholesterol test. Even more importantly, the old test only picks up about 45% of cholesterol problems, but the VAP test identifies about 90% or more of them.

    In addition to the basic scores – total cholesterol, HDLs, LDLs, and TGs – the VAP test includes new categories of the lipid profile, the most important of which are lipoprotein A, LDL pattern size, the metabolic syndrome, and lipid remnants. These extra data make the test much more effective in predicting heart attack or stroke. Data from the VAP test can help determine whether your cholesterol is actually dangerous or if it is present in your bloodstream but virtually harmless in terms of triggering a heart attack.

6. Here are some useful tips to interpret the LFTs: SGOT (aka AST) and SGPT (aka ALT) are the most sensitive tests for liver cell injury (as a result of alcohol, toxins, viruses or drugs):
    - mild elevation of SGPT (ALT) between 50 and 100 U/L, most likely due to fatty liver secondary to high glycemic index foods (especially in non-drinkers), body fat, and alcohol;
    - mild elevation of SGOT (AST) + SGPT (ALT) could be due to alcohol;
    - SGOT (AST) > 500 U/L is unlikely to be from alcohol use alone; consider acetaminophen (Dolipran/Tylenol) toxicity;

- isolated elevation of GGT: quite commonly due to fatty liver secondary to high glycemic index foods (especially in non-drinkers) or induced by alcohol (in drinkers);
- SGOT/SGPT > 2, with SGPT < 300 U/L indicates alcoholic hepatitis.

7. In a multi-institutional study published in 2003 in the *Journal of Urology*, PSA levels between 4 and 10 ng/mg were shown to be accurate in identifying prostate cancer only 19% of the time compared to the EPCA-2 test, which detected 94% of the men with prostate cancer.

The leader's brain: protecting the hardware

If the Brain were so simple that we could understand it, we would be so simple that we could not.

Lyall Watson, SuperNature

In this chapter, you will learn by illustrative example, how to first get it wrong and then get it right by:

1. Controlling blood pressure
2. Protecting the brain against strokes
3. Preparing the brain to avoid Alzheimer's disease
4. Learning the importance of prioritization
5. Learning the benefits of laughter

Abbreviations and acronyms that you will need to read this chapter smoothly include:

AGE	Advanced glycation end-product
EFA	Essential fatty acid
EPA	Eicosapentaenoic acid
TIA	Transient ischemic attack

INTRODUCTION

Hello, my name is Rachel. I am the 42-year-old director of the marketing division of a large IT company (in the UK) for northern Europe. I am the daughter of Richard (thin, heavy drinker, and hyperactive) and Joan (who subsequently developed symptoms of dementia, weight gain, and mild diabetes), and the youngest in a family of four children – three boys and myself.

My father was the owner of a shoe shop in own town, while my mother looked after the children. My memories of my childhood were the arguments about money, getting by, spending less, the price of food going up (my brothers and I held a yearly contest to see what vacations we were *not* taking that year). It seemed that my family was in a constant financial crisis.

As in the case of my three brothers, who are all accomplished scientists and businessmen (and musicians), I set out to construct the bridge between my reality and my dreams. There was a Christmas, after seeing the film *Gone with the Wind* for the first (of six) times, when I stood in front of my older brothers and, holding my chest, I stated:

As God is my witness, I'll never be hungry again!

PROFESSIONAL LIFE

Throughout my professional career (electrical engineer and MBA), I had always been thin and somewhat hyperactive, so never really suffered from any lack of energy, fueled by my own world view, plenty of sugary coffees, sweets, and diet colas.

My working days were intense, starting at 5.30 a.m. every day and finishing late (well after my son Adam had gone to bed). I had even made time for the gym and spent about 2 hours a week there, usually in my lunch hour.

Though I suffered occasionally from twinges of guilt, I wrote it off as "part of the territory" for a single professional mother and, God willing, a prospective leader in my field. As "down-payment" on this dream, I made sure that Adam had everything he needed and wanted, including a portable phone (at 10 years of age, against my better judgment), an MP3 player, and his own PC.

Nevertheless, true to his genetics, Adam would from time to time make off-the-cuff comments on Saturday mornings regarding my work priorities and lack of availability for his piano recitals. However, I felt deep down that, all things considered, I was successfully managing to juggle my personal and professional lives.

PRIVATE LIFE

In our family, complaining was not even an option. If there was a problem, you dealt with it, silently. Strangely, I felt quite comfortable with this arrangement, as I was not particularly eager to bare the intimate details of my soul's tortured ideations to my older brothers. In fact, while growing up in a family of boys, I can distinctly remember being constantly teased for being such a "tomboy": I reveled in the attention I received by refusing any interest in "girly" things (dolls, jump ropes) and felt immediately attracted to things my brothers were doing: science, business, sport, and career.

Throughout my adolescence, I excelled in my science studies and started running long-distance races (10K and half marathons). My family, to my pleasure, seemed to take my studies very seriously, as they knew full well that I was capable of obsessing myself with a subject that I enjoyed or in which I simply wanted to excel. At the dinner table, when we reached a heated impasse in an argument on practically any subject, my father would say "Stop! Let's ask Rachel. Rachel, what do you think?" As I scrolled mentally for the answer (that always seemed to be there waiting), I had to hide my smile, as I basked in the light of their attention.

As I started accumulating diplomas and running medals, and to my *secret* pleasure, my brothers called me "nerd," "geek," "hermit," "CD-ROM Rachel," the "Computer Kid," and so on. And, of course, the other signs of achievement started rolling in: the money, the baubles, gadgets galore – all indicating that I would never be as poor as my parents.

They even joked from time to time that I would never find a man who could keep up with me intellectually or physically. And they were not completely wrong in their assessments. I had subjugated all aspects of my social life to my career climb. However, I did finally get married (I found it excessively confining), had a beautiful son, Adam, and watched helplessly as the marriage slowly atrophied on the branch as our careers and personalities pulled us apart. The divorce was a "whatever" kind of decision, as insipid as the marriage had been. Although it came at a bad time for Adam, aged 10, he seemed to take it well.

HEALTH PROFILE

I had figured that, as a thin female, there could not be anything wrong. For the chronic headaches I got, aspirin and a little relaxation usually did the trick. For my insomnia, a couple of gin and tonics usually worked to get me relaxed and to sleep at night.

NUTRITION

Fast food, business lunches, sandwiches, Kit-Kats, diet colas, whatever, to keep the furnaces going, night and day.

PHYSICAL AND INTELLECTUAL ACTIVITY

I had made sure that whatever I had set myself to master, I would muster the focus to get it done. I would soon learn that it was a good character trait to have on the road to becoming a leader. I did sports: racquet ball, and tennis when a court was available.

Most important leadership quality	Confidence
My idea of great leaders	• Winston Churchill, as a wartime leader • Aung San Suu Kyi, Burmese activist • Mahatma Gandhi
My most inspiring quotation Never, never, never give up. <div align="right">Winston Churchill</div>	

MY FIRST WAKE-UP CALL: THE FIRST CHECK-UP

Eventually, as part of the corporate wellness efforts at work, I dutifully presented myself to the specialists for a complete medical check-up, albeit in a somewhat anxious state of mind. It was time to "take stock."

Rachel's baseline health and fitness report

	NORMAL/IDEAL RANGE	ME
Actual age (years)		42
Health age (years)	Actual age (or less)	49.5
Blood pressure (mmHg)	< 135/85	175/100
Resting heart rate (beats/minute)	< 60	82
Body fat %	< 20% men, < 23% women	15%
Waist-to-hip ratio	< 0.90 men, < 0.80 women	0.75
Total cholesterol (g/L)	< 2.00	1.85
High-density lipoprotein cholesterol (g/L)	> 0.50	0.55
Low-density lipoprotein cholesterol (g/L)	< 1.30	0.95
Triglycerides (g/L)	< 1.40	0.75
Fasting blood sugar (glucose) (g/L)	0.70–1.20	1.65
Homocysteine (micromoles/L)	7.0–10	30.5

In fact, I was quite concerned with the results, especially the blood pressure, fasting blood sugar (glucose) and homocysteine readings, which I assumed were due to excessive caffeine, sugary snacks, and stress (a bad time of year). But, as with numbers at work, the results did not seem that far off the standards and so I let the whole issue slide a bit into oblivion.

The doctor, however, was quite insistent that I should not take this too lightly, since my father had had a stroke at age 65 and Mother had early signs of Alzheimer's disease. Nothing could have prepared me for this news. I was *dumbstruck*. One of my concerns was what I would tell Adam to not make him nervous, as my divorce had had an effect of rendering my little bundle of laughter much more subdued, less joyous. After all, Adam was my son, not some fashion accessory or another task on my daily checklist of things to manage! Or was he?

Several months later, prompted by the untimely death a colleague at work who suddenly died of a heart attack, I decided to take stock at home, to see where I stood with my son. One calm Saturday afternoon, on the way back from a piano lesson, I asked Adam sitting next to me in the front seat of the car how he might describe me to friends. I expected nice words like "caring," "generous," "warm," or the like, I was flabbergasted when Adam, with his characteristic honesty (and bluntness), answered, "Well, Mommy, you're never around, you are always busy at work and traveling." He continued, "and sometimes when I interrupt you talking on the phone, you get cross and angry with me, but just *some* of the time, Mom. It's not really that important. Your *career* is more important. I understand. Don't worry about me." But the image of those two ideas, "absent" and "angry," etched into my tombstone started to haunt my dreams at night, and then even caught up with me during my daydreams.

MY SECOND WAKE-UP CALL

My next wake-up call came unexpectedly one morning just before setting off to work, while engaged in a heated conversation with a colleague over the kitchen phone. Given his recent reflections on my character, I was making an obvious effort to spare Adam the trauma of these kinds of daily intense conversations. Watching him as he munched his breakfast cereal, I tried hard to appear relaxed and centered as I spoke, smiling broadly and avoiding using my hand to point out my objections to what I was hearing.

I shall remember that day for as long as I live. As I spoke, I could feel my head pounding (which was quite usual) palpably as I spoke vividly with my co-worker. My head just behind my left eye started throbbing, and the pain grew steadily, in waves. Suddenly, my colleague's voice now resembled slow-motion gibberish, as if my life was slowing from 78 to 33 rpm. Suddenly the conversation came to an abrupt stop, there was a flash of something, my legs gave way, and I hit the floor. The phone receiver was on the floor, bleating in slow motion, growing more and more unintelligible with each passing moment, next to me. As I watched it, I could do nothing.

"Hello, hello? Rachel ... are you there? Hello ...?"

My mind tried to race to get the solution to my situation, but I was like a passive spectator, watching everything in slow motion as I slid to the floor. I could still see and hear Adam, as he ran to my aid, screaming, "Mommy, Mommy, are you OK?!" Nothing in my body would respond; I had lost control of my bodily functions. I couldn't lift my arm to regain the phone and the conversation, and then my whole life faded to black. I was gone.

MY JOURNEY OF AWAKENING

I woke up several hours later (as far as I could tell) in a hospital bed. As I scanned the room, I first came to the same worried look on Adam, my guardian angel, that he had had when I blacked out. I smiled inwardly at the relief that I was still alive and able to see him. I was in the hospital, not Heaven. But as I attempted to reassure him, my speech came out garbled, as Adam gently wiped the saliva off my lower lip.

"It's going to be OK, Mom. Don't speak now," Adam reassured me. He seemed older, more mature. Was that possible in just one day?

I decided then and there to not traumatize Adam and my family by trying to speak, but, rather, to attempt use my laptop computer screen in LARGE TYPE, as my chalk board, to communicate. I heard a strong voice from my left and above the bed where I was lying: "He is a very brave young man."

As I turned my head towards the familiar voice, I could see other people (two of my brothers, my Dad) at the foot of the bed, until my eyes fell upon an older man, dressed in white. My older brother jumped at the chance to shine the attention on Adam to break up the heavy ambience: "You might not have even made it here, had it not been for Adam's quick thinking. It was Adam that saved you by dialing the emergency number and getting the ambulance over to the house. Then he called us and here we are."

I rolled my eyes and attempted a lopsided smile at Adam, trying to say with my eyes, "That's *my* little man!"

The prognosis was not particularly cheery. An aneurysm had opened and bled over a small part of my brain. Though the hemorrhage had been stopped in time, I had temporarily lost my full mobility, my speech, and the use of the right half of my body (I am left-handed). While my thinking was still reasonably sharp in terms of raw cognition, calculation, and reading abilities, my memory was still somewhat cloudy. My neurologist warned me that one of my biggest challenges would be getting used to being fully aware of my disabilities and starting to do things consciously, as a child would have to do.

In the next several weeks I had my corrective surgery, followed by *many* months of rehabilitation, designed for regaining my speech, my walking, EVERYTHING. I was starting from the ground up, and I decided to use my rehab time to apply the same intense (though I didn't feel all that intense at the beginning) analysis that I had used on my studies.

Fortunately, I knew nothing of the challenges that awaited me in the weeks ahead because it would have been far too daunting to even start. Instead, I went straight at it, my way, breaking all the rules, no presumptions, asking whatever I needed to know. I had a second chance at getting this right and having a shot at a normal life with my son. This was my motivation.

My hospital room was a clean and very busy place, a whole new world. Yet despite this beehive activity, I felt somehow quite peripheral and lonely, so I opted *not* for a private room, but rather to share a room with another woman. I was given a shared room with another stroke victim, a middle-aged Chinese woman, Mrs Gladys Lim, a retired pharmacist. Just my luck! I am recovering in a hospital room with an elderly Chinese woman who is unable to speak and who spends most of her time smiling and shuffling about the ward, stretching and generally staying active. But though she was almost invisible in her discretion and silence, Gladys was a welcome presence, especially in the middle of the night when her gentle snoring reminded me of my cat's purring.

What I found out surprised, amazed, and even shocked me: sometimes all at once. First and foremost, I found out that one need not be a neurologist to begin to study the brain. In fact, during my rehabilitation, I had decided to use my time "off" (the first 6 months during the intensive phase of rehabilitation) to get to the bottom of this thing called the brain and, if possible, to develop a strategy to avoid this problem in the future. After all, Adam was my *career* now, not my job.

Little did I know that my fevered research into my brain was exactly what I needed to help the brain to recover its functionality. The actual investigation was helping the surviving brain cells compensate for the cells destroyed in the stroke.

One the day of the visit from the eminent Professor Epstein, of the neurology department, on his weekly rounds, trailed by obsequious residents and students, I thrust my computer screen around with my good arm to start the conversation.

"And good morning to you, Rachel," he said smiling. "First things first. Allow me to introduce my team this week who will try to learn from your case. Rachel, I see that you are using your laptop to communicate whatever questions you might have with the team here during your rehabilitation."

My mind, though cloudy still, started racing, and the questions came fast and furious, faster than I could type with one hand. I positioned my laptop on the bedside tray so that Professor Epstein could read my queries. "What happened to me?" I tapped on the computer.

Professor Epstein started, "People with untreated high blood pressure and diabetes suffer from periods of reduced blood flow to the brain due to clogged brain arteries, which, in turn, damages individual brain cells and set the stage for strokes and Alzheimer's. Now, let's see how sharp our student doctors are."

To start out with, I had divided the tropics of interest to me into just two general areas:

1. How does the brain get broken in the first place? How do we get strokes and Alzheimer's disease?
2. Will I fully recover?

Having finished reading my questions, the Professor scanned round his team above his reading glasses. "Any takers?" he taunted.

The students and even the resident physician didn't seem to have a clue and just shrugged off the question, while searching the crowd for someone who could come up with some regurgitated nonsense, meant to obfuscate. So much can be said about a team by its leaders and the followers. The students seemed intimidated by the attending physician. Was Professor Epstein a good leader? Seems not. His team was neither inspired, nor self-motivated, and seemed to cower at his challenges.

My musings were interrupted finally when one courageous student perked up, albeit timidly: "We don't really get into this in medical school, Professor Epstein, not even close. It's all memorizing and rote study, not much time for metaphysics ..."

The Boss cut him off. "Rachel, I am going to say something shocking to you. They don't know. In fact, the processes of learning, anticipation, planning, grieving, and so on remain a mystery to us.

"We don't really know, Rachel, and, in fact, any honest neurologist or even medical person would readily admit to being completely overwhelmed by the brain's complexity. But your questions are excellent and deserve more than some cursory treatment, and these students have loads of free time ... each student take a question and report back as the week progresses. Do you mind if we leave the laptop here so that the students and myself can make entries while you are at rehab or out?"

I had succeeded in completely engaging the team to do my research with me. I removed the entry passwords while they were there and left the pages open so that the team could make entries. I was delighted.

"Rachel, all your systems are back on track, as much as we can get them, in preparation for the surgery to remove the blood clot in 2 weeks. That is, your blood pressure and blood sugar are both well controlled. See you next Saturday, same time, same channel, and we shall let you know what we have found in our research."

So what *do* they know? What is known? What is knowable?

THE JOURNEY CONTINUES

In the days following the first visit of Professor Epstein, my research was very intense. Access to the Internet was automatic and gave me a feeling of being connected. I swung my bedside tray round, pulled my laptop over the bed, and started my special one-handed typing, as though I was beginning the analysis of some complex electrical circuits. That was my starting model: the brain is like a fancy computer, which is admittedly complex, but still somehow understandable and perhaps even *programmable*. The idea that the brain programs itself, that is, evolves as a function of environmental pressures, really intrigued me.

Consider the design specifications of the human brain. Humankind has been working on just that for centuries. The reason is quite simple yet profound: the brain is the gateway, the "door," between the body and the mind, between our outer macro-world and our inner micro-world, the interface between the stars and our imagination. Anything we do, think, reflect, dream, when we walk, make love, calculate, plan the future, eat, swim, caress, be caressed, mourn, and a myriad of other activities, would be impossible without it, and the better we can help the brain to function, the better we can function and prosper. One basic fact that I discovered about the brain filled me with awe and reverence.

This living beehive of electric activity is composed of roughly 150 billion neurons. Each neuron has the functional power of a PC, capable of $10^{2,783,000}$ connections, with 100 billion processes programmed per minute!

These neurons are constantly chatting, scolding, censuring, calculating, and conspiring, keeping score with an uncountable number of interconnections between them, while they receive and store, interpret, calculate and compare, analyze and respond to, and forward literally billions and billions of electrical signals that they receive from other neurons, the body, and the outside world. And they do this all quite automatically while you are reading this page on the way to work.

The neuron has two main parts to it:

- the **body** (containing the cell workings and DNA), which receives signals from other neurons via feelers (**dendrites**);
- a **tail** (**axon**), which carries the "signal" (stimulatory or inhibitory).

It works something like this. The brain sends a "message" in the form of an electrical charge at 100 km/hour down the length of the neuron (from millimeters up to a meter long), not unlike a telegraph wire. Once it reaches the end of one neuron, the electrical signal is converted to a chemical signal called a **neurotransmitter** (such as adrenaline, dopamine, serotonin, and so on), which travels across the space between neurons (a **synapse**), interacts with a specific antenna (**receptor**) and re-converts the chemical signal back into a electric signal – and down the nerve length it goes.

What I found out was that neurons have a universal language to construct words, images, emotions, tastes, and dreams. Each neurotransmitter has highly specific properties that will affect the information being relayed until the signal reaches a target (another nerve or organ).

So these electrical signals, as a function of the particular neurotransmitter, will deliver different messages from both the external and internal environments via the brain. Some, such as adrenaline, will send an excitatory message because the brain has been programmed to "fight or flee" when it perceives a threat or danger. Others, such as serotonin, send inhibitory messages. The brain is an organ engaged in constant chemical "chatter," regulating, refining, instructing, evolving, and growing, all quite automatically.

The beauty of the system is that, unlike even supercomputers, the brain constantly evolves in response to stimuli from the environment, constantly upgrading and becoming more efficient, constantly enriching itself *when properly stimulated*. Properly trained and nourished, the brain actually increases its neural connections when it learns "how to learn" new skills, such as playing music or learning a new language. That is, at any age, the brain is continually seeking out, even during sleep, the best methods for acquiring information to survive and thrive. The main determinant for making the brain becoming faster and more efficient was something my father used to remind me of while I did calculus: "Pay attention!"

As the week sped by towards its end, I greatly looked forward to the Saturday morning round with the students to get some feedback to my questions and my research. Wow! Finally Saturday came, and Professor Epstein stepped into my room and started to look at the computer – first from a standing position, then bent over, and finally seated with a frown on his face.

"OK, let's see what kind of answers the students have written. Ahhh! They have been busy. Here's what they have entered … Allow me to read the first entry. To Question 1, 'How does the brain get broken? How do we get strokes and Alzheimer's disease?,' the answer reads:"

First of all, there are *two* brains, in perfect symmetry: right and left. The two brains have different functions, different priorities, different ways of perceiving and processing information, and even different natures.

The right brain, let's call it RIGHTY, orchestrates the visual details of life, and through our senses, gives us a sense of the present time: its smell, its view, its feeling, texture, and so on. It is the "artist figure" that sees us all as connected through our collective consciousness. It is concerned with the integrity of the Universal Self, the soul. As such, it is really the hemisphere that connects us to other people, other beings …

The left brain, let's call it LEFTY, is much more scientific, more methodical, even more obsessed with details of survival. To be so, LEFTY concentrates its energy on past events, as a reference for future projections. LEFTY is the nagging "accountant figure" that gives us our identity as discrete individuals, complete with titles and accolades. It is chiefly concerned with the local self.

These two brains are connected by the corpus callosum, a thick band of roughly 300 million fibers that acts as a bridge between the two completely separate sides.

The Professor continued reading, slowly, incredulously:

As Dr. Jill Bolte Taylor,[1] a neuroanatomist who suffered a devastating hemorrhagic stroke at the age of 37, stated so eloquently:

We are the Life Force power of the Universe, with manual dexterity and 2 cognitive Minds … and we have the power to choose moment by moment who and how we want to be in the world. Right here, right now, I can step into the consciousness of my right hemisphere, where we are, I am the Life Force power of the Universe, the 50 trillion beautiful molecular geniuses that make up my form, at ONE with ALL it is.

OR

I could choose to step into the consciousness of my left hemisphere where I become a single individual, a solid, separate from the flow, separate from you …

… which do you choose? And when? I believe that the more time we spend CHOOSING to run the deep inner peace circuitry of our right hemisphere, the more peace we will project to the world and the more peaceful our planet would be.

Professor Epstein continued and looked somewhat disturbed at the answers.

Strokes are Nature's way of telling us to slow down. They are the result of too little attention to the messages sent between the body and the brain. Blood pressure is one of these often ignored messages.

Alzheimer's disease is another disease of prosperity, of our fast-food civilization, the result of a lifetime of being poisoned by stress and bad nutrition, particularly refined sugars ...

Professor Epstein continued to read aloud. He seemed curiously intrigued. "To Rachel's second query, 'Will I fully recover?,' the answer reads:"

You will most *certainly* recover and even start to rejuvenate the brain. Its ability to bounce back, create new cells until the damaged ones are healed, is proven.

It is a "use-it-or-lose-it" proposition. There are even exercises to start the process NOW: relaxing the brain (regularly and frequently), learning new languages, learning a musical instrument, exercising vigorously to oxygenate the brain, avoiding sugary and processed foods, taking supplements and so on. Though none of us seems to have any degeneration of the brain, these are disease processes that tend to smoulder insidiously and slowly. Waiting for manifestations or symptoms to arise may make it too late to stem the degeneration.

No one had come forward to own up to these answers so Professor Epstein put his foot down: "If the student doesn't come forward, I will be forced to ..."

Just then, a meek little voice came up from behind the curtain of the adjacent bed.

"It was me; I am sorry ..." – the first sound that I had heard from my roommate's mouth sounded more like a lisp than an articulated voice. Professor Epstein threw the curtain behind him open in a swoosh, as though he were doing the finale to a magic trick. "Gladys! Where ... when ... how ... did you re-learn how to talk?" he stammered.

"I cannot say for sure, but, several days ago, I started hearing my inner voice awakening, and while Rachel was at her physical therapy, I got online on her computer and looked around; most interesting ...."

"Gladys, that was one of the most interesting introductions to brain science I have ever seen, better than I could have done. Obviously, I have spent far too much time talking to LEFTY. I would advise the medical students and house officers to start exercising their right brain once in a while to counterbalance the heavy left-sided activities that are far too common in med school.

"Have you ever considered medical school?" the professor queried.

"I used to teach medical students in China, and anyway, at my age, there are other things more interesting to research!"

"Gladys and Rachel, you put us to shame with your optimism and never-say-die attitude. I predict another 30 years of vitality and good health for you, Gladys, and the same goes for you, Rachel. Soon enough, the neurosurgeons will have removed the blood clot from your brain, and your blood pressure continues to be stable. We on the team here look forward to seeing and exchanging with you when you come in for your rehabilitation and clinic visits. For all we have learned from you, we all owe both of you a massive thank you."

CASE DISCUSSION: LEADING YOURSELF OUT OF PRIVATE HELL

The case of Rachel deserves special attention as stroke is the one disease that has little warning, but there are devastating consequences for doing nothing. The term "stroke" refers to either:

- a ruptured artery (due to high blood pressure, such as in Rachel's case), causing the blood to destroy the surrounding brain tissue (a hemorrhagic stroke);
- a blockage of blood flow, due to a clot (an ischemic stroke).

In either case, brain damage can be arise from an increase in free radicals at the stroke site when the blood flow is restored. Free radicals are negatively charged oxygen molecules that harm cells. Moreover, thinking ability declines because high blood pressure impairs blood flow to the brain.

So, high blood pressure (> 135/85 mmHg) is a good clue that, down the road, a stroke may lie in ambush. Numerous studies demonstrate that lowering systolic blood pressure by 15 points and diastolic pressure by 8 points lowers stroke risk by almost 40%! Moreover, the common amino acid homocysteine has been implicated in strokes, as well as heart attacks and Alzheimer's disease.

Given her longstanding high blood pressure, Rachel would be considered, in the corridors of the neurological ward, to be one of the "lucky ones," someone who had lived to talk about surviving a hemorrhagic stroke. They are the distinct minority. More than 50% of people who have a large hemorrhage die within a few days. Those who survive usually recover consciousness and all or part of brain function over time. However, most do not recover *all* lost brain function.

Rachel was fortunate to have had a smaller bleed that was confined and the resultant clot easily removed at surgery, during which the aneurysm was repaired. But she should never had played Russian roulette with her brain and her life.

In the 3 years it took to fully recover, Rachel became nearly obsessed with learning all about this idea-generating machine and keeping it going. But her real exercises involved creating new connections to new neural circuits.

AN IDEAL HEALTH ACTION PLAN FOR PROTECTING THE HARDWARE

Develop a healthy approach to blood pressure

There are many brain-saving options available, backed up by real science (Table 4.1).

TABLE 4.1 *Table of lifestyle changes and their effects on blood pressure (BP)*

ADVICE	SPECIFICS	COMMENTS
Eat smart	Replace high glycemic index foods by fruit and nuts	BP drops 10–15 points
Exercise	Walk for 15–30 minutes/day after meals	BP drops 10 points
Lose abdominal obesity (body fat)	Use a tape measure weekly to gauge the decrease in abdominal girth	For every cm of waist lost or every 1% body fat lost, BP drops 2–3 points
Learn to breathe (meditate)	Five deep breaths several times per day, especially when feeling stressed, oxygenates the brain and heart	BP drops 15–20 points
Watch alcohol intake	No more than three glasses of red wine a day	Variable effect
Tea	More than four cups, split between black and green	BP drops 5 points
Essential fatty acids	Hempseed oil and flaxseed oil decrease inflammation	BP drops 10 points
Drop the salt	Switch to potassium chloride (KCl) and eliminate table salt (NaCl)	BP drops 10–15 points
Vitamin C	2–3 g/day	BP drops 7–10 points
Vitamin B complex	B_{12} 0.5 mg/day^2 and folate 500 mg/day	Lowers homocysteine
Ginkgo biloba	Terpenoids (ginkgolides) dilate blood vessels, improve blood flow, and thereby lower BP	BP drop variable

Walking

The great news for all of us is that *exercise helps to create and maintain new neurons*, called **neurogenesis**, perhaps by increasing the synthesis and secretion of brain-derived neurotrophic factor – BDNF). In this case, BURST walking would be a great place to start for oxygenating the brain. For controlling blood pressure, buy a pedometer and walk 5,000 steps a day on weekdays and 10,000 steps on each weekend day.

Researchers at Canterbury Christ Church University have found that walking at a steady pace is a more effective way to reduce blood pressure than walking at maximum intensity. The findings were that walking at 50% effort for 30 minutes was the most effective way to bring down the participants' blood pressure, compared to resting. It was also found that walking for 30 minutes at 50% effort was as effective as walking for 60 minutes at the same intensity. Findings support the American College of Sports Medicine's recommendation that healthy adults should undertake at least 30 minutes of moderate physical activity on at least 5 days per week.

Endorphins, which are the "euphoria" chemicals produced by the brain, are increased when we exercise, which in turn makes both the body and the mind feel better.

Essential fatty acids (EFAs)[3]

Together, omega-3 and omega-6 fatty acids play a central role in brain function, growth, and development. Specifically, there are some prospective studies that have examined the relationship to fish or omega-3 fatty acid intake:

- One Japanese study found that essential omega-3 polyunsaturated fatty acids were beneficial[4] and might help protect stroke patients from suffering a second ischemic stroke. The researchers noted that because this trial used *purified* eicosapentaenoic acid (EPA) instead of the fish oil used in previous studies, the preventative effects on stroke could be attributed to EPA. The exact mechanism remains unclear, however, because EPA has a variety of beneficial effects in the body, including lowering cholesterol and inflammation as well as the production of platelets, the blood components that promote the formation of blood clots. EPA also guards against heart rhythm disturbances that lead to sudden cardiac death.
- A Harvard study of strokes among 80,000 female nurses followed for 14 years reported in the *Journal of the American Medical Association* found that women who ate fish oil five or more times a week had a 52% lower risk of stroke than women who ate fish less than once a month. In sum, the Mediterranean diet containing fish and olive oil can lower your risk of coronary heart disease and possibly also lower stroke risk.

B vitamins (especially B_{12}, B_6, and folic acid)

These all help to keep homocysteine in the normal range. Patients with Alzheimer's disease have higher plasma homocysteine levels than controls, and higher plasma homocysteine levels are associated with more atrophy of the hippocampal *and* cortical regions of the brain.

Try ginkgo biloba

This may also protect against brain damage after a stroke. In a recent study, published in *Stroke* in October 2008, scientists gave rodents a 100 mg/kg oral dose of the extract for a week and then induced a stroke. Brain function and damage in the mice were assessed. Results showed those pretreated with the supplement had 50.9% less neurological dysfunction and 48.2% less brain damage compared to the mice who did not receive ginkgo biloba. Currently, there is only one US Food and Drug Administration-approved drug to treat stroke – tissue plasminogen activator – which dissolves blood clots but does not protect from cell damage when blood flow returns. Ginkgo biloba *could* provide a preventative treatment option.

Take vitamin C

A new 2008 Italian study found that intravenously delivered vitamin C could lower blood pressure by acting on an overactive central nervous system.

Early studies have already shown that vitamin C and potentially other anti-oxidants in the blood may help lower the risk of stroke.

The current study involved 12 patients with an essential form of high blood pressure who had not received any treatment for their condition. All the participants were intravenously administered 3 g of vitamin C during a period of 5 minutes and then monitored for blood pressure and sympathetic nervous system activity for 20 minutes. It was found that sympathetic nervous activity dropped by 11% and blood pressure was lowered by about 7% on average.

Tea

Tea – the leaf from which we have derived hundreds of hot beverages, *Camellia sinensis*. Compounds in the leaf provide protection to the brain (and heart) from *inflammation* ("glue") and *oxidation* ("rust;" see Chapter 1) and even block damage to our DNA. Dutch studies have concluded, in a study of more than 300 men and women, that those who drank four cups a day lowered their risk by 70%. It is also reported to help burn body fat.

Eat garlic

Studies have shown that garlic can, in large doses, reduce blood pressure and overactivity of the intestine, and can slightly lower blood sugar levels.

Use curcumin

This active ingredient of the Indian curry spice turmeric not only lowers your chances of getting cancer and Alzheimer's disease, but may also reduce the size of a hemorrhagic stroke because curcumin is a potent anti-inflammatory and antioxidant agent.

Chocolate

Chocolate, especially black chocolate, is loaded with all sorts of brain-enhancing chemical with strange names: PEA (phenylethylalanine), theo-bromine, 1MeTIQ (which inhibits the development of Parkinson's disease), and procyanidins (antioxidants that counter inflammation). There are even certain chemicals that increase anandamide, a brain chemical that binds to the cannabinoid receptors in our brain, therefore mimicking cannabis.

Beware of drinking distilled spirits

Use more dilute alcoholic beverages, such as wine and apple cider, to reduce the dramatic and deleterious effect of alcohol on blood pressure.

Get rid of the belly

A new study from Germany in the journal *Stroke* in late 2008 suggested that belly size and other markers of abdominal fat are a better predictor of stroke and transient ischemic attacks (TIAs, or "mini-strokes"), Alzheimer's Disease, and heart disease than body mass index is.

This case control study matched 379 adults with stroke and/or TIA with 758 controls of the same age and sex living in the same region. It showed that large bellies were strongly linked to risk of stroke/TIA, regardless of other risk factors. In fact, participants with bigger waists (more than 102 cm [40 inches] for men and 89 cm [35 inches] for women) had four times the risk of developing a stroke or TIA compared to those with more typical waist sizes. Those with the largest waist-to-hip ratio had nearly eight times the risk of developing a stroke or TIA.

Quit tobacco

The World Health Organization estimates that about 17 million people a year die of cardiovascular diseases, particularly heart attack and strokes. A great number of these can be attributed to tobacco smoking, which increases the risk two- or threefold.

HEALTH ACTION PLAN SUMMARY FOR RACHEL

1. Walk (with a pedometer): 5,000 steps on weekdays, and 10,000 on Saturdays and Sundays (golf counts!).
2. Learn to meditate: just 3 minutes in the morning and just before bed.
3. Eliminate added salt use.
4. Take supplements:
   - green tea
   - EFAs
   - vitamin C
   - ginkgo.

Three parameters along the way to heart fitness will signal your progress: blood pressure, fasting blood sugar, and homocysteine. Make use of the grid below to mark your progress, every week over 1 month. Then measure every month regularly – there is no need to measure more often than that.

	IDEAL	BASELINE	FOLLOW-UP 1	FOLLOW-UP 2
Blood pressure (mmHg)	< 135/85			
Fasting blood sugar (g/L)	0.70–1.20			
Homocysteine (micromoles/L)	7.0–10			

Rachel's second health and fitness report

	NORMAL/IDEAL RANGE	ME (BEFORE STROKE)	ME (18 MONTHS AFTER STROKE)
Actual age (years)		42	43.5
Health age (years)	Actual age (or less)	49.5	41.5
Blood pressure (mmHg)	< 135/85	175/100	125/70

	NORMAL/IDEAL RANGE	ME (BEFORE STROKE)	ME (18 MONTHS AFTER STROKE)
Resting heart rate (beats/minute)	< 60	82	58
Body fat %	< 20% men, < 23% women	15%	16%
Waist-to-hip ratio	< 0.90 men, < 0.80 women	0.75	0.75
Total cholesterol (g/L)	< 2.00	1.65	1.85
High-density lipoprotein cholesterol (g/L)	> 0.50	0.55	0.76
Low-density lipoprotein cholesterol (g/L)	< 1.30	0.95	0.95
Triglycerides (g/L)	< 1.40	0.75	0.75
Fasting blood sugar (glucose) (g/L)	0.70–1.20	1.65	0.84
Homocysteine (micromoles/L)	7.0–10	30.5	9.6

CLOSING WORDS FROM A LEADER ... A STROKE OF GOOD LUCK

Looking back over my experiences of the past year, I must admit that the stroke temporarily devastated my life and my career in business. Just prior to the stroke, I had had a fabulous career, full of promise and prosperity. So here's my message from the front lines.

To all you young and not-so-young turks out there spending far too much time in your left brain, scratching your way up the side of Golden Mountain, fear not crossing the bridge to the right brain. You will be safe there. In my experience, it would have been a little less scary during my stroke if I had been there before, to my right brain.

> When your Ego (LEFTY) cries at what it has lost, the spirit (RIGHTY) laughs at what it has gained.

So live your life in such a way that anything can happen from one day to the next. An old phobia or scary memory from infancy could pop up and haunt you into real humility. *Because it happened to me.*

During the 3 years that it took me to fully and completely recover (we never become the same person after something like a stroke, and in some ways, that's a very good thing), I had plenty of "blue" moments, feeling unfortunate. As fate would have it for me, I "stumbled" upon an essay by the humorist Erma Brombeck, which I would like to share with you. While coping with cancer, Ms. Brombeck needed an organ transplant and, even though she could have been moved to the head of the waiting list due to her social standing, she declined and ultimately died of organ failure.

IF I HAD MY LIFE TO LIVE OVER AGAIN

I would have talked less and listened more. I would have invited friends over to dinner even if the carpet was stained, or the sofa faded. I would have eaten the popcorn in the "good" living room and worried much less about the dirt when someone wanted to light a fire in the fireplace.

I would have taken the time to listen to my grandfather ramble about his youth. I would never have insisted the car windows be rolled up on a summer day because my hair had just been teased and sprayed. I would have burned the pink candle sculpted like a rose before it melted in storage.

I would have sat on the lawn with my children and not worried about grass stains. I would have cried and laughed less while watching television – and more while watching life. I would have shared more of the responsibility carried by my spouse. I would have gone to bed when I was sick instead of pretending the earth would go into a holding pattern if I weren't there for the day. I would never have bought anything just because it was practical, wouldn't show soil, or was guaranteed to last a lifetime.

Instead of wishing away nine months of pregnancy, I'd have cherished every moment and realized that the wonderment growing inside me was the only chance in life to assist God in a miracle. When my kids kissed me impetuously, I would never have said, "Later. Now go get washed up for dinner."

There would have been more "I love you's" ... more "I'm sorry" ... but mostly, given another shot at life, I would seize every minute. Look at it and really see it ... live it ... and never give it back. Stop sweating the small stuff. Don't worry about who doesn't like you, who has more, or who's doing what. Instead, let's cherish the relationships we have with those who do love us. Let's think about what God HAS blessed us with. And what we are doing each day to promote ourselves mentally, physically, emotionally, as well as spiritually.

Life is too short to let it pass you by. We only have one shot at this and then it's gone. I hope you all have a blessed day.

> Throughout all your successful weeks and months, when everything seems to go your way, don't forget to say "thank you" so that when you have dark times, your "pleases" are answered.

So, at the end of the day, this is the most important aspect of my story you can remember as you go through the various aspects of your career: If I was able, through grit and desire, to lead my life and son back from this devastating brink, you, in your lonely hours, can find your way back to your humanity too. In short, life is the career, not survival, and may your **right** brain hijack your life and career just long enough for you to see love *not* as a transaction to be managed like an emotional budget, but as a precious gift to be treasured and shared.

I, for myself, have reordered my thinking and have decided to spend next summer going around the world with the person without whom I would not have had a world, my teenage son and guardian angel, Adam.

◼ LEADERS' TOP FAQS ON BRAIN HARDWARE

What is the best way to consciously empower your children to start their journey?

Start by walking down any street in the world with an eye to studying children. The streets and schools are teeming with children whose inner joy has been stifled by angry cynical adults. The love they have missed out on shows in their walk, their smile, their speech. The cycle to the next generation is complete. The love you are investing every day in your child will ensure that later their joy will be yours to share.

Lastly, don't tell your kids that they are intelligent or gifted. More than three decades of research shows that a focus on effort and hard work – not on intelligence or ability – is key to success in school and in life.

What is more important: the systolic blood pressure (the higher number) or the diastolic blood pressure (the lower number)?

If you're over 50, systolic pressure matters more than diastolic. Once you're over 50, your systolic blood pressure starts to climb because the blood vessels get more clogged and stiffer. Systolic pressure measures how hard the blood is pumped against the artery walls when your heart beats. Normally the arteries should dilate, or expand, as much as in younger people, but due to the rigidity, the pressure rises.

On the other hand, the diastolic pressure (which measures the pressure against artery walls *between* heartbeats) may be too low in older people because when blood flows out of the large arteries and into the smaller vessels, the arteries should be supple enough to contract. However, the stiffness prevents this and so blood pressure drops more than it should.

Is the Internet changing the way our brains work?

Use it or lose it. That's the credo when it comes to brain function. How could it be any other way? As the brain ages, it can shrink and decrease in cell activity, which can decrease on performance.

It has always been believed that brain activities, such as crossword puzzles and reading, frequent social interactions, regular aerobic exercise, and having a balanced diet can also reduce cognitive loss. No question about it: for middle-aged and older people at least, using the Internet helps boost brain power, research suggests. The filtering of information, making snap decisions, Internet searching, and text messaging has clearly improved functionality in parts of the brain that control language, reading, memory, and visual abilities. Surfing the Internet, which is really one gigantic collective brain, stimulates areas that control decision-making and complex reasoning. But only in those who are experienced web users.

We are becoming detached bionic processors all in our own right. These improvements may even prevent the brain changes that cause the brain's functions to deteriorate with age. The latest UCLA study was based on 24 volunteers aged between 55 and 76. Half were experienced Internet users, the rest were not. Each volunteer underwent a brain scan while performing web searches and book-reading tasks.

Lead researcher Professor Gary Small said, "The study results are encouraging, that emerging computerized technologies may have physiological effects and potential benefits for middle-aged and older adults. Internet searching engages complicated brain activity, which may help exercise and improve brain function." The downside is that these the tech-savvy people (dubbed "digital natives" by Dr. Small) are less capable of the social skills such as interpreting facial messages and subtle gestures that characterize their parents, the "digital immigrants."

The smart way ahead is to surf the net and increase brain connections, but once every couple of hours, get off your seat, go for a walk, and chat with someone in the park about what you found while you were surfing.

My auntie has diabetes and has been diagnosed as having early signs of Alzheimer's disease (memory loss, disorientation, inappropriate judgment, language issues, misplacing common things). Is there any connection between these two diseases?

Yes, there is a connection between diabetes and Alzheimer's disease. In fact, we are rapidly approaching what has been called a unified theory of health and disease, wherein diseases previously thought to be unrelated are found to share many common points.

Take heart disease and Alzheimer's. These two share very common risk factors: abdominal obesity, high blood pressure, smoking, the metabolic syndrome, and high insulin (due to high glycemic index foods).

Further evidence of the *intimate* relation between insulin and Alzheimer's disease is the build-up of what is known as advanced glycation end-products (AGEs). These AGEs, toxic byproducts of protein and sugar (high glycemic index foods), have been identified in the neurofibrillary tangles and plaques that characterize Alzheimer's disease.

This is all good news in the sense that it provides a starting point that we can do NOW. Get off sugary foods, not just for your waistline, but for your blood pressure and memory as well.

Is there any connection between sugar consumption and cancer?

It has been well documented since the 1980s that up to 85% of cancers can be prevented through lifestyle changes.[5] In the cited reference, the authors concluded that *nutrition*, and in particular *refined sugar*, "positively correlated with both the incidence of and mortality from" colon, rectal, breast, kidney, prostate, testicular, and ovarian cancers. This has been confirmed by literally thousands of research papers since then.

Why do brains sleep and dream?

We, as adults, spend a third of our time in the bizarre world of sleep. Newborn babies spend about twice that. It is extremely difficult to remain awake for after a full day–night cycle. It must be of profound importance, as sleep exposes many mammals to much time being relatively defenseless. The three primary functions for sleep are:

- pure rest, not just to restore energy stores, but also to relieve the back of further vertical balancing acts;
- to allow dreaming and fantasies to occur, as a natural extension of our conscious day: this permits planning and decision-making;
- to prioritize what must be remembered and what must be forgotten, as lessons throughout the day. That is, a good night's sleep consolidates what was learned during the day.

How does stress affect the brain?

Prolonged periods of stress or depression may actually lead to the damage or even the death of certain neurons, especially those within the memory centers of the brain.

Those people who are prone to anger, anxiety, and depression, and who suffer from low self-esteem, are far more likely to experience damage to the brain than their calmer, more relaxed peers. Doctors have recently reported that as many as 50% of patients who experienced periods of major depression also possessed high levels of cortisol, which, as we know, can have negative effects on the brain and cells.

Is exercise useful in shrinking our stress?

It is well known that stress may result in feelings of being overwhelmed or out of balance, and can lead to anxiety and depression. The effects on the body include shortness of breath, headaches, stomach upsets, sleep problems, high blood pressure, backache, fatigue, changes in appetite, increased cortisol secretion (the so-called "stress hormone"), changes in weight (loss or gain), increased resting heart rate and respiratory rate, muscle tension, sweaty palms, and cold hands and feet. The mental benefits that can be gained from regular working out are:

- feeling good or peaceful;
- better mental health (less depressive episodes);
- playfulness or communion with Nature/others;
- less loneliness;
- increased sexual satisfaction;
- distraction from daily affairs;
- a spiritual awakening of potential;

- preparing the body (the "temple") for meditation;
- improved self-confidence;
- better socialization skills;
- less anxiety;
- improved sexual expression;
- less symptoms of depression;
- better sleep;
- healthful distraction from "affairs;"
- better preparedness for change;
- increased energy and stamina.

What are benefits of laughter?

The benefits are numerous and enduring:

- Heart and lungs:
  - Lowers blood pressure
  - Increases vascular blood flow.
- Nervous system: decreases pain perception.
- Hormonal: decreases blood levels of stress chemicals:
  - Beta-endorphins
  - Corticotrophin
  - Cortisol
  - Growth hormone
  - Prolactin
  - Adrenaline compounds.
- Immunological system:
  - Decreases blood levels of immunosuppressive chemicals: cortisol and adrenaline compounds
  - Increases activity of natural killer cells (which fight tumor cells)
  - Increases interferon-gamma activity, which activates T, B, and natural killer cells and immunoglobulins
  - Increases salivary immunoglobulin A, which protects the respiratory tract against infectious invaders.
- Muscles: tones the diaphragm and accessory respiratory muscles.
- Respiratory system: increases oxygen to the muscles; laughing, coughing, and hiccoughing help to clear the airways of mucus.
- Mind:
  - Laughter is cathartic: it allows pent-up tension to be released.
  - Shameless hamming (such as a stand-up comic or performing karaoke) is an excellent tool to build confidence and control the ego.
  - Laughter helps us temporarily to forget anger and fear, the first step to reconciliation.
  - Laughter provides the opportunity of starting over: a "reset button" after a long hard day.

- Laughter can, by helping us to detach from a stressful situation, create a feeling of power and hope.
- If you can laugh at it, you can survive it.

NOTES AND REFERENCES

1. See the extraordinary story of neuroanatomist Dr. Jill Bolte Taylor, who, at the age of 37, suffered a hemorrhagic stroke about the size of a golf ball on the left side of her brain and lived to talk about it. Go to http://www.ted.com/index.php/talks/jill_bolte_taylor_s_powerful_stroke_of_insight.html

2. This high dose is needed due to the variable absorption of oral vitamin B_{12} in doses of 500 μg or less. This regimen has been shown to be safe and well tolerated. Lederle FA. Oral cobalamin for pernicious anemia. Medicine's best kept secret? *JAMA* 1991; **265**: 94–5.

3. Wainwright PE. Do essential fatty acids play a role in brain and behavioral development? *Neurosci Biobehav Rev* 1992; **16**: 193–205.

4. Keli SO, Feskens EJ, Kromhout D. Fish consumption and risk of stroke. The Zutphen Study. *Stroke* 1994; **25**: 328–32. See also: Gillum RF, Mussolino ME, Madans JH. The relationship between fish consumption and stroke incidence. The NHANES I Epidemiologic Follow-up Study (National Health and Nutrition Examination Survey). *Arch Intern Med* 1996; **156**: 537–42.

5. Doll R, Peto R. The causes of cancer: Quantitative estimates of avoidable risks of cancer in the United Staes today. *J Natl Cancer Inst* 1981; **66**: 1191–308.

Programme the software from a normal brain to a superb brain

In this chapter, you will learn, by illustrative example, how to first get it wrong and then get it right by:

1. Controlling counterproductive emotions
2. Developing a regret-free life
3. Preventing stress from permanently damaging your health
4. Learning how to relax (especially when it is most needed)
5. Learning how to build up a mind that better resists business stresses
6. Learning to identify the signs and symptoms of depression
7. Learning to shrink your memory of negative thoughts down to size
8. Beating the blues before they become depression

INTRODUCTION

Hello, my name is Miguel. I will tell you my story, which anyone can learn early in life but took me years and years.

I grew up on a farm in Extremadura, Spain, with four brothers and a sister, where we were all expected to contribute and slacking off was severely punished. My father, José, was a tough but fair man of the earth.

I am the 42-year-old director of new products at a telecom company based in Barcelona. I had three children, Jorgé, Adriana, and Emilia, with my wife, Maria (a lawyer), from whom I am divorced. I have never remarried.

PROFESSIONAL LIFE: "LEADING BY TITLE ONLY"

As the director of my division, I am expected to make tough choices. I cannot say that I have made all of them with an eye to my base values, values that my parents and culture had instilled in me from an early age: trust, honesty, diligence. But, if I really am honest with myself, I would say that I have also been involved in more dubious judgment calls that helped to make the company a fortune, though the products were inferior or dangerous. These compromises inevitably led to often violent arguments at work and at home.

Since an early age, I remember my father telling me: "Son, there is nothing on God's green earth that can resist the power of man's mind."

As with everyone else, I felt deep boredom once I got to the place of "no return" in my career. The point of no return is that place in our career, as defined by a fellow MBA, where we realize that we have a job where we can advance no further, but where we are being paid enough to stay put.

I *do* have a temper and pride issue at work, leading to me being nicknamed "the Dictator" by co-workers. Somehow, I felt they were not referring to Charlie Chaplin's masterpiece, but to something much more ominous. Early on, I was clearly distracted by home issues, but more so by my own internal issues. I was a leader by title only, not by moral integrity.

> Leadership is action, not position.
>
> Donald H. McGannon
> *Media pioneer and former CEO, Westinghouse Broadcasting Co*

PERSONAL LIFE

This has at times been very lonely and, frankly, very sad. There would be times after long business trips that I would return home bone-tired and really quite inconsiderate of Maria's needs. Since she had been stuck at home for all these years, I would feel obliged to take her out in town for a nice dinner, in an effort to smooth over the rough areas. Well, those dinners were often quite painful too. Nice restaurant and all, both of us just sitting there without really much to say, looking past one another, as if we were both waiting for the whole thing to pass. Totally humorless and devoid of any real intimacy. Something was lost, at least temporarily.

My marriage to Maria was, even from the beginning, flawed for sure by my absence from home due to my ambitions to get ahead. But there was also a nagging feeling I had that Maria had started to drink more heavily than usual during parties, social events, and when I was away. As the time passed, marked by birthdays and anniversaries, I found myself falling into a routine of getting up, going to work, coming home late, eating something totally forgettable, washing it down with plenty of wine, falling asleep in front of the TV, getting up – and the routine continued for years like that, slowly chipping away at the house mortgage, but with no real deep sense of fulfilment or success.

During our arguments, Maria would say, "Just look at the rut you have been in for the past 4 years, doing the same thing every day, the gray days just melting into one another. It is not living you are doing, it's just basic existence."

To my surprise, the effect of having more children never really sealed our relationship. As the time passed, my doubts as to our couple's survivability started to grow, especially when Maria's drinking combined with her lively personality to make her very flirtatious in public. Of course, the next morning she would deny everything and denounce me at the breakfast table in front of the children as "paranoid" and "obsessed."

Despite the fact that I had had my own youthful indiscretions with my secretaries and several co-workers, I could not accept Maria's behavior. My mind seethed with the idea that Maria was doing to me what I had been doing to her for all these years.

But none of this mattered as long as Jorgé, my pride and joy, considered me his "hero." To make up for being so absent from his life, I spoiled him with attention in the form of gifts. As he passed through the stages of infancy and childhood, I noticed his personality traits starting to resemble my own, both good (confidence and persistence) and bad (arrogance and insensitivity towards others, stubbornness). Coming home to him was the only way for me to forget my work hassles.

But that all changed radically once he started adolescence: "You are doing to us now exactly what you have been doing to Mama all these years, and don't think for a second we all don't know about all your running around. We have never really been 'on your agenda,' so why fake it now?"

A perverse thought flashed through my mind – "Why indeed?" – but I gave the thought no voice in front of Jorgé.

Things got progressively worse with Jorgé. I remember when he was about 16, while vacationing by a quarry, Jorgé and the girls were playfully jumping off the rocks into the water below, while Maria prepared the picnic and I sat reading my mails on my Blackberry. As Jorgé, my only son, jumped off the rocks to the water below, he bellowed: *"Suicide is an alternative!"*

It took a brief second to register it, and when its meaning dawned on me, I turned to Maria, now visibly distraught, and said, "What did he just say?"

"You heard him perfectly well, and don't pretend that you don't know that he is drinking and using hard drugs. You are blind!" she said, wiping away the tears welled up in her eyes with the inside of her index finger.

"Pretend to not know what?" I queried. I wasn't pretending not to know. I did not have a clue, but, in life, when it comes to problems of children, I have learned, either you *do* know about it and you deny it or you *don't* know and you are ignorant. Either way …

Over the following months, Jorgé admitted to me that he had only tried cannabis and ecstasy, but nothing harder. I had my doubts when I looked into his eyes, but I stifled the doubts: too much effort to follow up. It was only a passing stage in his life, I reasoned.

Our messy, almost violent divorce after three children, at my own admission, clearly traumatized the children, especially Jorgé, who was 17 at the time. He seemed to put the blame for the verbal violence squarely on *my* shoulders alone.

In fact, in retrospect, I had had quite a few of these rather painful wake-up calls. When Jorgé told me, "I never asked to be born," I realized that this was a major turning point in my life. Outbursts became more common and more embarrassing, the arguments got louder, more violent, and more public. Another time, while waiting with him in the car at the train station for the train to arrive, I started, "What's going on with you these days? You seem so detached …"

He cut me off. "What's going on with ME!? What is YOUR problem?"

In fact, despite how painful the conversation was, at least he was talking, or should I say screaming. "What did I do to get you to hate me like this? What crime did I commit?"

"You just don't get it do you? It is not about YOU! Is it true that before you guys got married, when Mom got pregnant with me, you rejected her and me? You told her something like, 'It's not mine. Deal with it.' Did you really say that to Mom with me still in her belly?"

"Jorgé, it was not that simple. Your mother at that time …", I feebly tried.

"BULLSHIT!! And you know it. When you guys got divorced, you left her high and dry. That's one reason she is drinking so much! I was born in a public hospital and your name was not even on the birth certificate! Mom told me everything."

I was speechless and defenseless.

"Have you even spoken to Mom lately? Do you have any idea what private hell she is going through?"

When I asked him to try to help the situation with his mother and sisters, by doing a little PR for me, he didn't miss an opportunity to empty his bag.

"You are already doing the PR for yourself. Fight your own battles, Dad. And that's not all," – he was practically screaming at me, emboldened by my incredulity – "you have done nothing but undermine her and try to discredit her over the years. Until you excuse yourself for how you treated my mother and make it up to her, we have nothing to say to each other!"

With that, he stormed out of the heated car, turned and slammed the door hard. I never saw him again. Months passed. I heard that he was seriously involved with a girl, living together …

As the silence and space between us grew and grew, I swung between anger and depression. My frustration grew and smouldered into fiery anger, and I didn't know where to direct it. I felt betrayed, but where was the traitor? Here I had been, working like a beast for all these years to provide for the family, and this is what I got in return. The only solace I could get from the whole picture was the fact that I was now free, free to explore. Somehow, though, I felt trapped from within, anything but free.

It had become increasingly clear to my colleagues at work that I could not adequately contain the tension at home from spilling over at work. After calls from home, I would be distracted at work, forgetting appointments and meetings. Even without my customary three cafés expressos before 10 a.m., my heart rate started accelerating, my breathing became labored, and my legs became jittery. Something was way off; was I getting sick?

NUTRITION

For me, nutrition, and life in general, comes down to this: God put the animals (and the entire earth, for that matter) at the disposal of human beings (made in His image) so I accept the offer. I adore pork chops, bacon, all charcuterie, pâtés …

PHYSICAL AND INTELLECTUAL ACTIVITY

I enjoy playing soccer, running long distances, and hiking. Staying active was never an issue for me. I had a body fat of 15%, normal blood pressure, but what really irritated me was my concentration and memory. They were effectively shot to hell. Thanks God for these hand-held ectopic brains – the iPhone, Blackberry, and so – on to cover my lapses in memory.

Most important leadership quality	Humility

My idea of great leaders	• Mahatma Gandhi • Barack Obama • Lee Kuan Yew

My most inspiring quotation

I claim to be a simple individual, liable to err like any other fellow mortal. However, I have **humility** *enough to confess my errors and retrace my steps.*

Mahatma Gandhi

Miguel's baseline health and fitness profile

	NORMAL/IDEAL RANGE	ME (BASELINE)
Actual age (years)		42
Health age (years)	Actual age (or less)	56.7
Blood pressure (mmHg)	< 135/85	125/75
Resting heart rate (beats/minute)	< 60	82
Body fat %	< 20 % men, < 23% women	15%
Exhalation count (seconds)	> 100	25
Photographic memory (items)	> 10	4
Numeric memory (items)	> 10	3
Concentration (numbers)	> 14	5
Reflexes (ruler test) (cm)	< 3	11
Homocysteine level (micromoles/L)	7.0–10	56.8
High-sensitivity C-reactive protein (mg/L)	< 1	Not done
Psoriasis	None	Florid
Early prostate cancer antigen-2 test (EPCA-2) (ng/mL)	< 30	35
Nightmares	Infrequently	Every night

Every time Jorgé and I would have heated disputes (especially in his teens), my skin would break out in an ugly itchy rash – psoriasis.

MY FIRST WAKE UP-CALL

Finally, after many months of struggling with depression and its symptoms (fatigue, withdrawal, and libido issues), I met Carmen at a party after an art gallery opening in Barcelona. Things seemed to start to change for the better. Carmen was an artist, 27 years old, from Barcelona whose presence breathed new life and confidence into my own. Her life was anything but a bowl of cherries: daughter of a devout Catholic mother and an abusive father (who never appreciated her wild artistic side), she had survived both the death of her brother (in a car accident), as well as a near-fatal cancer in her early 20s (chemotherapy, hair falling out, surgery, the whole mess). With her calm demeanour in the face of crisis, she had the unflinching courage of a war veteran.

In fact, I would have been quite "happy" to have had just a nice relationship with Carmen. It certainly would have simplified things for me, though even with her, I found myself scheming; even after making love, my mind would drift away to my thoughts.

But once we got past the "just for sex" stage of our relationship, I could feel the scene shifting. She wanted to know *all* about me, my past, my divorce, my children. She asked me if it were alright to contact Adriana, if I didn't mind.

I had to be careful about Carmen. She was an artist and a free thinker, well versed in literature and Eastern philosophy, yoga, and all sorts of such activities. On several occasions, she would arrange an "Evening of Discovery," as she called them. Although I resisted, I could, in fact, instinctually feel that all this, all these crazy activities Carmen instigated, were really good for me. The nightmares were fewer, less intense.

MY SECOND WAKE-UP CALL

About 18 months later, while riding horses with Carmen in Andalucía, yet another *real* (real because I couldn't ignore it) wake-up call came by telephone. It was my daughter, Adriana. Her voiced trembled. She was always so sensitive.

"Papa, it's Jorgé. He is sick. He is in the hospital with advanced hepatitis C."

"Adriana, you know your brother and I have not been speaking for years now, and we have separate ways of living, but still … that's too bad. When will he be getting out? Shall I send chocolates or a letter?"

"Papa, when I say that Jorgé is sick, I mean really sick this time. His girlfriend has already died of AIDS and I know you don't want news of him, but this time he is really sick and very vulnerable. He may not be getting well any time soon, according to his doctor. You had better come here. Can you come to Barcelona to make a visit?"

"I can't just now, I am in the middle of something important. Adriana, you know I love you, baby."

"Can you at least call him?" she begged me. I could never resist her.

"Baby, he and I … he doesn't want to hear from me …"

"Yes, he does!" she screamed at me, now crying, "yes, he does, papa. He needs you!" She was sobbing uncontrollably.

"OK, OK, OK, I'll call him tomorrow afternoon to please you, just stop crying please! Give me the number at the hospital."

Immediately after hanging up, I regretted it, as I didn't have the heart to call him. I did not even feel as though I knew my own son, but I *did* care for him, as a person.

I did my best to keep Carmen in the dark, as usual, and waited for her to go out for food before I called Jorgé. As I dialled, I felt acid in my stomach, and I watched as my hand trembled with the numbers. Waiting for him to pick up, hoping he wouldn't.

The weak voice of an older man pick up at the other end. "Hello?"

"Yes, um huh," I hesitated, "Is Jorgé Fernández there, please?"

"It's me, Papa." He hadn't called me "Papa" in years. I had an instant lump in my throat. He continued feebly, but serenely. "How are you? *Where* are you? Are you in Barcelona?" His voice was raw, vulnerable.

"I'm fine. You sound tired. And you? Adriana mentioned to me that you were having a rough time. You OK?" I asked, hoping to deflect his question as to my whereabouts.

"Not too great. The doctor says my liver is sick. But I am tough, you know. I come from you and Grandpa, don't forget, eh? Can you come for a quick visit?"

"How long do you think you will be there? I have to check my agenda. There's is a lot going on over here. I may have to stay put. Maybe I can come next week?" That would be more convenient for me to get back to Barcelona, and for Carmen.

"Sure, sure, not to worry, Papa, whenever you can," he put up a brave front. "See what you can do. If you make it, great, if not, no big deal. There was just one last thing I've been wanting to say to you. Ummm ...," he hesitated.

I was not in a hurry to dig too deeply with Jorgé after so many years of not talking. For me, having just spoken to him was enough, regardless of content, to score points with Adriana and Carmen.

"Jorgé, let's do this. Let's speak when I come next week ...," I tried to nip the conversation in the bud, but Jorgé persisted.

"No, listen, Papa." He seemed determined. "Listen, we spoke a long time ago about what went down between you when you guys split up, as to whether you thought I was your son or not ..."

"Jorgé, Jorgé, Please let's not get into that," I attempted.

"Papito," Jorgé was in charge and firm, "I can't afford to argue with you at this point. I just wanted to tell you that, even if you are still doubting us, I'm *not* doubting anything! YOU are my father and I am your SON. Now it's your turn to 'Deal with it.' I'll see when I do."

As I hung up from my call with Jorgé, the door opened and Carmen walked in, smiling. As we embraced quietly, I could not recall the last time I felt that good, that alive. That warm feeling would not last long; once again I had made another bad bet.

Only by joy and sorrow does a person know anything about themselves and their destiny. They learn what to do and what to avoid.

Goethe

MY THIRD WAKE-UP CALL

Three days later, as I came walking back into the house, Carmen was holding her portable phone, crying. "Check your messages, Miguel. Jorgé has died, early this morning. His mother and sister were with him. They had the traditional honour of cleaning and dressing his body. Oh, Miguel I am so sorry. Let's call the girls."

As I dialled Adriana's number, I noticed, sure enough, here I was notified by text message. An already difficult call turned even more so when Maria, Jorgé's mother, answered Adriana's phone.

"Hello, Miguel. Sorry we missed you here. Jorgé asked for you before he died. I told him you had tried to make it. Where were you?" Her voice was full of the fire and reprimand reserved for a naughty son.

"Please, Maria, don't start. It's not really the time for that."

"It's precisely the best time for this. Miguel, the facts speak for themselves and you need to hear them. You were not there for his birth, you missed his wedding, and you were absent when he closed his eyes."

Not awaiting my response, she added, "I'll pass you to Adriana."

"Hi, Papa. I can't talk right now, the scene is pretty heavy here. There's one more thing: Jorgé and his girlfriend had a baby boy together, who is now 2 and a half years old. I just want to say that I love you and I really regret you missed Jorgé."

After a brief uncomfortable moment, we hung up, and the only thing that stuck in my head was that last phrase of Adriana's, the news of Jorgé's son, a detail I decided to keep secret, for the time being, from Carmen.

I HIT ROCK BOTTOM

Jorgé's death hit me much harder than I could have ever anticipated, and I did a free-fall into depression. It felt like falling into a prehistoric tar pit: sticky and black. In the days and weeks after Jorgé's passing, Maria's words weighed heavily on my shoulders. I just couldn't get my head around the basic truth in everything she said. In life, basically parents want to be there for their kids when they are born, when they get married, and get sick. I had missed my only son's entire life. Someone could manage that feat only if they really tried.

Carmen had no trouble noticing my state of mind. As the days dragged on after Jorgé's death, my spirits plunged further, my psoriasis lit up like a Christmas tree, and, worst of all, my libido flagged, soon to be followed by a severe attack of the "blues" – "los diablos azules."

"What's up, *querido*?" Carmen would hazard. "You are getting stuck somewhere, it seems."

"No, nothing really, just working through some ideas ..." I had realized that Carmen was as objective as any of the lovers I had been with. She listened carefully and attentively, and then responded with the same cold thinking as if she were analyzing an electrical circuit. I had to tread gently here.

"Stop it. You are hiding something. Do you think I am blind or just stupid?" She was ruthless in her compassion.

"No, it's not that so much as what Maria said to me that doesn't stop echoing in my mind. She has been sabotaging me from the beginning with the children. It seems that there is nothing I can do right." I could feel the tears welling up.

"Right, I have the antidote for those 'diablos azules,'" she offered. "We are going, just you and me, on a trip to India! Let's get away from all this crazy tension for a while. You know, charge our batteries, see the sights, meet some people, do some yoga, breathing, have some fun ..."

I resisted. "Don't know about that. Not so sure. I just want to be left alone, not be surrounded by a billion people. Some of my friends told me that India is dirty and you cannot even get a good beef steak there. Not just that, I am a dyed in the wool Cartesian: don't ask about meditation – it's just not my culture!"

"What the hell are you talking about, 'your culture'? What is that supposed to mean? What's 'your culture'?" she was on the attack.

"You know what I mean by 'our culture': Western, Christian, God-fearing, law-abiding ..." I was frankly at a loss as to where I wanted to go with this. I hadn't really thought it through completely.

"You mean the whole predictability of the collective ant colony climbing all over each other to get a German car, hoarding, child abuse, war for oil. Miguel, culture is not necessarily a friend of your evolution, but also a force of conformity and uniformity. That is not necessarily positive. Look at the Inquisition or Communism or political assassinations: colossal efforts were made to keep any free-thinking people in fear, their hopes suppressed to keep the average human being cowered.

"Culture is not just going to museums and the opera. It is a constantly shifting, constantly changing collective consensus about what neurotic behaviour is deemed 'normal.' The 'normal' of now is different than the normal of 200 years ago. And that's just for the West." I had no good argument to counter all that, so I gave in. Anyway, the nightmares were getting worse.

Eventually, out of desperation, I allowed myself (for the first time) to go to India, to be guided to the inner world by Carmen and start the painful dredging and sorting process. There I was able to try some new things out, like meditation, yoga, and just letting go of my sadness and anger.

MY VISIT TO INDIA AND BEYOND

The mind creates the abyss and the heart crosses it.

Nisargadatta Maharaj

Carmen and I travelled to India, partly on vacation, partly to search, just to be exhaustive. I was already testy when we arrived at the dusty Rishikesh rail station: the air was thick with flies and the ground smeared with cow dung. My search for a simple answer had become decidedly complicated.

After settling into the ashram where Carmen had stayed years earlier, we drifted over to the meeting hall to hear a speaker, a swami, a holy man. The swami (everyone called him "Swamiji") just sat there, unconcerned with the din around him. After the audience settled down, the mostly Western participants looked nervously around the room. There was one Westerner dressed in a holy man's garb, smiling in a very calm, wise manner. Swamiji asked him:

"What is your name, Sir?" calmly asked the Swami.

"My name is Rama Dama. It's been 10 years and I still have enormous tension inside of me, but cannot find the solution."

"Jealousy (the rejection of self or station) is the source of all mental anxiety. Your anxiety is a symptom of low mental discipline, of lack of conviction in yourself and the ideas and methods that you have been trying these past 10 years. Why dress like an Eastern holy man? Has it gotten you closer to where you need to be in this world? Of course not! These are external props for weak convictions. Real change comes from within, not without.

"You are searching for water, but you dig one hole, then move on to dig another. If you want peace, stick to something like breathing and see where it takes you. You want peace, but you do everything to prevent it."

I raised my hand during the silence and asked, "What is the ultimate source of all this suffering in the world?"

Carmen knew instinctively that I wanted to impress her by asking a question of the swami in front of her.

"What is your name, Sir, and where do you come from?" calmly asked the Swami.

"My name is Miguel and I am from Spain."

"Miguel, all suffering, whatever form it takes, such as anxiety and sadness, is present in this world as a teacher – we call it the Ultimate Guru. Where would we be without it? Could you imagine life without the Great Teacher?

"Life's suffering and stresses push us to act, to rely upon our wits to solve our everyday problems, whatever they are about, family, money or work. Soon enough, the body slowly starts to break down, blood pressure, chronic infections, sleeplessness, back pain, emotional swings – all are viewed as hassles or a betrayal instead of an alarm bell that needs tending. We desire to be once again fixed and whole, but are unable or unwilling to take a moment and decipher the message. Life is a continuous series of messages, often subtle or even subliminal, but real messages just for us. To start to 'get the messages,' we need to refocus the mind, like an antenna.

"Success in this endeavor begins with you and how well you can direct your mind and the interplay of deep fears, imprints, and emotional conflicts buried so deep in our psyche that we are not even aware of them. We are all aware of the manifestations of these deep wounds in everyday life, the tension, the anxiety, the depression, but how to escape them is the mystery." He finished his phrase by adding, "You should be more selfish."

This statement from a holy man came as a bit of a shock to me. "What do you mean by 'be more selfish'?"

"You have to love your self a bit more, and by your self, I mean love your eternal self, what you in the West call your soul. If you think of the mind as a *projector*, here's how it works: it is quite simple, at least to explain. It's all *your* projection. Like everyone, you view life through tinted lenses. Tinted by what? By your parents, your culture, your past experiences, your desires, your pain, which then seem to color, change, and twist the reality. You eventually become blinded by preconceptions, leading bad emotional habits and compulsions, like anger, that are all 'local' phenomena particular to you and have nothing to do with any universal reality.

"The result is that you live without actually appreciating the Grand Design and *all* of the beautiful manifestations of it in our world. Your borders stop at your skin. You're missing out on a lot, it seems. One may ask, 'Why would anyone agree to have less than a complete view of reality? Why allow our emotions, like anger and cynicism, to blind us from seeing the whole?' Because, the scheming *left* brain, wherein resides the ego, has calculated it that way. There is always an ulterior motive if the *left* brain is involved. The ego is a good servant but a terrible master. Never forget:"

> Intentionality is everything! The results – the fruits – are nothing.

"A man who tries to kill and fails is still a killer in his heart." So I asked, "And what is this Grand Design, and who designed it?"

"Well, *you* designed it. Or I should say, your software or your inner divinity, your *right* brain, did it for you to learn from, if you pay attention. Basically, the universe, your universe, is designed for your growth and entertainment, to prevent you from dying stupid, because that's the whole point. But you are not following the course, the curriculum. It is not really much more complicated than that – at least from where I am sitting," said the swami gently.

"No matter what you hear and see, and no matter where you go or who you listen to, *there is only one way* I know that can help you to remove these imprints and remove the misery that goes with them. But before I tell you, you have to know that it is hard work, probably the hardest work anyone could do. It is a life's work."

"What is the technique: meditation? Because my girlfriend here has already tried that ..."

"No, meditation can help, but this is far more difficult than sitting quietly: it is to know your mind, how it works, fails to work, reacts, just know your self. That is all." He spoke and then stopped and closed his eyes as if he were waiting for another message, another transmission.

I looked at Carmen, my eyes saying, "Is that it? What am I supposed to do with *that*?"

"Miguel, why don't you ask the questions of me?" asked the Swamiji, his eyelids still closed.

"Where would someone like me start this process of self-discovery?"

"Just start to learn to RELAX, to let go. Start with meditation, or pranayama or deep breathing. You see, Miguel, it just takes a break from the robotic hypnotic activity that is what modern life is about. Most people are sleep-walking when it comes to self-awareness because their entire awareness is preoccupied with survival issues, feeding mouths, paying bills, getting by. They are too tired to explore the origins of the problem and get tied up in the manifestations of those conflicts: a vicious cycle indeed.

"The modern world seems to be calling for anything but that, but a careful view of the matter reveals that the world's problems can be traced back to the mind of humankind."

It started to dawn on me that the whole point of all the running around, all the keeping busy, was only to never have the time to reflect on what to do in my life, my own mountain to climb. The trips to the East, the mistresses, the rest, all classic tactics to get around those empty feelings.

I felt as though I had compromised my basic values a long time ago and since had been trying to find myself. I *knew* it. The reason I was staying so fit, I admitted, was to buy time to forestall the inevitable.

The swami continued, "You are so wrapped up in the activities of constantly identifying yourself with your body/mind complex. That takes a lot of energy! We live our lives through a prism of our fears. Miguel, please tell me: what is your greatest fear in life?"

I barely hesitated or reflected at all: "To not be useful. To be irrelevant," I said, rather sure of myself.

"You want love, but you – your actions – produce the exact opposite. You see, people are like neurons. They want to connect. The more they connect, interface, and feed back, the smarter they get. That's what physical love is all about, what music and prayer are all about, what drug use is all about, connecting with another to forget your loneliness.

"That's what all of mammalian life is about: forgetting your absolute lone-liness by migrating from your analytical *left* brain to your transcendent *right* side. You must accept the transience of all life forms: look all around you – nothing lasts. The only way is to live fearlessly because fears reside in the ego, which you must cross over to the left side. You, as an instrument of the Life Force, will be more formidable because you will become bigger than the ego, the devil.

"As you know, the stresses of modern life can lead to many diseases and states of inflammation, such as heart attacks, brain dementia, and cancer. You should practice pranayama (controlled breathing[1]) and yoga nidra (the "yoga of sleep") with complete sincerity and earnestness. I can say without hesitation that the exercise of controlled breathing and yoga nidra will heal you of whatever ails you, inside and outside. That would be the most effective and enduring practice towards a full healing that I can recommend.

"It is interesting – we here are constantly aware that whatever we do, whatever act we perform, it must be sacred because it will cause problems for us later, so to speak. Above all, we want to be sure to get that right, even if it means being wrong, from an ego point of view.

Take responsibility where you need to take responsibility: in your thoughts. Don't care what others think about you; care only for your thought parade, where it's going and why. Worry as much as you can, but remember that you are but an actor on the stage. You must study the great writers. Didn't Shakespeare say:

> All the world's a stage,
> And all the men and women merely players;
> They have their exits and their entrances;
> And one man in his time plays many parts,
> His acts being seven ages. At first the infant,
> Mewling and puking in the nurse's arms;
> Then the whining school-boy, with his satchel
> And shining morning face, creeping like snail
> Unwillingly to school. And then the lover,
> Sighing like furnace, with a woeful ballad
> Made to his mistress' eyebrow. Then a soldier,
> Full of strange oaths, and bearded like the pard,
> Jealous in honour, sudden and quick in quarrel,
> Seeking the bubble reputation
> Even in the cannon's mouth. And then the justice,
> In fair round belly with good capon lin'd,
> With eyes severe and beard of formal cut,
> Full of wise saws and modern instances;
> And so he plays his part. The sixth age shifts
> Into the lean and slipper'd pantaloon,
> With spectacles on nose and pouch on side;
> His youthful hose, well sav'd, a world too wide
> For his shrunk shank; and his big manly voice,
> Turning again toward childish treble, pipes
> And whistles in his sound. Last scene of all,
> That ends this strange eventful history,
> Is second childishness and mere oblivion;
> Sans teeth, sans eyes, sans taste, sans everything.

"You see here where East meets West, where Swamiji meets Shakespeare, with the same message:

> Don't take all this so seriously. Life is a test if you do it right, but it's a trap if you cannot lead yourself.

"Enjoy the ride if you can," the swami continued. "If not, there will be another time. The Chinese have an expression that the wise of this world are Confucian in good times, Buddhist in bad times, and Taoist in old age. Essentially, that means to take it easy. You are getting too old to not have figured that one out.

"Reflect on this. Your reason for coming has been addressed. We have planted the seeds. You no longer need to be here. The bridges you need to cross are back in your home country, in your garden. There are no accidents in this regard. Return to your country and be at peace. I think there is someone very special waiting there for you," he said as his eyes glimmered.

MIGUEL'S THREE-POINT HEALTH ACTION PLAN FOR A HEALTHY MIND

1. Learning to relax.
2. Controlling depression.
3. Programming the mind.

Today's business environment (hostile takeovers, acquisitions, mergers, deregulation, downsizing uncertainty, and new technologies) can produce changes in our lives with more speed and violence than ever before. Who will survive? Who will thrive? Aspects of our life that once provided shelter and refuge (job security, our health, marriages, and other relationships) are all now vulnerable. This chapter not only addresses the classic external sources of stress, but also presents tried and true strategies for surviving our own internal neuroses.

The modern doctor's office or emergency room is a living testimony to the prevalence of the tense mind:

- High blood pressure.
- Heart attacks, at younger ages and more deadly every year.
- Increased suicide rates, even among teens.
- Alcohol and drug-related deaths (homicides, car accidents).
- Irritable bowel syndrome.
- Ulcers and heartburn.
- Domestic violence and break-ups.

Unfortunately, the way Western medicine and psychiatry are set up, we are trained to react to the symptoms and not respond to the person. Instead of teaching people who are hurting to listen carefully to their particular symptoms, their "inner voice," we smother the annoying symptoms with drugs, check off the patient, and move on to the next one.

The case of Miguel is all too common, nearly ubiquitous, in professional circles of work, in the setting of obsession with productivity, less time, less resources … But the way out is clear and the methodology sound. It involves step-by-step progress in learning first to lead yourself.

Logical and precise, left-brain thinking gave us the Information Age. Now comes the Conceptual Age – ruled by artistry, empathy, and emotion.

Dan Pink, *A Whole New Mind: Why Right-Brainers Will Rule the Future*

Step 1: Explore the battlefield of the mind

All that we are is a result of what we have thought. It is founded on thought. It is based on thought.

Buddha, *The Dhammapada*

The *objective* here is to relax long enough to use these tried-and-true methods first to identify whatever negative thought forms there might be in the subconciousness and then to consciously substitute them for those that create a greater chance for harmony in your world.

The battle within the human mind is for the high moral ground between "opposing moral tendencies," as Gandhi called them. The real battle in life is, of course, internal: constantly raging within us between the forces of *good* (truth, kindness, generosity, authenticity, impeccability, sincerity, justice, hope, humor, patience, and especially love) and *evil* (greed, humorlessness, cynicism, intolerance, selfishness, laziness, ignorance, mediocrity, meanness, and especially fear).

The whole game of life and self-mastery has more to do with mastering our own anger and negative emotions, and really nothing to do with oppression of or violence towards others. It really has more to do with the internal battle of right choices and self-mastery than with bloodshed and violence.

I learned that courage was not the absence of fear, but the triumph over it. The brave man is not he who does not feel afraid, but he who conquers that fear.

Nelson Mandela

But how can we approach the mind *with* the mind? Will the mind's software even permit our corrective approach? Or will the mind, fearing its own change, reject our efforts? One can only tell by trying.

Start by understanding the basic workings of the mind. Equipped with a memory of past events (traumatic and pleasant), the *left* brain takes "data" coming in now and compares them to what we have learned from past events, such as lessons from various authority figures in our lives (parents, teachers, schoolmates, cousins, and so on). This includes various acquired fears and phobias, which color our thinking process every day.

Based on this earlier programming, the mind and body react to current life situations in two basic ways. Either:

- the present "data" fit into the pattern of previous experiences and no tension or conflict is experienced; *or*
- the new "data" do not fit somehow and confusion arises, leading to an unresolved conflict and tension. This particular interplay between the limbic system and the cerebral cortex is designed to protect us from the "foreign," to protect us in turn from potentially dangerous threats.

Even when powerful or painful sensory messages occur, we tend to stick with our thinking minds, the analytical *left* brain – "my mind, right or wrong" – which, of course, is a main source of tension. With this as background, one fact becomes clear: we are all at the mercy of the contents of our minds. Our overreaction to various external life stressors starts the activation of the "fight or flight" physiology: panic (Fig. 5.1). Once we move the focus of our investigation from the interior world to the exterior world, our ability to control our lives quickly slips from our hands.

As an example how our mind affects our body, consider how any *acquired* fear (snakes, dark, failure, flying, death of a loved one or loss of a job) impacts on our physiology. (Note that fear is the mere thought of the object, and NOT the object itself.) According to Dr. Murphy, there are only two **innate** fears: the fear of falling and the fear of loud noises.

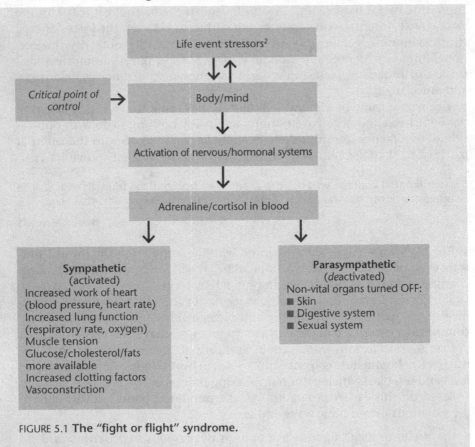

FIGURE 5.1 **The "fight or flight" syndrome.**

As can be seen in Figure 5.2, the starting point for all diseases and ailments, physical and mental, is the *left* brain and how it (over)reacts to standard life events. The problem is that we are using more and more psychological energy, because we are perceiving life as a series of threats, to react in a knee-jerk fashion, instead of using opportunities to respond. Because we have been designed to be neophobic (to have a fear of new or "foreign" things), we must, to become a complete person, a true leader, override this primitive hardware.

All religious leaders – Jesus Christ, the Prophet Mohammed, Buddha, and others – have taught the same ideas over the centuries: change your mind towards others ("Love thy neighbour as thyself"), instead of trying to change others.

But, in fact, very little of all this actually gets to the conscious level as the brain (in particular the reticular activating system) in effect defends the brain by allowing only a small proportion of information to actually get our conscious attention at the level of the ego. If it is an emergency or if it "fits" our previous mental programming ("what we know" and "who we are"), it gets "air time" in the consciousness. If the reticular activating system cannot make a match between past and present events, tension occurs. This is the general rule, that the outside world is simply not concerned with our previous programming. Accordingly, the "fight or flight" system of survival is triggered, increasing tension further.

> **TIP** Steps to being your own psychiatrist:
> - The **first** step is to achieve greater self-mastery: learn to RELAX.
> - The **second** step is, once relaxed, to explore the mind.
> - The **third** step is to remove the causes of tension.

Step 2: Learning to relax is not an option for psychic healing, it's a necessity!

Why learn to relax? Quite simply, so as not to miss out on so many of life's lessons, as happened to Miguel.

In ancient days, merely getting a good night's sleep was enough to refresh the mind and body. However, in modern business life, with its inherent stresses and tensions (basic job dissatisfaction, isolation from loved ones for prolonged periods of time, and artificial deadlines), the mind and body remain tense all the time. No amount of sleep can relax us. For this reason, learning to relax is a self-mastery tool to help reduce anxiety and manage tension. Learning to effectively relax from within, without help from the old standard methods (alcohol, pills or conflicts), revitalizes and rejuvenates the body and mind.

Most importantly, we must relax from within, by removing the deep-seated fears embedded, perhaps since youth, in our minds. We then avoid entering, for the rest of our life, into the vicious cycle that characterizes modern life: tension leading to illness to negative thinking and back to more tension.

Imagine a hurricane: on the periphery there is violence, while at the centre there is peace. To know the mind, you must relax enough to get back to the centre, where psychic healing takes place through exploration of the mind. Learning to center the mind is the key to psychic and physical health and self-mastery. Anatomically speaking, the center of the hurricane is the critical zone. It is the calm, cool right brain, and the periphery of the hurricane is the detail-oriented, ego-based, "I am" left brain.

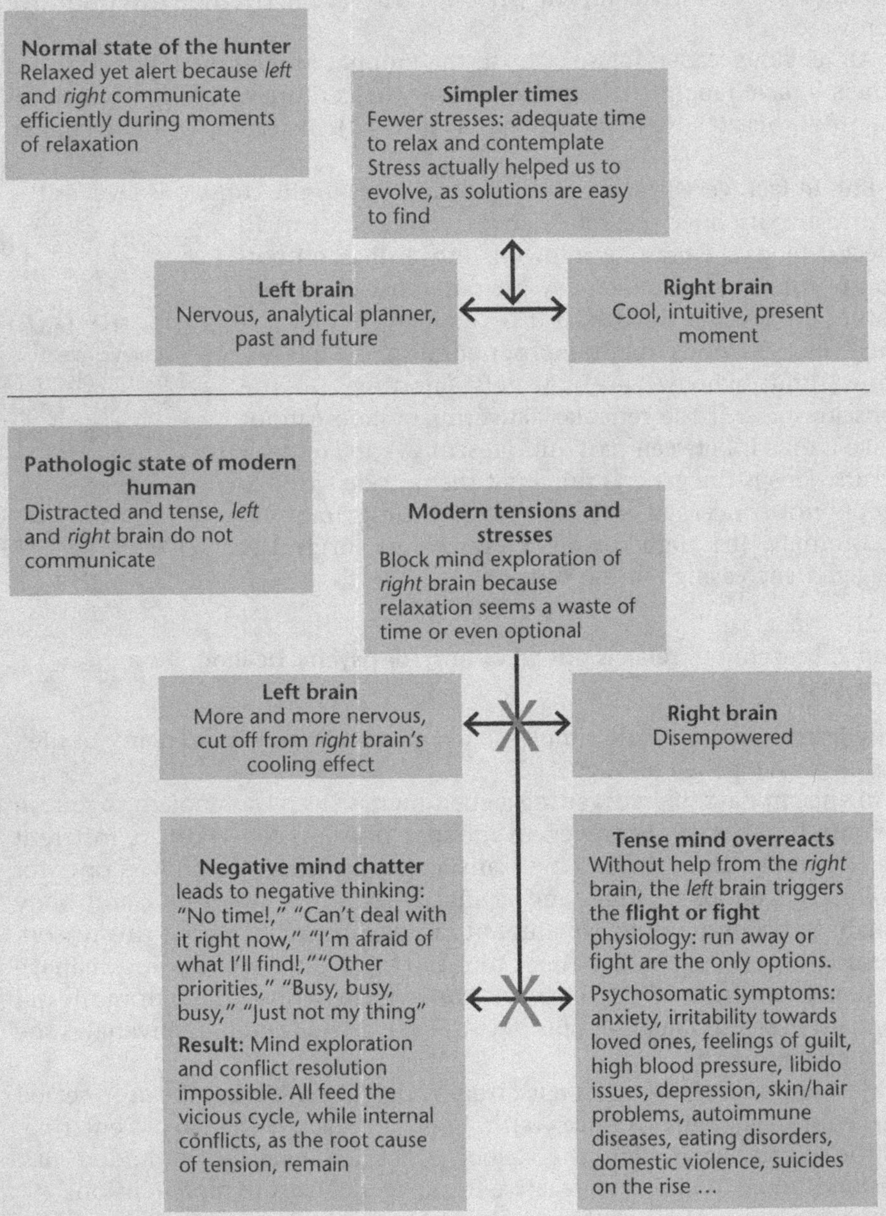

Normal state of the hunter
Relaxed yet alert because *left* and *right* communicate efficiently during moments of relaxation

Simpler times
Fewer stresses: adequate time to relax and contemplate
Stress actually helped us to evolve, as solutions are easy to find

Left brain
Nervous, analytical planner, past and future

Right brain
Cool, intuitive, present moment

Pathologic state of modern human
Distracted and tense, *left* and *right* brain do not communicate

Modern tensions and stresses
Block mind exploration of *right* brain because relaxation seems a waste of time or even optional

Left brain
More and more nervous, cut off from *right* brain's cooling effect

Right brain
Disempowered

Negative mind chatter
leads to negative thinking: "No time!," "Can't deal with it right now," "I'm afraid of what I'll find!,""Other priorities," "Busy, busy, busy," "Just not my thing"

Result: Mind exploration and conflict resolution impossible. All feed the vicious cycle, while internal conflicts, as the root cause of tension, remain

Tense mind overreacts
Without help from the *right* brain, the *left* brain triggers the **flight or fight** physiology: run away or fight are the only options.

Psychosomatic symptoms: anxiety, irritability towards loved ones, feelings of guilt, high blood pressure, libido issues, depression, skin/hair problems, autoimmune diseases, eating disorders, domestic violence, suicides on the rise …

FIGURE 5.2 **The critical role of relaxation in primitive vs modern humans.**
(The gray Xs indicate the blockage between the left and right brain)

When we are centered, we feel a sense of peace that is impossible with drugs, vacations or alcohol. It is during this *critical period* at the figurative center of the hurricane, when we are alert and relaxed, that we imprint, we learn better.

Humans spend the bulk of their time dealing with the *manifestations* (psychosomatic symptoms) caused by *inter*personal conflicts which very often come from deep *intra*personal conflicts. We feel the tension without really knowing what has caused it: the pain is real, but the underlying cause remains shrouded in mystery, often for our entire lives.

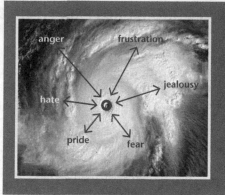

When we are relaxed and our mind is centered, our outlook on life is radically different than when we are feeling anger or frustration. When we are calm, free from anxiety and stress, we manage to laugh at and understand life's lessons, which only hours before gave us dangerous blood pressure and a violent attitude.

When we are relaxed, we see life's challenges in a new light, with new understanding. This understanding starts to bring other positive changes in our lifestyles as well. Confused and dazed by the constant stresses of modern life, we reel from crisis to crisis, overreacting to the pain and anxiety that these conflicts cause. Pills, alcohol, and anger only exacerbate the conflicts further, while weakening our ability to respond effectively.

Moreover, we do not want to completely avoid life's stressful moments (life's challenges, impossible deadlines, incompetent and insensitive people, money issues, endless hours in traffic, separation from loved ones, and evil of all sorts) for the simple reason that nothing worthwhile really gets done without them.

Exploration of the mind can happen only when we are relaxed and centred, free of emotions. This is the critical zone where we gain all the insights we need to solve life's problems, when we *relax* long enough to extricate our thinking processes from the day-to-day survival pressures so that we can direct in towards the interior, where the solutions to the problems are to be found.

Life's stresses make it very difficult to explore the mind to discover and remove the causes of these tensions. Often our culture rewards dysfunctional behaviour such as workaholism, aggression, and even depression:

> The intuitive mind is a sacred gift and the rational mind is a faithful servant. We have created a society that honors the servant and has forgotten the gift.
>
> **Albert Einstein**

In sum, stop thinking, stop feeling, stop moving, take a few deep breaths, and see what happens. As the Buddhists say, "Everything is impermanent." So learn to detach yourself from the stresses and relax to gain the proper perspective on life. Then you can respond to the world, not react. Eventually, peace of mind flashes by.

CLOSING WORDS FROM A LEADER ... CHANGE THE WORLD OR CHANGE YOUR MIND

While I was in India, I met a yoga teacher from Belgium who passed me an article written anonymously in a yoga journal by an ex-convict that changed me as much than anything there. I share this with you here. Read the passage slowly, trying to put yourself in the prisoner's place.

The beginning was a disturbed childhood, a habit of drinking and no good purpose in life. At 18, I landed in jail on a charge of petty theft, which started the cycle of theft for easy money, a good time, arrest, trial, prison sentence, hate for society, release, and again theft and thoughts of murder for revenge.

After 8 months, I began to feel the effects of imprisonment. Luckily, sickness came – insomnia, constipation and headache and a daily routine of visiting sick bay. Drugs were given without much relief and even more symptoms appeared. I began to think that it was the prison food, so I obtained a book on dietetics.

One time I accidentally visited the prison butchery and received a terrible shock. Hanging upside down was half an animal, frozen nine years earlier. From then on, I stopped eating meat. This was indeed difficult to manage inside a prison. While others were trying to get alcohol and medicine, I was trying to obtain fresh and healthy food.

Slowly I began to feel better, which assured me that I was on the right path. Then I discovered yoga and began practicing from a book. It was the only physical exercise possible in the confines of a cell. As I performed different asanas, I felt a transformation taking place, not only outwardly, but also inwardly. I suddenly realized that my life had been a succession of mistakes and that hate was a much heavier burden for myself than for those who were the object of it.

I was still drinking alcohol and smoking nearly 3 packets of cigarettes a day. I learned that this was weakening my heart and destroying my lungs. It was the reason I was coughing and spitting. Over one week, I decided not to smoke during my waking hours and it was quite an ordeal. Progressively I reduced the number of cigarettes daily. I thought finally "I will get rid of this smoking habit," and repeated this sentence again and again. Then I began breathing more deeply and with awareness for the first time. Finally I exchanged my cigarette provision for sweets. However, this need slowly disappeared and, with my success in giving up smoking, I decided to win over my alcohol habit also. Gradually, I got rid of many unhealthy habits and this improved all levels of my being – physical, mental, emotional and psychic.

Here I was, however, still a slave to my negative thoughts, so I consciously decided to transform my thinking and my mind. Now I understand that the first steps of transformation started with taking responsibility for my own health and habits. My conscious efforts started with one of the most destructive emotions in man – hate. Where there would be hate, there would be love, where there was selfishness, there would be generosity, etc. I wrote these maxims down and repeated them like a sankalpa every day.

I realized then I was the only one responsible for my evil tendencies. No matter what injustice I felt in the world, I decided to forget all ideas of revenge. It felt good to live without hate but in peace with all. Even my cell seemed larger and more pleasant. A new life was blooming before me – one of love for others and nature, for everything, in fact, that made up our existence. The metamorphosis resulted in a new and happy man with inspiring friends made through continual study of health, yoga and dietetics. This revealed to me that the outer world changes as one's inner world evolves.

After 5 years in jail, a warden came to my cell and told me "You are free." I smiled. I was already free – free of the ideas that bound me more than anything else. The reason I am relating this today, is for anybody suffering in similar circumstances, living in hate, or thinking it's too late to change. It is possible to change the world – that is, our view of the world – to a more beautiful and positive one. You can expand your health, awareness and happiness with fresh nourishing food, yogic discipline and a balanced lifestyle. This is not the first time that yoga and a higher life has been discovered inside prison walls. Being 'inside' is a time when one can reflect on one's life, to think, to meditate, to make decisions to change, or to continue the downward spiral of self-destruction. In the words of Tagore:

I was asleep and dreaming
That life was only joy.
I woke up and saw
That life was all service
I served and saw
That service was pure joy.

Since I returned from India, things are getting better, slowly but surely. But the journey of inner healing and self-mastery, while long and difficult, has been one of the most stimulating and rewarding endeavors that I could be doing. While there have been plenty of pitfalls of self-loathing, jealousy, and bitterness along the way, I have been able to recognize them as "tests" or "imposters" and I have been able to move on, hopefully a little wiser for it all.

Moreover, I've seen a lot of benefits in my professional life from all these various mental exercises, as I have learned to actively listen (as if I actually cared – because I do!). One of my most useful pointers is that my health is a combination of physical health and spiritual health.

I have had a very interesting life up to now: lots of "ups" and "downs." But in all honesty, I have wasted a lot of time and have only just recently realized that I have made bad decisions and lost many opportunities (thinking of Jorgé here). In fact, in retrospect, by not accepting my family for what it was, I charted a course of despair and tragedy.

But, thanks to many friends and enemies alike along the way, I now take full possession of my software, my "bullshit" (as Carmen would call it), my destiny. I have a lot of meaning in my life now. I am involved in the payback period of my life. Giving freely of my time to the community, my church, and Jorgé's son helps me to feel in service to others and keep my depression at bay.

It is not the mountain we conquer but ourselves.

Sir Edmund Hillary

Miguel's second health and fitness report

	NORMAL/IDEAL RANGE	ME (BASELINE)	ME (FOLLOW-UP)
Actual age (years)		42	44
Health age (years)	Actual age (or less)	56.7	45.7

	NORMAL/IDEAL RANGE	ME (BASELINE)	ME (FOLLOW-UP)
Blood pressure (mmHg)	< 135/85	125/75	125/75
Resting heart rate (beats/minute)	< 60	82	56
Body fat %	< 20 % men, < 23% women	15%	18%
Exhalation count (seconds)	> 100	25	110
Photographic memory (items)	> 10	4	10
Numeric memory (items)	> 10	3	10
Concentration (numbers)	> 14	5	14
Reflexes (ruler test) (cm)	< 3	11	5
Homocysteine level (micromoles/L)	7.0–10	56.8	9.6
High-sensitivity C-reactive protein (mg/L)	< 1	Not done	Not done
Psoriasis	None	Florid	Quiet
Early prostate cancer antigen-2 test (EPCA-2) (ng/mL)	< 30	35	14
Sleep Quality	10/10	2/10	10/10
Nightmares	Infequently	Every night	Every week or two

When I was asked to write about my leadership qualities, I hesitated but then agreed. You see, I experienced (and caused) so much private pain that I hope to inspire you to do the *opposite* of what I did. I finally understand several critical facts of life:

- That the only thing I need, or indeed can, control is the interior world: my reactions to anxiety and stress. Approaching any personal conflict from anywhere but the inside is an illusion and a time-waster. I am fed up with "just not getting it." I deserve better from myself.
- That to give *higher meaning* (meaning beyond the game of material survival) in my life, is to give back the love I have been given, thereby multiplying it. That's the miracle. I realize that we are defined by how we react in a crisis.
- I now feel a strong sense of connection to both of my daughters and am determined to allow these relationships to bloom from the ashes of these very trying times. I am committed to helping in any way possible with Jorgé's son, Franck. I may get a second chance at this yet.
- Now in arguments, I don't pour oil on the fire, I listen to what the other person is trying to say. This has helped *a lot* at work. After all, a Leader's Mind is a Beginner's Mind: always ready to learn.

And always remember: Life is not measured by the numbers of breaths you take but by the moments that take your breath away.

Quantify to improve

Just remember the key rule to progress: quantify to improve. In my particular case, there are several health parameters along the way to fitness that act as gauges to my progress:

- Blood pressure
- Exhalation count
- Sleep quality
- Concentration;
- Memory: – photographic and numeric
- Anger.

I can monitor all these using the grid below:

Date	Ideals			
Blood pressure (mmHg)	< 135/85 mmHg			
Exhalation count (seconds)	> 85			
REM sleep: presence of dreams – yes/no?	Dreams twice a week			
Concentration (items)	> 10 items			
Memory (items)	> 10 items			
Anger (number of episodes)	Rare			

The best ...

- The best time to laugh ... when you are afraid or hurt
- The best way to keep from crying ... laugh
- The best stimulant for the brain ... oxygen
- The best mind/body work-out ... yoga, martial arts (karate)
- The best path to serenity ... daily meditation
- The best way to tie up loose ends ... write a LifePlan
- The best mantra ... "Thank you" 25 times on arising and going to sleep
- The best way to let go ... humor
- The best way to get to sleep after a stressful day ... repeat at bedtime: I have done my best, now I shall take my deserved rest; may the morning sunshine bring answers to my worries.

LEADER'S TOP FAQS ON BRAIN SOFTWARE

When should I meditate? How much is enough? And what should I expect?

Upon arising, do a 3-minute meditation to center your mind and resolve NOT to be provoked by anyone or anything today. In general, do meditation for as long as it takes you to smile widely and promise yourself that nobody at the office or home will pull you "off center."

Are type A personalities mentally tougher?

When challenged, research shows that type As have higher adrenaline and cortisol levels and, in fact, recover more slowly than type Bs. The key to coping appears to be a selective type A picture: type A empowered. Although type As may have more challenge-seeking behavior, if this is accompanied by the classic type A profile (hostility, anger, and depression), they tend to crack under the load. The solution is the classic type A (go-getter + perfectionism + success-driven) minus the hostility = type A empowered.

Is there an historical gender difference in coping?

In a recent report, researchers studied the calamities that beset the westward-bound settlers in 19th-century America. Most striking was the finding that nearly twice as many men died as women (57% vs 28%). Of those settlers who tried to snowshoe out of the mountains where they were stranded, all the men died and all women survived. Possible reason: better insulation (body fat), plus less panic.

Stress and nutrition: what can be done?

A University of Alabama study found that rats subjected to stress had lower levels of the stress hormone cortisol when they were fed the human equivalent of several grams of vitamin C a day. Cortisol can also suppress your immune system, which is why stress has been known to increase the risk of getting ill. Taking large daily doses of vitamin C (over 2 g/day) may also counteract that effect and help keep you healthy during times of stress. The study results also suggest that current governmental guidelines for vitamin C intake (60 mg a day) may be too low.

Meanwhile, a recent Californian study found that alcohol empties your brain of chemicals that make you feel good – neurotransmitters such as dopamine, serotonin, and gamma-aminobutyric acid, which affect your brain's pleasure pathways. The brain attempts to compensate by dramatically increasing corticotrophin-releasing factor, a stress chemical that leads to depression. This combination of decreased neurotransmitters and increased corticotrophin-releasing factor leaves your brain in a state of dependence – it wants more alcohol to get things back to normal.

So if you're under major stress, load up on vitamin C – take the supplements periodically throughout the day, because your body flushes out excess vitamin C every time you urinate. And lastly, go easy on the after-work drinks – they're not as relaxing as you might think.

What is meant by "nervous breakdown," and what general warning symptoms can be perceived?

"Nervous breakdown" is a lay term, not an official diagnosis, so there is no specific definition and its meaning may vary. The general public seems to use it as a catch-all term to describe an acute emotional or psychological collapse.

What is the physiology of nicotine?

At lower blood levels, nicotine causes mild sedation and relaxation, which is precisely why most people use cigarettes during acute anxiety attacks. The sedative effect gives way to a stimulatory effect at higher dosages, thereby delaying the onset of sleep. The half-life of nicotine, that is, the time it takes for half the amount to be cleared from the body, is 2 hours. An average to heavy smoker sleeps between 30 and 60 minutes less than a non-smoker.

Does smoking directly affect my blood pressure?

In addition to "thickening" the blood, smoking cigarettes causes an explosion in blood pressure due to a radical oxygen mismatch (abruptly decreasing oxygen availability combined with critical increases in demand during stressful moments). Try checking your blood pressure during a cigarette smoke to see what the heart is witnessing. This is one of the reasons why cigarette smoking is responsible for 21% of all mortality from heart disease.

Is passive smoking dangerous?

Because of the toxins and carcinogens (marked * below) in cigarette smoke – nitroamines ammonia, cyanhydric acid (used in gas chambers), acetone/toluene (solvents), methane (swamp gas), naphthalene, carbon monoxide (a constituent of car exhaust fumes), phenol, DDT (an insecticide), toluidine*, urethane*, dimethylnitrosamines*, naphthylamines*, pyrene*, polonium-210* (radioactive), cadmium* (a heavy metal found in car batteries), vinyl chloride* (a plastic), and benzopyrene* – passive smoking is associated with respiratory illnesses, asthma, and lung cancers. Passive smoking is responsible for over 3,000 deaths a year in the US. Studies following the babies of mothers who smoked showed a "dose-related increase" in hospitalizations (three times if the mother smoked one pack per day), more asthma (a twofold increase), increased ear infections, a higher incidence of sudden infant death syndrome, and an increased incidence of lung cancer as adults.

Do smoke-free policies work?

Absolutely. In a study based on a company with 15,000 employees that developed a no-smoking policy, 25% of smokers quit outright (peer pressure in reverse), and there were 13% fewer medical visits for respiratory complaints and an annual saving of US$110,000. Such policies work for the people, whether smokers or non-smokers.

I have heard that we use only 10% of our brains. What is happening to the other 90%?

The full answer is not yet clear, but one thing is certain: Nature, in her economical manner, does not make trivial decisions. She has bestowed upon us, in a relatively short time from an evolutionary point of view (10 million years), a massive cerebral cortex with limitless potential and capacity. For what function? Certainly not mere physical survival. In the book *Doors of Perception*, Huxley invites his readers to leave behind the noise of the marketplace of everyday life and use that brain capacity to expand the mind, build rooms in our soul for future refuge, and develop our true potential, as well as gain a greater understanding of life and each other. As Oscar Wilde once wrote: "We are all in the gutter, except that some of us are looking at the stars."

Is depression more common in heart attack patients?

According to *Circulation*, the journal of the American Heart Association, depression and withdrawal are very common among heart attack patients. Depressed patients are approximately three times as likely to die when compared to non-depressed patients. The single most important factor in alleviating depression is strong social support, which may protect patients from the negative aspects of depression and improve their overall prognosis.

What is the relation between smoking and aging?

Both smoking and high blood pressure accelerate the normal aging processes, accounting for 15% of the damaged abnormal brain tissue seen on magnetic resonance imaging scans. Behavior in mid-life can make a difference to what faculties we have to enjoy later on.

Stress and asthma: what is the connection?

Studies have shown a clear causal relationship between anxiety, attack frequency, the medications required to control asthma, and asthma hospitalizations. Not only can stress trigger an asthmatic attack, but it also worsens the severity of the attack.

Does poorly controlled stress make us stupid?

Yes. A report presented at the Neuroscience 2000 Conference, suggests that chronic release of the stress hormone cortisol actually kills brain cells, an effect of chronic stress that is particularly evident in the memory centers. These hormones – glucocorticoids – also induce diabetes, high blood pressure, high triglycerides, and colitis.

NOTES AND REFERENCES

1. Modern physical and psychological stresses act on the individual to produce oxidative stresses in the form of free radicals. The aim of this study was to assess the effect of yogic breathing exercises (pranayama) on these oxidative stresses. The study group consisted of 30 young male volunteers, trained for the purpose of this study, and an equal number of controls. The free radical and superoxide dismutase (an antioxidant) levels were measured before and at the end of the study. The free radicals were decreased significantly in the study group, but the superoxide dismutase was increased insignificantly compared to the control group. Yogic breathing exercises not only help in relieving the stresses of life, but also improve the antioxidant status of the individual. An improvement in antioxidant status is helpful in preventing many pathological processes that are seen with impaired antioxidant systems of body. Bhattacharya S, Pandey US, Verma NS. Improvement in oxidative status with yogic breathing in young healthy males. *Indian J Physiol Pharmacol* 2002; **46**: 349–54.
2. Holmes TH, Rahe RH. The social readjustment rating scale. *J Psychosom Res* 1967; **11**: 213–18.

Epilogue

THE STEPS TO BECOMING A LEADER ... OF YOURSELF

The only way to go is forward. After teaching at INSEAD and within corporations for 20 years, where we had the privilege to teach over 75,000 senior managers, an effective five-step formula to develop a self-led futuristic leader has emerged:

1. The first step is to **Decide who you are**. Know thyself. You "are" that part of your make-up that you identify with most:
   a. The *body*: all desires and appetites should be subjugated to the mind's control.
   b. The *mind*: thoughts, ambitions, passions, and emotions should be subjugated to the spirit's control.
   c. The *spirit*: leaders are distinguished by sufficient inner discipline and courage to control the mind and the body, as parents "control" their children, *gently but firmly.*

2. The second step is to **Take stock** honestly of your resources before starting the climb. Know, in hard numbers, where you stand with regard to blood pressure, body fat, cardiofitness, cholesterol, and the 30 other critical parameters of health? Do you know what provokes your left brain to spike your blood pressure or to eat sugary foods? Time to set specific goals.

3. The third step is to **Accept the challenge** to overcome the inertia inherent in business life and life in general. This decision is the hardest part, as the basic law of inertia states:

   a body (or a mind) at rest, stays at rest, unless acted upon by an external force. a body (or a mind) in motion, stays in motion, unless acted upon by an external force.

   Once the inertia has been overcome, indispensable *momentum* will have been achieved. The rich get richer ....

4. The fourth step is to **Keep track of everything**. To do this, one must *quantify to improve*, to avoid the twin devils of denial and doubt. Develop and write down a Health Action Plan that sets concrete goals on the road to self-mastery. This is a time-honored exercise in *personal accountability*. This involves a bit more than just woefully looking in the mirror after your

morning shower. You can only begin this journey of awakening from where you are NOW.

5. **Develop personal momentum** by applying 1–4 to *all* challenges. Practice real yoga. Not just the twisting and sitting yoga. Yoga means bending the "outside" reality to the "inside" ideals. You can dramatically increase your psychic momentum to overcome the bumps in the road ahead by uniting your body and your mind with the spirit to overcome this inherent inertia. There will be tough moments and stressful days when you drag yourself back to the hotel, but bear in mind that having a body and mind that are strong and supple is the first grand step towards that new human being that Maslow described.

Throughout the centuries, paradoxical though it may seem, virtually all spiritual and secular cultures have found reason to use the analogy of war to signify the greatest of battles. History is replete with excellent examples of the leader spirit. Whether one studies Christianity (the Crusades), Hinduism (the Bhagavad Gita) or Islam (the Jihad), the concept of "holy war" and warriors abound. Over 2,000 years ago, Sun Tzu compiled the Art of War in China, which sprang from the great spiritual tradition of Taoism. The Japanese developed and idealized the whole concept of the samurai and, in fact, leaders ruled Japan for seven tumultuous centuries, starting in the late 12th century and lasting until 1868. Native American Indians, revered around the world for their noble spiritual traditions, had a tradition of leader. Even nowadays, everywhere you look, the leader mindset is revived. But what, indeed, is the nature of *true* leader? On this issue, above all others, we *must* get it right.

Throughout the years, we have all been taught that the war is "out there." We have to just face it. Life is war: an invigorating and prolonged conflict, composed of a constant series of battles, not just for power, money, land, food, water, but also in preservation of happiness, lofty principles, and love. Territory is gained and territory is lost, and you revel in the game. Sure we all take some tough "hits" now and again in the process, which may temporally send us into a tailspin, but that will never deter us, but only spur us on.

In the material world of business, the generation of new visions, bringing them to reality, and getting them exposed in the market alongside (or in front) of those of the competition is a real satisfaction to be savoured. The "enemies" are well identified and the battle lines are drawn clearly in the sand. Any self-respecting professional, either in the academic context or out there "on the front line" would admit to the thrill of engaging one's talents and skills in pursuit of something meaningful, particularly if competition is involved. And you, as the modern descendants of these ancient leaders, all love it that way.

You can divide the world into two basic types of people: leaders and worriers. The leaders prepare themselves for the battles, while the worriers, crippled by self-doubt, spend precious resources fretting over a self-fulfilling prophesy. War has been part of the human experience from time immemorial, and we have all had flashes of strategic brilliance on life's battlefields. As it turns out, the greatest of all battles will be the internal battles against all sorts of devils: fears of being ourselves, hatred for our brothers and sisters, choice of the "easy" way instead of the "right" way, self-deprecation, self-doubt, and feelings of unworthiness.

At every juncture and in *every* decision of life, however trivial (from saying "Good morning" to the cleaning lady in the hotel to serious ethical decisions at work), forces within us are constantly in opposition, in conflict. Both sides of this classic dichotomy are *essential* halves of the whole human experience. The "fire" of the conflict between good and evil forces provides not just the heat, but also the light necessary for personal growth. The true leader is aware of that and is undaunted by the battle. In the leader's words, "We're always going to take some hits, but we'll come through in the end." There is no backing down from the "battle" because it is the essential human experience, waiting for you at every juncture, every instant.

In the course of life, everybody goes through certain experiences when, often quite by chance when we least expect it, we experience an awakening, a flash of the real fragility of life. This comes to us through some special experience, such as the illness of a child, a near-fatal car accident, a dead bird in our driveway, glancing through the obituaries and noticing the death of a contemporary, or the death of a close friend. With death is only right around the corner, life goes from a chore or penance to something delicate. Leaders know that there are many things in life that can "go wrong," that, quite often, horrible things happen to very good people, but they are undaunted by the task. They are not paralysed by their vulnerabilities because they know how to handle certain mental, physical or spiritual turbulences that ultimately stem from identification with transitory aspects of life. Leaders are not easily deluded by false idols.

Patients on their deathbed become extremely lucid and conscious. Their priorities are clear, they have little time to waste. Nobody on their deathbed ever wishes that they had spent more time at the office. You see, lying in a hospital bed recuperating from heart surgery, "wired for sound," completely dependent on strangers and uncertain of your fate does indeed have *definite* benefits. You are thrown back upon yourself, you are afforded a reluctant pause for reflection to take stock of your life. Questions come up like:

- What role does dignity play in my life?
- Am I respecting my body, the temple of my soul?
- Am I really doing what I want to do? Why am I here?
- At every juncture of life, am I making conscious decisions to do "the right thing"?
- If, as Gandhi asserted, "Your life is the Message", what is your message?
- Am I honoring those with whom I am in daily contact (children, spouse, colleagues) by giving them undivided attention?
- Am I winning this game called "life"?

A LAST WORD OF ENCOURAGEMENT

The key to awakening the inner leader is to start from where you *are* because, above all, to be a leader is to be unafraid of who you *really* are. The good news is that once "awakened," the leader cannot be crushed or smothered. Whether on the golf course, in the conference room or resting quietly at night, just quieten the chatter and you will find that leader.

Self-led individuals realizing know full well in their heart that life's playing field is extended to include the greatest battlefield of all: that *within*. You are the modern counterparts of the leader of old, with a slight twist. That leader within is the immutable, unspoiled and original essence of a human being prior to all the conditioning: a flame that can *never* be extinguished.

So, never fret. We are all on the path to becoming a leader. Some of you are further along that path, some getting there faster, and some are just better actors. No matter. Never be discouraged. If you don't get there now, it will be later. Sooner or later, we will *all* arrive. Just keep on trying and enjoy the ride.

Nutritional tables, self-assessments, and exercises

appendix

The contents of this appendix are:

1. The glycemic index (GI) of various common foods
2. Superfoods every day for super performance
3. One-stop shopping at the health shop
4. Supplements for optimal health
5. The best of the best ...
6. Tips for preparing meals
7. Fast foods, slow digestion, fast death

THE GLYCEMIC INDEX (GI) OF VARIOUS COMMON FOODS

TABLE AI.1 *Glycemic index (GI) of common foods*

COMMON FOODS AND DRINKS	GI	COMMENTS
High-GI foods (GI 70–105)		
Maltose	105	
Glucose	100	Glucose is given an arbitrary value of 100 and other carbohydrates are given a number relative to glucose
Distilled alcohol	95	Prefer red wine
Most candy	95	
French baguette	95	Prefer wholegrain seed bread
Dates/raisins	93	GI effects are offset though by the powerful antioxidant effect
White bread	81	Choose a really grainy bread full of seeds, sourdough bread or soy and linseed bread
Cornflakes	83	
Potato, red, baked	80	Reduce the number of potatoes you eat, unless for survival
Commercial breakfasts	65–83	Replace high-GI cereals (they spike blood glucose levels) with low-GI natural muesli, traditional porridge oats or bran
Doughnut	76	Eat two a day for rapid fat gain
Gatorade	76	Even 'gators won't drink it
Fries (chips)	75	Worst possible nutrition: trans-fats + high GI
Beer	73	

COMMON FOODS AND DRINKS	GI	COMMENTS
Raisin bran	73	
Bagel, plain	72	
Watermelon	72	
Life-Saver candy	70	
Mid-range-GI foods (GI 56–70)		
Croissant	67	
Canteloupes	65	
Pineapple	66	
Rye bread	64	
Colas	65	
Couscous	65	
White sugar (sucrose)	64	Pure, white, and deadly
High-fructose corn syrup	64	Present in colas, energy drinks, and snacks
Pizza, cheese and tomato	60	
Basmati rice	58	Use lower-GI rices such as basmati, Doongara Clever Rice, Moolgiri medium-grain rice or wild rice. White rice GI = 69
Bananas	56	
Low-GI foods (GI < 55)		
Honey	55	
Mixed grain bread		Use breads with wholegrains, stone-ground flour, sour dough
Mango	55	
Kiwi fruit	52	High vitamin C makes kiwis Superfood
All-Bran	51	
Cheese tortellini, linguini	50	Enjoy pasta, noodles, and quinoa
Pumpernickel	49	
Oatmeal	48	Use breakfast cereals based on oats, barley, and bran
Spaghetti, 5 minutes boiled	44	
Red wine	44	Full of antioxidants
Plums	39	
Apples, tomato soup	38	
Vermicelli pasta	35	
Milk, low fat	32	Take off the delicious fat and the sugar (lactose) rushes in
Milk, full fat	30	Great pre-bed drink for wonderful sleep, with honey

COMMON FOODS AND DRINKS	GI	COMMENTS
Black beans	30	
Lentils, green or brown	30	Ideal food
Red lentils	27	
Fructose	23	Fructose is OK when packaged as a fruit
Black chocolate[1]	23	Dark chocolates have low GI and are full of antioxidants and heart-protective magnesium
Agave nectar	19	Cactus sugar
Nutella	33	Free of preservatives and artificial colors
Yoghurt, plain	14	Superfood, Supersnack

The rule of thumb is to avoid high-GI foods to avoid high insulin, which causes us to store fat and increases our risk for diabetes (Table AI.2), weight gain, high triglycerides, heart disease, and cancer. Table AI.1 shows compiled GI figures from several research labs, and often from more than one study; as such, these GI figures will be approximate and may not be identical to other GI figures.

TABLE AI.2 *The prevalence of diabetes worldwide: note the progression of cases as a function of sugar intake*

	DIABETES INCIDENCE: 2000	DIABETES INCIDENCE: 2030 (PROJECTED)
Worldwide total	171,000,000	366,000,000
European total	33,332,000	47,973,000
Austria	239,000	366,000
Denmark	157,000	232,000
Finland	157,000	239,000
France	1,710,000	2,645,000
Germany	2,627,000	3,771,000
Greece	853,000	1,077,000
Hungary	333,000	376,000
Ireland	86,000	157,000
Israel	257,000	500,000
Italy	4,252,000	5,374,000
Netherlands	426,000	720,000
Norway	130,000	207,000
Poland	1,134,000	1,541,000
Portugal	662,000	882,000
Russian Federation	4,576,000	5,320,000
Spain	2,717,000	3,752,000

	DIABETES INCIDENCE: 2000	DIABETES INCIDENCE: 2030 (PROJECTED)
Sweden	292,000	40,4000
Switzerland	219,000	336,000
Turkey	2,920,000	6,422,000
United Kingdom of Great Britain and Northern Ireland	1,765,000	2,668,000
SE Asia total	46,903,000	119,541,000
Democratic People's Republic of Korea	367,000	635,000
India	31,705,000	79,441,000
Indonesia	8,426,000	21,257,000
Nepal	436,000	1,328,000
Sri Lanka	653,000	1,537,000
Thailand	1,536,000	2,739,000
Bangladesh	3,196,000	11,140,000
America total	33,016,000	66,812,000
Argentina	1,426,000	2,457,000
Brazil	4,553,000	11,305,000
Canada	2,006,000	3,543,000
Chile	495,000	1,047,000
Colombia	883,000	2,425,000
Mexico	2,179,000	6,130,000
United States of America	17,702,000	30,312,000
Mediterrean and Middle East total	15,188,000	42,600,000
Egypt	2,623,000	6,726,000
Islamic Republic of Iran	2,103,000	6,421,000
Iraq	668,000	2,009,000
Lebanon	146,000	378,000
Libyan Arab Jamahiriya	88,000	245,000
Morocco	427,000	1,138,000
Pakistan	5,217,000	13,853,000
Saudi Arabia	890,000	2,523,000
Somalia	97,000	331,000
Sudan	447,000	1,277,000
Syrian Arab Republic	627,000	2,313,000
Tunisia	166,000	388,000
United Arab Emirates	350,000	684,000

	DIABETES INCIDENCE: 2000	DIABETES INCIDENCE: 2030 (PROJECTED)
Africa total	7,020,000	18,234,000
Algeria	426,000	1,203,000
Cameroon	70,000	171,000
Congo	14,000	39,000
Côte d'Ivoire	264,000	636,000
Democratic Republic of the Congo	291,000	910,000
Equatorial Guinea	8,000	21,000
Ethiopia	796,000	1,820,000
Kenya	183,000	498,000
Lesotho	31,000	4,2000
Liberia	40,000	154,000
Madagascar	100,000	301,000
Malawi	55,000	118,000
Mali	140,000	405,000
Mauritius	111,000	233,000
Mozambique	133,000	273,000
Namibia	25,000	60,000
Nigeria	1,707,000	4,835,000
Rwanda	30,000	77,000
Senegal	143,000	421,000
South Africa	814,000	1,286,000
Swaziland	13,000	21,000
Uganda	98,000	328,000
United Republic of Tanzania	201,000	605,000
Zambia	70,000	186,000
Zimbabwe	108,000	265,000
Western Pacific total	35,771,000	71,050,100
Australia	941,000	1,673,000
China	20,757,000	42,321,000
Japan	6,765,000	8,914,000
Malaysia	942,000	2,479,000
New Zealand	179,000	307,000
Papua New Guinea	152,000	392,000
Philippines	2,770,000	7,798,000
Republic of Korea	1,859,000	3,378,000

	DIABETES INCIDENCE: 2000	DIABETES INCIDENCE: 2030 (PROJECTED)
Singapore	328,000	695,000
Viet Nam	792,000	2,343,000

Source: http://www.who.int/diabetes/facts/world_figures/en/

SUPERFOODS

These protect us from toxins and cancer by several different mechanisms of action:

- *Directly killing or shutting down:*
  - bacteria or viruses that may cause cancer;
  - tumor cells: bioflavonoids, vitamin C, B_{12}, K, and garlic help here;
  - the oncogenes (cancer genes) in human cells: soybeans and vitamin A and D help here.
- *Binding up substances:*
  - bile acids, which can decay into a carcinogenic substance: fiber is a champion here;
  - carcinogenic heavy metals, in a process called chelation (say "key-lay-shun"), and carrying these toxic minerals out of the body. Bioflavonoids, vitamin C, and garlic help this way;
  - vegetables and fruits: a good rule of thumb is, the deeper the color of the vegetable, the more nourishing it is.
- *Stimulating the body's defenses:*
  - to produce more toxin scavengers, like glutathione peroxidase from indoles in cabbage;
  - the immune system. Once the external therapies of chemotherapy, radiation therapy, and surgery have eliminated the visible tumor, the real and final cancer battle is totally dependent on the immune factors. Many foods and individual nutrients are influential here;
  - certain detoxifying enzyme systems, like the liver's cytochrome P450 and antioxidants: selenium and vitamin C help here.

Superfood No. 1: the Allium family (onions, garlic, chives, leeks, shallots, and scallions)

Garlic, onions, leeks, and chives contain flavonoids that stimulate the production of glutathione (the tripeptide that is the liver's most potent antioxidant). Glutathione enhances the elimination of toxins and carcinogens, putting the Allium family of vegetables at the top of the list for foods that can help prevent cancer. Here are just a few benefits from members of this family; they:

- inhibit the growth of cancerous cells;

- cause an increase in high-density lipoprotein (HDL) cholesterol (especially when eaten raw);
- reduce total cholesterol levels;
- increase blood-clot dissolving activity;
- good source of beta-carotene, vitamins B and C, potassium, and selenium, and they contain small amounts of prostaglandins A1 and E which help lower high blood pressure;
- stimulate the immune system;
- reduce the risks of diabetes;
- have antibacterial and antifungal properties;
- reduce the risk of certain cancers;
- help relieve stomach upset and other gastrointestinal disorders.

Onions and leeks

Onions contain two powerful antioxidants, sulphur and quercetin – both help neutralize the free radicals in the body, and protect the membranes of the body's cells from damage.

Leeks have all of the healthy properties of the Allium family as described above. However, leeks also contain vitamin B_6, vitamin C, folate, manganese, iron, and fiber. This particular combination of nutrients makes leeks particularly helpful in stabilizing blood sugar, since they not only slow the absorption of sugars from the intestinal tract, but also help ensure that they are properly metabolized in the body. Remember, the stabilization of blood sugar is one of the most important goals. Spikes in blood sugar accelerate aging, wrinkles, and a host of degenerative diseases.

Garlic

This stinky little vegetable has been used for 5,000 years in various healing formulas. Pasteur noted that garlic killed all of the bacteria in his petri dishes.

More importantly, garlic has been found to stimulate natural protection against tumor cells. Researchers have found that white blood cells from people fed garlic were able to kill 139% more tumor cells than white cells from non-garlic eaters. One of the most common form of cancer worldwide is stomach cancer: Chinese researchers found that a high intake of garlic and onions cut the risk for stomach cancer in half.

Garlic also provides the liver with a certain amount of protection against carcinogenic chemicals. Scientists have found that garlic is deadly to invading pathogens or tumor cells, but is harmless to normal healthy body cells, thus offering the hope of the truly selective toxin against cancer that is being sought worldwide.

Garlic bulbs contain hundreds of components, including allicin, an amino acid byproduct that is released when raw garlic is crushed or cut. The creation of allicin, a self-defense mechanism in the plants, is what makes garlic so pungent; it's also the secret behind garlic's healing and medicinal properties.

In addition to reducing the clotting tendency of platelets, garlic can be used as an antiseptic and antibacterial because it stops microorganisms such as bacteria from reproducing.

Important note on freshness: One problem is the unstable nature of natural extracts of allicin. Garlic's effectiveness also is affected by the way it is processed. Cooking can destroy some of the active compounds – microwaving appears to completely ruin them – and preparations formulated to be odorless might be inactive. Still, garlic has plenty of proven healing benefits and few side effects, aside from an off-putting aroma.

Superfood No. 2: red-hot chili peppers

The term "peppers" encompasses a diverse group of plants, ranging from the popular sweet green or red bell pepper to the fiery hot habanero or the even more lethal Scotch bonnet. Peppers – whether sweet bell or hot chili – are members of the plant genus *Capsicum*, a term that comes from the Greek word kapto, which means "to bite." All peppers contain compounds called capsaicinoids. This is especially true of chili peppers, which derive their spicy heat – as well as extraordinary anti-inflammatory, analgesic, anticancer, and heart-healthy effects – from very high levels of capsaicinoids, the most common form of which is capsaicin.

In addition to capsaicin, chilies are high in antioxidant carotenes and flavonoids, and contain about twice the amount of vitamin C found in citrus fruits.

Superfood No. 3: yoghurt

Yoghurt is an impressive *immune stimulant:*

- In both humans and animals, yoghurt in the diet tripled the internal production of interferon (a powerful weapon of the immune system against tumor cells), while also raising the level of natural killer cells.
- Yoghurt has been shown to *slow down the growth of tumor cells* in the gastrointestinal tract, while improving the ability of the immune system to destroy active tumor cells.
- Yoghurt can *block the production of carcinogenic agents* in the colon. When scientists looked at the diet of 1,010 women with breast cancer and compared them to an equally matched group without breast cancer, they found an inverse dose-dependent relationship: the more yoghurt consumed, the lower the risk for breast cancer.
- In several European studies, yoghurt in animal studies was able to *reverse tumor progress*. A 1962 study found that 59% of 258 mice implanted with sarcoma cells were cured through yoghurt.
- A more recent American study found a 30% cure rate through yoghurt. While it is doubtful that yoghurt is going to cure advanced human cancer, it is likely that yoghurt can better fortify cancer patients' immune systems.

Superfood No. 4: green tea (*Camellia sinensis*)

Green tea:

- prevents cancers by blocking the growth of blood vessels to tumors (> 4 cups/day);
- increases HDL and decreases total cholesterol, low-density lipoprotein (LDL), and triglycerides (TGs), due to decreasing intestinal absorption or upregulating hepatic LDL receptors;
- contains epigallocatechin gallate, which increases the liver's uptake of LDL cholesterol by 300%, for a decrease in LDL blood levels of 30%! Therefore, it reduces heart disease and the build-up of plaque in arteries, detoxifies, scavenges free radicals, and protects against the formation and growth of cancer. Drink at least four cups each day.

Superfood No. 5: cruciferous vegetables[2]

Broccoli, brussel sprouts, cabbage, and cauliflower were involved in the original discovery that nutrition is linked to cancer. Dr. Lee Wattenberg of the University of Minnesota found in the 1970s that animals fed cruciferous vegetables had markedly lower cancer rates than matched controls. Other other evidence has been accumulated too:

- Scientists at Johns Hopkins University found that lab animals exposed to the deadly carcinogen aflatoxin and then fed cruciferous vegetables had a *90% reduction* in their cancer rate. Cruciferous vegetables are able to increase the body's production of glutathione peroxidase, which is one of the more important protective enzyme systems in the body.
- Moreover, in the case of cabbage, it contains sulforaphane, a chemical that increases your body's production of enzymes that disarm cell-damaging free radicals and reduce your risk of cancer. In fact, Stanford University scientists have determined that sulforaphane boosts your levels of these cancer-fighting enzymes higher than any other plant chemical.
- When we eat vegetables like broccoli, our body breaks down the broccoli's nutrients. One compound in vegetables is particularly important: glucobrassicin metabolizes into a valuable compound called indole-3-carbinol (I3C). I3C plays an active role in purifying the body of cancer-causing chemicals, but is naturally broken down in the digestive tract.

Superfood No. 6: legumes

The multi-faceted nutritive and preventive powers of beans – a category that encompasses common beans (e.g., kidney, black, navy, and pinto), chickpeas (garbanzo beans), soybeans, dried peas, and lentils – make them an anti-aging dietary necessity.

The health benefits of bean are as follows:

- Beans are *low in fat* (except for soybeans), calories, and sodium, but high in complex carbohydrates and dietary fiber, and they offer modest amounts of essential fatty acids – mostly omega-6s (only soybeans having significant amounts of omega-3 fatty acids). They are also an excellent source of *protein*, needing only to be combined with grains such as barley or oats to provide all the amino acids necessary to make a complete protein for vegetarians who do not have other sources of protein for their meals.

- Beans are extremely beneficial in an *antidiabetes diet* because they rank low on the glycemic index, which means that they do not cause the inflammatory, hunger-inducing spike in blood sugar levels associated with refined grains and baked goods.
- They are a good source of *potassium*, which may help reduce the risk of high blood pressure and stroke. More than 80% of American adults do not consume the daily value for potassium (3,500 mg); just half a cup of cooked dry beans contains as much as 480 mg, with no more than 5 mg of sodium.
- Dry beans are a good source of *folic acid*, which protects against heart disease by breaking down the amino acid homocysteine. (One cup of cooked dry beans provides about 264 µg of folate, or more than half the recommended daily intake of 400 µg.) High levels of homocysteine in the blood, or inadequate amounts of dietary folate, can triple the risk of heart attack and stroke. Folate is also key in preventing birth defects, and may help reduce the risk of several types of cancer because it plays an important role in healthy cell division and is crucial to the repair of damaged cells.
- In a large study of almost 10,000 men and women, those who ate beans four or more times a week *cut their risk of coronary heart disease* by about 20% compared to those who ate beans less than once a week. Other studies show that, within 2–3 weeks, diets high in either canned or dry beans (85–115 g/day) reduce blood cholesterol levels by 10% or more, an effect that can result in a 20% decrease in the risk of coronary heart disease.
- Beans and lentils have the same potent *anti-inflammatory* antioxidants – through flavonoids and flavonols – that are found in tea, fruit (especially grapes), red wine, and cocoa beans. In particular, the reddish flavonol pigments in bean and lentil seed coats exert antioxidant activity 50 times greater than vitamin E, protect against oxidative damage to cell membrane lipids, promote healthy collagen and cartilage, and restore the antioxidant powers of vitamins C and E after they have battled free radicals.
- Beans are among the richest food sources of *saponins*, chemicals that help prevent undesirable genetic mutations.

Generally speaking, the larger the bean, the longer they need to soak; and the longer you soak beans, the faster they cook. Dried chickpeas, beans, and whole dried peas need about 8 hours of soaking.

If you forget to soak the beans the night before, just do it before you leave in the morning and they'll be ready to cook when you get home. Or add three times the amount of water as beans, bring them to a boil for a few minutes, remove from the heat, and let them sit for an hour. Throw out the soaking water, and cook as normal. You can also use a pressure cooker, which will reduce the cooking time by more than half and reduce nutrient loss. (Of course, you can just drain and rinse canned beans, and add them directly to salads, soups or curries.) You can also prepare large batches to freeze in meal-sized portions, as cooked beans freeze well.

Well-soaked beans take 45–60 minutes to cook, depending on the variety. Cook beans until soft, and then rinse them thoroughly, because the residual starch on the surface feeds the harmless bacteria in your gut, which then release gas. Some of the gas-producing starch stays in the soaking water, so don't cook with it.

Superfood No. 7: prunes

Prunes contain high amounts of neochlorogenic and chlorogenic acids, antioxidants that are particularly effective at combating the "superoxide anion radical." This nasty free radical causes structural damage to your cells, and such damage is thought to be one of the primary causes of cancer.

Eat them as a snack mix complete with raisins and almonds.

Superfood No. 8: pumpkin seeds

These jack-o'-lantern waste products are the most nutritious part of the pumpkin. They are healthy because of the high level of magnesium they contain. This is important because French researchers recently determined that men with the highest levels of magnesium in their blood had a 40% lower risk of early death than those with the lowest levels. And on average, men consume 353 mg of the mineral daily, well under the 420 mg minimum recommended by the US Department of Agriculture.

Eat the pupkin seeds whole, shells and all. (The shells provide extra fiber.) Roasted pumpkin seeds contain 150 mg of magnesium/oz (28 g); add them to your regular diet and you'll easily hit your daily target of 420 mg. Look for them in the snack or health-food section of your grocery store, near the peanuts, almonds, and sunflower seeds.

Superfood No. 9: purslane *(Portulaca oleracea)*

Purslane has the highest amount of heart-healthy omega-3 fats of any edible plant, according to researchers at the University of Texas at San Antonio. The scientists also report that this herb has 10–20 times more melatonin – an antioxidant that may inhibit cancer growth – than any other fruit or vegetable tested.

Superfood No. 10: fresh ginger

To be used with honey and lemon for a delicious alternative to coffee. There is a wide range of benefits of ginger such as for nausea, digestive problems, circulation, and arthritis. Treating nausea caused during pregnancy or by traveling is one of the uses of ginger root. Ginger is also known to have the ability to calm an upset stomach and promote the flow of bile.

Superfood No. 11: apple cider vinegar

Mix two tablespoons each of apple cider vinegar and honey in a glass of warm lemon water and drink. The benefits include the following:

- *Help for gout.* Apple cider vinegar contains malic acid, which is very helpful in fighting fungal and bacterial infections. This acid dissolves uric acid deposits that form around joints, helping relieve joint pains. This dissolved uric acid is gradually eliminated from the body with increased water intake.
- Pectin in the vinegar is a fiber that helps reduce bad cholesterol and helps in *regulating blood pressure.*

Superfood No. 12: cinnamon

US Department of Agriculture researchers found that people with type 2 diabetes who consumed 1 g of cinnamon a day for 6 weeks (about a quarter of a teaspoon each day) significantly reduced not only their blood sugar, but also their TG and LDL cholesterol levels. Credit goes to the spice's active ingredients, methylhydroxychalcone polymers, which increase your cells' ability to metabolize sugar by up to 20 times. Drink cinnamon tea with honey during Ramadan or any fasting.

Superfood No. 13: eggs

Organic eggs are one of the most affordable high-quality proteins in the refrigerator, with remarkable anti-infammatory properties.

Superfood No. 14: spinach – Nature's green gold

When compared calorie for calorie to other vegetables, nothing is as nutrient-dense as spinach:

- Spinach has a large nutritional value, especially when fresh, steamed or quickly boiled. It is loaded with such antioxidants as vitamins A, C, E, K, B_1, and B_6, minerals like potassium, calcium, and zinc, and so much more.
- Recently, opioid peptides called rubiscolins have also been found in spinach.
- It is a source of folic acid, and this vitamin was first purified from spinach. To benefit from the folate in spinach, it is better to steam it than to boil it. Boiling spinach for 4 minutes can halve the level of folate.
- The folic acid also helps neutralize harmful homocysteine (an important marker of heart disease, high levels also being associated with elevated risks of stroke).
- Spinach is packed with over a dozen phytonutrients. These phytonutrients are potent substances that have properties that can fight cancer.

- Spinach contains lutein, which is a nutrient that has been extensively shown to protect against not only macular degeneration, but also cataracts.
- Spinach was also the most potent in protecting different types of nerve cells in two separate parts of the brain against the effects of aging.

Superfood No. 15: honey

Honey offers numerous antiseptic, antioxidant, and cleansing properties for our body. When taken prior to bed with whole milk or yoghurt, honey speeds up fat-burning metabolism, eases stress hormones, and help us get a better night's sleep. This natural sweetener has many vitamins – B_6, B_1, B_2, and B_5 – minerals such as calcium, copper, iron, magnesium, manganese, phosphorous, potassium, sodium and zinc, antioxidants, and amino acids, the building blocks of proteins. Moreover, honey's GI of 55 compares favorably to sucrose's GI of 64.

Superfood No. 16: essential fatty acids (EFAs; flaxseed and hempseed)

The human body cannot function properly without two polyunsaturated fats – linoleic and alpha-linolenic acid. These fatty acids, which are found in flaxseed oil and other healthy oils, are truly vital to normal cell structure and body function. Flaxseed may prove useful in the nutritional management of patients with autoimmune diseases.

EFAs can:

- lower cholesterol;
- improve brain function;
- slow the aging of cells;
- protect the cardiovascular system;
- improve flexibility of the joints;
- provide a more resistant immune system;
- regulate the heartbeat;
- "thin" the blood;
- lessen the risk of heart disease;
- aid in treating depression.

Symptoms of EFA deficiency are:

- high blood pressure;
- high TG levels;
- sticky platelets;
- eczema-like skin eruptions;
- loss of hair;
- behavioral disturbances;
- impairment of vision and learning ability;
- weakness;
- immune dysfunction.

Superfood No. 17: almonds and other nuts

Just more good news: these are full of the good fats that lower LDL cholesterol and reduce your risk of developing heart disease. Studies have shown that by exchanging some of the sugar snacks with almonds and other nuts, a significant risk reduction for heart disease of up to 40% can be achieved. Almond skins contain 20 flavonoids, some of which are comparable to those found in well-known health foods, such as catechins in green tea. Lastly, nuts have even been studied in relation to gall stones, with research demonstrating that women who eat them regularly can have up to a 25% lower risk of developing gall stones.

Superfood No. 18: sprouted seeds

First of all, sprouts are grown in your home and are therefore organic – they have no additives, preservatives, pesticides, fertilizers or chemicals: pure Mother Nature!

Sprouts, as baby plants, are extremely nutritious and healthful, as they have greater concentrations than at any other point in the plant's life, even when compared to the mature vegetable, of:

- vitamins and minerals;
- proteins and enzymes;
- phytochemicals;
- antioxidants;
- trace minerals;
- bioflavinoids and chemo-protectants (sulphoraphane and isoflavone), which work against toxins, resist cell mutation, and invigorate the body's immune system.

ONE-STOP SHOPPING LIST

(Photocopy this page to use when shopping.)

Organic Superfoods

- Onions, leeks, and garlic
- Hot chili (Cayenne) peppers
- Yoghurt (one-pot "seed" culture)
- Green tea
- Cruciferous vegetables
- Beans, lentils, and red beans
- Prunes
- Pumpkin seeds
- Puslane
- Ginger, fresh
- Apple cider vinegar
- Cinnamon
- Organic eggs
- Spinach
- Honey
- EFAs: flaxseed and hempseed oil
- Almond and hazel nut pastes
- Oatmeal

Useful machines

- Powerful juicer: we recommend the home juicer Champion 2000+, which extracts the juice and cell walls of the fruit.
- Wheatgrass kit.
- Yoghurt maker.
- Apple cider vinegar-making clay pot.
- Sprout maker. The nutritional value of sprouted seeds was discovered by the Chinese thousands of years ago. Recently, in the US, numerous scientific studies have shown the important benefits of sprouts in a healthy diet.[3]

USEFUL SUPPLEMENTS FOR OPTIMAL HEALTH

Table AI.3 details some useful supplements.

TABLE AI.3 *Useful supplements*

SUPPLEMENTS	DOSAGE	COMMENTS
Hempseed oil[4]	1 tablespoon/day	On salads and in soups
Flaxseed oil	3000 mg gel caps/day with meals	Stimulates DNA fat-burning genes
Co-Enzyme-Q10	100 mg/day. Take the soft gel capsules, with a meal, for high blood pressure. Eat some kind of fat or oil with your Co-Q10 or your gut won't absorb it well	There are more than 100 studies showing the heart benefits of Co-Q10. In one study, patients with high blood pressure began taking a Co-Q10 supplement. Within 1 month, the person's average blood pressure began to improve. At the end of the study, 51% of patients were able to discontinue their blood pressure medication[5]
Magnesium capsules	Recommended maximum daily dosage is 100–300 mg. Best to take it at bedtime with calcium in the ratio of two parts calcium to one part magnesium	For muscle cramping. Protects the cell from heavy metals such as aluminium, mercury, lead, cadmium, beryllium, and nickel
Vitamin C crystals	At least 2–3 g/day. Build up slowly	Antioxidant par excellence: use crystals
Vitamin E[6]	400 IU of mixed tocopherols and tocotrienols per day	Increases circulation and reduces plaque in the arteries
Selenium	50 µg of selenium per day	Keeps your lungs elastic. Found in garlic, liver, fish, and brazil nuts. Protects against heart disease and cancers of the lung, colon, liver, and prostate
Chromium	28 g of brewer's yeast supplies up to 200 µg of chromium	Maintains proper blood sugar level by increasing the sensitivity to insulin

SUPPLEMENTS	DOSAGE	COMMENTS
Tribulus terrestris (gokshura)	250 mg of standardized extract per day	Used in ayurvedic medicine to increase sex drive
Vitamin B complex[7]	Vitamin B_3 (niacin) 100 mg once a day, *plus* a combination of folate, vitamin B_{12}, and vitamin B_6	B_3: if your LDL stays high (> 1.30 g/L), your TGs stay high (> 1.40 g/L) or your HDL stays low (< 0.50 g/L), try B_3 100 mg + aspirin 30 mg with dinner. Monitor blood glucose B_6, B_{12}, and folate lower plasma homocysteine
Saw Palmetto (men)	300 mg/day	Stops the multiplication of prostate cells and reduces tissue swelling
Blue–green algae (spirulina)	2 g algae per day	Contain gamma-linolenic acid
L-Arginine	500 mg once a day	This is a precursor of nitric oxide, which helps the cells lining your heart and blood vessels dilate: good for your heart and your libido

Notes on special supplements

Vitamin E

Vitamin E really comprises eight related substances: four tocopherols and four tocotrienols. Several studies deserve attention:

- Recent research from Finland gives us the first study demonstrating that vitamin E prevents prostate cancer, following over 29,000 men for up to 8 years. The men took either vitamin E or a placebo daily. Those taking the vitamin E had a 32% lower rate of prostate cancer. Also, these men had a 41% fewer deaths from prostate cancer than those men not taking vitamin E.
- Another report, from the well-recognized Physician's Health Study, supports the Finnish findings. The study was a randomized, double-blinded analysis of over 22,000 men. It concluded that vitamin E was successful at inhibiting cancer.[8]
- A 10-year follow-up in a large nurses' health study revealed that vitamin E was associated with a 34% drop in heart disease.

The researchers believed that vitamin E prevented cancer in several ways, by:

- neutralizing free radicals in the body;
- protecting the cells from oxidation;
- aiding in cell membrane stability;
- stopping damaged cells from multiplying.

Vitamin E is an excellent choice for the brain and heart as:

- it blocks the oxidative modification of LDL;
- it delays aging of the brain and immune system – it prolongs the life of the cells by blocking oxidative damage;

■ the very best forms of vitamin E come straight from Mother Nature. It is found in a wide variety of foods: cold-pressed vegetable oils, fish oils, eggs, organ meats, molasses, seeds, nuts, nut oils, wheat germ, avocados, seeds, apples, and spinach.

Beta-carotene (a precursor of vitamin A)

■ *Mechanism of action.* By neutralizing free radicals, it lowers the risk for cancers and heart disease (by 50%) in those with the pre-existing disease state.[8]
■ *Found naturally in:* carrots (25 mg, a therapeutically effective dose, is found in two large carrots), green cabbage, spinach, cantaloupe, broccoli, and fruit. As a supplement, take 25,000 IU/day (10 IU of beta-carotene = 1 mg retinol), with breakfast.

Selenium

■ *Mechanism of action.* There are several forms of this soil-based trace mineral, of which the most powerful is methylselenol. It is essential in the enzyme activities of antioxidants and has an ability to kill cancer cells themselves while inhibiting the growth of blood vessels that feed tumors; it shows particular promise against breast, colon, and prostate cancer. It is very toxic at dosages of 100 μg.
■ *Found naturally in:* mushrooms, meat, tuna, herring, sesame seeds, poultry, grains, nuts, garlic, and eggs.

Ascorbic acid/calcium ascorbate

Take 3–4 g/day (crystals are more efficiently absorbed). This is a well-researched antioxidant to help repair micro-damage to the tissues caused by smoking, pollution or stress.

The best …

■ The best blood thinners … aspirin, red wine, the EFAs EPA/DHA (eicosapentaenoic acid/docosahexaenoic acid), garlic and onions, flaxseed oil, hempseed oil, apples, cherries, and carrots
■ The best sleep inducers … whole milk (warmed) with honey
■ The best cooking oils … palm and ghee (clarified butter)
■ The best cancer busters … broccoli, carrots, spinach, and artichoke hearts
■ The best eating oils … hempseed, flaxseed, olive, and safflower
■ The best non-alcoholic drinks … water, kiwi juice, fresh lime/lemon juice (without sugar), and tomato/carrot juice
■ The best fat-burning exercise … BURST walking (see Chapter 1) after eating a meal with flaxseed oil
■ The best hotel work-out … yoga, jump rope, and a 4-minute BURST work-out

- The best hors d'oeuvres ... olives (black, green or stuffed), humus, cherry tomatoes, guacamole, and raw carrots with homemade mayonnaise
- The best alcohol ... red wine ... it has a GI of only 44, which causes a very low insulin surge. In a word, drinking wine makes you thin
- The best juices ... water or, for taste, try a tall glass of honey, lemon ginger or freshly sqeezed carrot, kiwi, grapefruit or any fruit juice that has no added sugar (check the label) and has retained the pulp or fiber: carrots, apples, kiwi, grapefruit or tomato. Avoid high-fructose corn sugar (HFCS) by eliminating processed foods and sugary drinks, including commercial low-fiber, high-HFCS juices, teas or "health drinks" (the same as colas!). Fruit-flavored drinks made from concentrates are virtually the same HFCS-containing problem as commercial soft drinks
- The best breads ... the best choices include any breads that fill you up with wholegrains or seeds (sunflower, poppy, and sesame), such as those found in German bakeries: dark moist breads, covered with seeds
- The best snacks ... by far and away walnuts, followed by nut mix (especially almonds, cashews, and sunflower seeds) and fresh fruit (kiwis, apples, and cherries). Walnuts have more omega-3 (alpha-linolenic acid) than any other nut. They:
  - lower your LDL cholesterol naturally and reduce joint pain (with natural anti-inflammatories);
  - prevent heart disease by lowering blood pressure;
  - are also high in an antioxidant (a flavonoid) called ellagic acid, which inhibits the growth of cancer cells;
  - are very high in arginine. Arginine helps make more nitric oxide. This helps your blood vessels to dilate, which increases blood flow – great for your heart; it also helps men get erections, and is how Viagra works!
- The best sugars ... honey or syrup of agave. You need energy from a variety of sources, but not from refined sugars. If your body fat is greater than 5%, you have adequate stores without resorting to refined sugars such as those found in pastries
- The best proteins ... the best choices include two poached/boiled free-range eggs, with grilled tomatoes (and beans, as optional), or omelette d'Orvanne (cheese and avocado)
- The best fats ... the best choices include any fats that are not excessively saturated. The fats commonly found at breakfast are, in order of decreasing benefit (i.e., best first), fatty fish (herring, mackerel, and salmon), butter, beef, pork, bacon, and lard.
- The best antioxidant[9] foods ... oxygen radical absorbance capacity (ORAC) is a measure of the total antioxidant power of foods. So eating plenty of high-ORAC fruits and vegetables (Table AI.4) – such as spinach and blueberries – slows the processes associated with aging in both body and brain.

TABLE AI.4 *Oxygen radical absorbance capacity (ORAC) of fruit and vegetables*

FOOD	SERVING SIZE	ORAC
Cinnamon, ground	100 g	267,536
Small red bean	½ cup dried beans	13,727
Wild blueberry	1 cup	13,427
Red kidney bean	½ cup dried beans	13,259
Pinto bean	½ cup	11,864
Blueberry	1 cup (cultivated berries)	9,019
Cranberry	1 cup (whole berries)	8,983
Artichoke hearts	1 cup, cooked	7,904
Blackberry	1 cup (cultivated berries)	7,701
Prunes	½ cup	7,291
Raspberry	1 cup	6,058
Strawberry	1 cup	5,938
Red Delicious apple	1 apple	5,900
Granny Smith apple	1 apple	5,381
Pecan	28 g	5,095
Sweet cherry	1 cup	4,873
Black plum	1 plum	4,844
Russet potato	1, cooked	4,649
Black bean	½ cup dried beans	4,181
Plum	1 plum	4,118
Gala apple	1 apple	3,903

Effect of high-ORAC foods

In the studies mentioned above, eating plenty of high-ORAC foods had the following effects:

- It prevented some loss of long-term memory and learning ability in middle-aged rats.
- It maintained the ability of brain cells in middle-aged rats to respond to a chemical stimulus – a function that normally decreases with age.
- It protected rats' tiny blood vessels – capillaries – against oxygen damage.
- In one study, eight women gave blood after separately ingesting spinach, strawberries, and red wine – all high-ORAC foods – or taking 1250 mg of vitamin C. A large serving of fresh spinach produced the biggest rise in the women's blood antioxidant scores – up to 25% – followed by vitamin C, strawberries, and, lastly, red wine.
- In the second study, men and women had a 13–15% increase in the antioxidant power of their blood after doubling their daily fruit and vegetable intake compared to what they had consumed before the study. Just doubling

intake, without regard to the ORAC scores of the fruits and vegetables, more than doubled the number of ORAC units the volunteers consumed.

■ Rats fed daily doses of blueberry extract for 6 weeks before being subjected to 2 days of pure oxygen apparently suffered much less damage to the capillaries in and around their lungs, one researcher said. The volume of fluid that normally accumulates in the pleural cavity surrounding the lungs was much lower compared to the group that did not get blueberry extract.

TIPS FOR PREPARING MEALS

When it comes to preparing a meal for friends and family, there are only a few absolutes, as follows:

1. Keep it raw. When it comes to extracting energy and nutrients from foods, it is best to eat them as close as possible to their natural state. Heating the food completely destroys the catalysts of many biochemical reactions – the enzymes – which act as "spark plugs" to ignite the metabolism.
2. Use fresh ingredients: nothing canned or stale.
3. Cooking with butter or oil?
   – If you have to fry, use more stable, less reactive fats (butter, palm or lard).
   – Optimally, to keep your free-radical load to a minimum, bake or boil.
4. In general, it is preferable, whenever possible, to cook together with a loved one while chatting about the day's events and listening (and humming) to soft background music with a glass of wine.
5. Never rush the preparation of a meal! That defeats the whole purpose: a meal in France is a pleasure, starting from mincing the garlic to sipping the Armagnac. Fine dining with loved ones is one of the primary reasons for working hard.
6. Lastly, your meal is your offering of love to your friends and family. Keep this in mind while cooking.

Breakfast

Breakfast is a very important meal. After all, you have been fasting all night long, while maintaining a high metabolic rate by engaging in plenty of REM fantasies and dreams. You will not see a great variety of recipes for breakfast because it is a meal with little time to prepare. However, it is a meal when we should strive to get the daily dose of roughage or fiber into the system.

For optimal health and energy, here are some breakfast suggestions for the heart and palate:

■ fresh blended kiwi juice, jasmine tea, wholewheat toasts with fresh butter and homemade jam;
■ cottage cheese or fromage blanc with fresh pineapple, Earl Grey tea with raisin or rye toast;
■ fresh pineapple juice, wholewheat cereals with fresh yoghurt and fruits, green tea;

- freshly squeezed orange juice, green tea, and wholewheat rye bread with fresh butter and homemade apple-spread;
- fresh apple juice, a big fruit salad with green or jasmine tea;
- poached eggs with grilled tomatoes and mushrooms, wholewheat toasts with fresh butter, tea, and fresh juice;
- scrambled eggs with some sliced tomatoes and onion;
- a cheese, onion, and tomato omelette. Wholewheat rye with fresh butter, tea, and freshly squeezed fruit juice;
- wholewheat or rye bread with butter, coffee or tea without sugar;
- yoghurt with non-acid fresh fruits, coffee or tea without sugar;
- freshly squeezed orange juice and fresh fruit salad;
- wholewheat cereal with yoghurt, banana, and raisin;
- snacks and miscellaneous: humus and taramasalata.

Homemade mayonnaise

Place an egg yolk (separated from the egg white) in a bowl and, using a whisk, whip a teaspoon of Dijon mustard into the egg yolk. Continue the whisking while starting to drip olive or hempseed oil in. You know if it is going to work if you see "strings" appear in the mixture as you drip in the oil. The best mayonnaise is made from a mixture of oils (sunflower, olive, and hempseed).

Lunch and dinner

If you cannot go for a walk afterwards, the following options are optimal: roast chicken with green peas; a leg of lamb with beans; or an onion and mushroom omelette.

If you can have a walk afterwards, these options are fine:

- pasta cooked with olive oil, garlic, and fresh tomatoes;
- wild rice with onions and mushrooms;
- potato stew with green beans, onions, and tomatoes;
- vegetable soup with garlic bread.

FAST FOOD, SLOW DIGESTION, FAST DEATH: LOSS OF RITUAL – MODERN FOODS

These modern fast foods may actually taste good during consumption, but they may cost dearly in health terms. Don't make your arteries pay for the caprices of your palate.

Match the foods 1–10 with their ingredients a–m in the list below the grid:

FOOD:		INGREDIENTS:
1.	Potato chips (crisps)[10]	
2.	Diet soda drink (cherry)	

FOOD:	INGREDIENTS:
3. "Natural" candy bar	
4. Instant pancake mix	
5. Dog food	
6. Lite Italian salad dressing	
7. Breakfast cereal	
8. Instant soup	
9. Colored candies for kids	
10. "Natural" cookies ("< 40% fat")	
11. Throat lozenges	
12. Instant tea drink	
13. Isotonic drink	

a. Bleached flour (wheatflour, niacin, reduced iron, thiamine mononitrite, riboflavin), sugar, soyflour, leavening, vegetable shortening (partially hydrogenated soybean and cottonseed oils), dextrose, eggs, buttermilk, salt, soy lecithin (an emulsifier), non-fat milk.

b. Maltodextrin, malic acid, instant tea, aspartame (phenylalanine), natural lemon flavour.

c. Sugar, butter, whole milk powder, cocao mass, whey powder, lecithin (emulsifier), flavouring, may contain nut tracings.

d. Beef, mutton, poultry, bone, gels, food colouring, vitamins and minerals.

e. Potatoes, palm oil, spices, salt, glutamic acid, citric acid.

f. Carbonated water, sucrose, glucose, citric acid, sodium chloride, potassium phosphate, sodium benzoate, E211, vitamin C, calcium phosphate.

g. Sugar, corn syrup, dextrose, glycine, gelatin, artificial flavour, vegetable gums, colours include red 3, red 40 lake, blue 2 lake.

h. Water, distilled vinegar, salt, sugar, < 2% garlic, natural flavours, soybean oil, xanthan gum, sodium benzoate, potassium sorbate, calcium-disodium EDTA (preserves freshness), yellow 5, red 40.

i. Wheat flour, palm and sesame oils, freeze-dried mushrooms, dehydrated sweetcorn, leeks, carrots, seaweed, sugar, monosodium glutamate (MSG).

j. Corn, oat and wheat flours, vegetable oils (soy, cottonseed sunflower) salt, sugar, natural colours (carmine).

k. Enriched wheat flour, raisins, rolled oats, fructose, polydextrose, soybean oil, water, apple and pineapple juices, powered cellulose, corn syrup, dough conditioner (lecithin), < 2% apples, corn starch, leavening agents, ammonium bicarbonate, bicarbonate of soda, sodium aluminium phosphates, natural and artificial flavours, spices, pectin, citric acid.

l. dextrose maltose, dextran corn syrup, malic acid < 2% artificial and natural flavours, calcium stearate, colour additives, wax, blue 1, blue 1 lake, red 40 lake, yellow 5 lake, yellow 6 lake, yellow 6.

m. Carbonated water, sugar, citric acid, sodium benzoate E 211, caramel E 150, colour (E122).

■ NUTRITIONAL SELF-ASSESSMENT

Now, try the following self-assessment.

1. Body fat % should not exceed:
   a) 1–5% ☐
   b) 10–20% ☐
   c) 15–23% ☐
   Key concept: _____

2. Dieting (calorie deprivation) is clearly the best and most efficient way to control weight:
   a) True ☐
   b) False ☐
   Key concept: _____

3. What is the most efficient way to burn body fat?:
   a) BURST (or another high-intensity) work-out
   b) Jogging ☐
   c) Walking ☐
   Key concept: _____

4. It is better to eat fruit:
   a) At the beginning of meals ☐
   b) At the end of meals ☐
   c) Between meals ☐
   Key concept: _____

5. Drinking water during your meal aids the digestion of food:
   a) True ☐
   b) False ☐
   Key concept: _____

6. Performance (physical and psychological) declines when as little as _% of our total body water is lost (60% of body weight is water: 40% of body weight as intracellular fluids, and 20% as extracellular fluid):
   a) 5% ☐
   b) 10% ☐
   c) 30% ☐
   Key concept: _____

7. Losing excess body fat lowers blood cholesterol:
   a) True ☐
   b) False ☐
   Key concept: _____

8. Protein, fats, carbohydrates and alcohol have caloric values of: _cal/g, _cal/g, _ cal/g, and _cal/g, respectively:
   a) 4, 9, 4, 7 ☐
   b) 4, 9, 9, 4 ☐
   c) 4, 9, 4, 9 ☐
   d) 4, 7, 4, 7 ☐

9. Snacking promotes weight gain:
   a) True ☐

b) False ☐
Key concept: _____

10. Muscle turns to fat when we stop using that muscle:
    a) True ☐
    b) False ☐
    Key concept: _____

11. The best low-GI cocktail snacks include:
    a) Olives ☐
    b) Salty crackers ☐
    c) Potato chips ☐
    d) Nut mix ☐
    e) Green vegetables and cheese dip ☐
    Key concept: _____

12. The best low-GI alcohol drinks include:
    a) Wine (red) ☐
    b) Distilled spirits ☐
    c) Champagne ☐
    d) Beer ☐
    Key concept: _____

13. The best fats for cooking include:
    a) Safflower oil ☐
    b) Palm oil ☐
    c) Coconut oil ☐
    d) Butter ☐
    e) Olive oil ☐
    Key concept: _____

14. The best oils for longevity are:
    a) Organic and unrefined ☐
    b) To be stored in dark bottles in the refrigerator ☐
    c) Corn/grapeseed ☐
    d) Sunflower/sesame ☐
    e) Hempseed/flaxseed/walnut ☐
    Key concept: _____

15. The best blood thinners include:
    a) Aspirin ☐
    b) Water ☐
    c) EFAs ☐
    d) Red wine ☐
    Key concept: _____

16. The best cooking methods include:
    a) Boiling ☐
    b) Steaming ☐
    c) Baking ☐
    d) Deep frying ☐
    e) Stir frying ☐
    f) Microwaving ☐
    Key concept: _____

NOTES AND REFERENCES

1. Benefits continue to accumulate for dark chocolate:
   - One study showed positive blood-sugar control effects in people with high blood pressure who ate 100 g of dark chocolate per day. Grassi D et al. Cocoa reduces blood pressure and insulin resistance and improves endothelium-dependent vasodilation in hypertensives. *Hypertension* 2005; **46**: 398–405.
   - A Swedish study in diabetic adolescents replaced a "diabetic" snack with milk chocolate and actually produced a lower blood glucose response. Cedermark G, Selenius M, Tullus K. Glycaemic effect and satiating capacity of potato chips and milk chocolate bar as snacks in teenagers with diabetes. *Eur J Pediatr* 1993; **152**: 635–9.

2. Auborn K et al. Indole-3-carbinole is a negative regulator of estrogen. *J Nutr* 2003; **133**(7 Suppl): 2470S–5S. Le H et al. Plant-derived 3,3-diindolylmethane is a strong androgen antagonist in human prostate cancer cells. *J Biol Chem* 2003; **278**: 21136–45.

3. Sprouts like, radish, mung bean, broccoli, alfalfa, clover, and soybean have concentrated amounts of phytochemicals (plant compounds) that can protect us against disease:
   - Studies on canavanine, an amino acid in alfalfa, has demonstrated benefit for pancreatic, colon, and leukemia cancers.
   - Alfalfa sprouts also contain saponins that lower LDL and stimulate the immune system by increasing the activity of natural killer lymphocytes.

   Sprouts also contain an abundance of highly active antioxidants that prevent DNA destruction and protect us from the effects of aging.

4. In the largest randomized controlled trial of supplemental omega-3 fatty acids to date, coronary heart disease patients who received supplements providing 850 mg/day of EPA + DHA for 3.5 years had a risk of sudden death that was 45% lower than those who did not take supplements, and a risk of death from all causes that was 20% lower. Dietary supplementation with n-3 polyunsaturated fatty acids and vitamin E after myocardial infarction: results of the GISSI-Prevenzione trial. Gruppo Italiano per lo Studio della Sopravvivenza nell'Infarto miocardico. *Lancet* 1999; **354**: 447–55.
   - Results of a meta-analysis that pooled the findings of 11 randomized controlled trials of dietary or supplementary omega-3 fatty acids indicated that increased omega-3 fatty acid intakes significantly decreased overall mortality, mortality due to myocardial infarction, and sudden cardiac death in patients with coronary heart disease. Bucher HC, Hengstler P, Schindler C, Meier G. N-3 polyunsaturated fatty acids in coronary heart disease: a meta-analysis of randomized controlled trials. *Am J Med* 2002; **112**: 298–304.
   - A larger trial of 223 patients found that supplementation with 3.3 g/day of EPA + DHA for 3 months and 1.65 g/day for an additional 21 months resulted in a modest decrease in the progression of coronary atherosclerosis compared to a placebo. von Schacky C et al. The effect of dietary omega-3 fatty acids on coronary atherosclerosis. A randomized, double-blind, placebo-controlled trial. *Ann Intern Med* 1999; **130**: 554–62.

5. Langsjoen P et al. Treatment of essential hypertension with coenzyme Q10. **Mol Aspects Med** 1994; **15**(Suppl): S265–72.

6. ATBC Cancer Prevention Study Group. Incidence of cancer and mortality following a-tocopherol and B-carotene supplementation. *JAMA* 2003; **290**: 476–85.

7. To lower homocysteine levels in people with high levels and keep homocysteine levels low in others – that is, by getting plenty of folic acid in the diet or in supplements – the recommendation would be for everyone to get at least 400 µg per day in the diet (asparagus, avocados, beans, broccoli, brussel sprouts, spinach, and collards) and take a 400 µg supplement.

8. Christen W et al. Design of Physician's Health Study II – a randomized trial of beta-carotene, vitamin E, and multivitamins, in prevention of cancer, cardiovascular disease, and eye disease, and review of results of completed trials. *Ann Epidemiol* 2000; **10**: 125–35.

9. Antioxidants explained: the science is clear – plant foods are good for you. And the credit often goes to chemicals they produce called antioxidants. Just as the name suggests, antioxidants help protect our cells against oxidation. Think of oxidation as rust. This rust is caused by free radicals, which are unstable oxygen atoms that attack our cells, inducing DNA damage that leads to cancer. Thankfully, antioxidants help stabilize free radicals, which keeps the rogue atoms from harming our cells. So by eating more antioxidant-rich foods, we boost the amount of disease-fighting chemicals floating in our bloodstreams. The result: every bite fortifies your body with all-natural preventative medicine.

10. The British agency found that some of the products had acrylamide levels 1,280 times higher than international safety limits. Those products included supermarket potato chips and fries, Walkers crisps, crackers, Kellogg's Rice Crispies and Pringles crisps. While raw and boiled potatoes tested negative for the chemical, French fries had some of the highest readings. Acrylamide is a white odorless compound that comes from heating starch. Waste-water treatment plant operators use this same compound in the treatment of sewage, waste, and drinking water, and manufacturers use it to produce organic chemicals and dyes. But, as the study found, it is also a byproduct of cooking foods at high temperature, foods such as potato chips, French fries, bread, rice, and cereals. Source: New tests confirm acrylamide in American foods, from the Center for Science in the Public Interest.

Answers to interactive exercises
Fast food, slow digestion, fast death: loss of ritual – modern foods
1. e; 2. m; 3. c; 4. a; 5. d; 6. h; 7. j; 8. i; 9. l; 10. k; 11. g ; 12. b; 13. f.

Nutritional self-assessment

1. b (for men) or c (for women). Key Concept: follow body fat %, not absolute weight, for effective weight control.
2. False. Key Concept: calorie deprivation, of ANY sort, *slows* metabolism and conserves calories.
3. a & c. A logical approach to fat control is more frequent low-grade exercises, such as walking, particularly after meals, and BURST exercise during the day.
4. c. Key Concept: fruit between meals accomplishes three key objectives: 1) its "clean" calories help to maintain a high metabolic rate and energy level while controlling hunger, 2) It provides an excellent source of fibre to keep us "regular", and, 3) It is an excellent water source.
5. b. Key Concept: water with meals dilutes digestive juices. Rather, opt, for fermented drinks, such as wine.
6. a. Key Concept: our bodies are constantly losing water: usually 2–3 L/day. In a 70 kg person, 42 kg (60%) are water. Five percent of that amount equals 2+L. A loss greater than that without replacement will result in impairment of both physical and psychological performance.
7. True. The first thing to do if total cholesterol is > 200 mg/dL OR TGs:HDL ratio is > 2 is to get the body fat % < 20% (low-GI food plus BURST) and re-check the TGs:HDL ratio in 3 months.
8. a. These are the calorie/gram values for each food type. Note how calorifically dense alcohol is.
9. False. Snacking intelligently (fruits, nuts, wheatgrass juice) maintains a HIGH metabolic rate, burns calories, and promotes weight LOSS.
10. False. One cell type (muscle) cannot be transformed into another cell type (fat). What happens when you become more inactive is that the metabolic rate drops, and excess calories are deposited as FAT.
11. a, d, e.
12. a
13. a, b, e.
14. a, b, e.
15. a, b, c, e.
16. a, b, c, d.

The objective to training the brain is for the reader to start to TRUST the miraculous workings of the *left* brain. While the left brain is useful in that it calculates, plans, and schemes, it is also where the ego "resides," and that means stress, fear, and anxiety from time to time, which must be effectively managed before real damage to one's confidence occurs. So the stakes, and the rewards, are high.

Life is a testing ground, a classroom, and we are getting as tense as teenagers in a physics exam because we have not tested and trusted our brains. The first step in trusting the brain is to learn to perceive all problems as linked (sometimes invisibly) with their solution: just like with a coin, "heads is the problem and tails is the solution."

We can only trust a brain that has been conditioned, like we can trust a heart that has been made more efficient by going through a rigorous training program. The objective to training the brain is to RELAX and let the 150 billion neurons, *each one of which* has the functional power of a PC and is capable of $10^{2,783,000}$ connections, function optimally, helping us to develop and engage our talents in pursuit of a meaningful life.

There are five general aspects of one's lifestyle that can help to maintain *left* brain health:

1. Understand the emotions[1] and the other social aspects of life:
   - Master fear
   - Develop a regret-free life: the LifePlan
   - Demystify death: DABDA
   - Control existential angst: worrying effectively
   - Control anger and guilt
2. Realize that the hardware does not always see "reality" as it is
3. Depersonalize life as a classroom
4. Find antidotes to stress: more people die of this than of heart disease!
5. Discover how to make yourself miserable and live foolishly
6. Practice yoga of the eyes: healing the brain with sun power

Trust yourself, then you will know how to live.

Goethe

UNDERSTAND THE EMOTIONS THAT WE ARE RUNNING ON IN OUR BRAINS

These emotions (fear, anger, guilt, and regret) are common to us all in society. Unfortunately, the brain functions very poorly when clouded by anger, hate, guilt or fear. They are like clouds in our psychological sky. Increase the number of social events in your home. This includes meetings, parties, and simply having friends or family over. Remember that brain health is a lifespan issue so all age groups need a little attention and love (socialization).

Mastering fear: hostage no more

Some would argue that fear is the key sign that your faith in the Grand Design is weak and faltering. Faith, simply put, is a re-perception of your self (all that you identify with your body and mind within the borders of your skin) as a real part of the self (the Life Force, Atman, God). Fears, therefore, are just a reminder that perhaps you are not as grand and infinite as you originally thought. As such, fears, if consciously handled, should represent an invitation to strengthen faith, to do internal battle with negative feelings or impulses. Fear could be the starting point of humility over arrogance.

> **TIP** The best strategy is to move from the *left* brain to the *right* brain during stressful moments.

Always keep some aces up your sleeve against fear. One effective fear-buster is the expression: "And so?" Many of our acquired fears stem from a lack of self-confidence in the face of loss: for example, what if I lose my job? With a well-developed sense of adventure, trust in yourself, and the driver, and you'll manage just fine. Newborns have two innate fears (again, very useful): the **fear of falling** (being dropped) and the **fear of loud noises**. The rest we develop as we come up through the stages of life.

Fear is the height of arrogance as it presumes that we have to control something that is not ours to control. Fear is another flawed mindset, left over from adolescence, that presumes that we are the prime mover of everything around us. The US philosopher Ralph Emerson wrote, "Do the thing you are most afraid to do and death of that fear is certain." Though confirmed throughout the ages, it is an experiment that few of us have taken the few minutes to do.

Make your own audit by listing all fears, both imaginary (including neurotic unfound fear such as going broke or becoming bald) and real (falling over a cliff). Now ask yourself: what is worse – fear of baldness or baldness itself? Strive not to become a lifelong hostage to fear. Start today to fight fears by standing on your own feet. When problems arise, spend the first 5 minutes gathering all the facts of the matter. Then ask, "What's to be done?" or try to get the resolution of the affair under way; then go on to something else. Never worry for more than 15 minutes about an affair of money, fame, power, pride or other such earthly triviality.

A REGRET-FREE LIFE

Get on the fast track to a regret-free life by using the Top Effective Strategies for Minimizing Regret (or stark examples of managers' wisdom compiled over 20 years at INSEAD):

- Always carry with you a recording device (besides your brain). It could be a cell phone, a pen and pad, or a wet palm, because great ideas have a way of surfacing when you least expect it.
- The best time to worry ... just before doing a meditation or mantra.
- The best time to meditate ... just after worrying.
- The best way to jump-start a relationship ... learn to forget and start over.
- The best way to success ... know what you want, be early to bed and to rise, and categorically refuse to associate with negative people.
- The best attitude ... life is the career: stay alert for opportunities.
- The best definition of success ... growing old without any regrets.
- The best way to confuse the enemy ... love and forgiveness.
- The best defense against depression ... gratitude for life's lessons.
- Yesterday was history, tomorrow is a mystery and today is a gift, appropriately called the "present".
- Start and finish the day with "Thank you."
- It's OK to get angry once in a while, but re-center quickly. Anger is a tempest; it will pass.
- Great achievements and great love involve great risks.
- Communicate anger before it smolders into hostility.
- Never make important decisions while angry.
- Unwind between work and home to prevent "overflow."
- Don't let an argument ruin a great friendship. It's not worth it; just let go.
- Teach by example: they are watching, not listening.
- Realize early in life as possible that *not* getting what you wanted may be an act of providence.
- Living well is the best revenge: fine dining, wine tasting.
- Being free of anger is better than being "right."
- Become master over loneliness.
- Gauge successes by what you had to give up to get it.
- In disagreements with loved ones, deal just with the present. Forget the past.
- Practice random acts of kindness.
- Simplify life: LESS IS MORE, live within your means.
- Life is designed to maximize your growth and entertainment.
- Follow the four R's:
  - Respect for self
  - Respect for others
  - Respect for the earth
  - Responsibility for actions.
- Marital squabbles: in this Game of Idiots, don't try to win. Let the storm pass; the kids are watching.

Demystify death

To override our cultural death phobia, get as comfortable with loss as you are with gain, on a daily basis. After all, loss is always going to be an inherent part of the life cycle. It gives the whole process of life meaning. Dr. Elisabeth

Kübler-Ross[2] has written of the five stages of death and dying. Here is the DABDA model to be applied to experiences in everyday life:

STAGE	MIND CHATTER
Denial (D)	"Not me! Can't be ..."
Anger (A)	"Why me?!?"
Bargaining (B)	"Listen, God, it's been a while since we've spoken, but I was wondering ..."
Depression (D)	"The 12 bar-blues"
Acceptance (A)	"New start to the cycle of learning," "The phoenix rises from the ashes" – gratitude

During our brief stay on this planet, we experience many "deaths" in the figurative, but nonetheless real, sense. We call it "growing up," "coming of age" or maturing. It starts as a youngster "I" that dies into the adolescent "I," which through an often painful "death" leaves the nest and is born into a sort of adulthood and so on.

This same cyclic nature of life–death–life is ubiquitous throughout literature, as seen in Herman Hesse's 1922 novel, *Siddhartha*. The main character, Siddhartha, leaves the comfort of princely life in the quest for enlightenment. His life is a series of living through, and then dying through, life's various chapters: from prince to ascetic to solitary sadhu to sensual creature, full circle to the rich man and so on, until the middle way of the Buddha:

> The world, Govinda, is not imperfect or slowly evolving along a path to perfection. No, it is perfect at every moment; every sin already carries grace within it, all small children are potential old men, all sucklings have death within them, all dying people — eternal life.

It was as if Siddhartha learned what needed to be learned and then died and was reborn, a changed man, into the next higher stage. Life and death have more to do with the ego's living and dying than that of the physical body.

In fact, the important thing is recognition of the various stages of what is called "ego death." We can also see all of these stages in each of our daily experiences of loss, profound and trivial. Is it possible that the daily experiences of loss are actually "dry runs" or rehearsals for the real thing, designed to help teach us acceptance, dignity, and good humor? Are we missing one of the great lessons of life while we chase convenience as a lifestyle?

There have even been applications of the DABDA model to the business arena, where it has been expanded to include Denial, Anger, Bargaining, Depression, Openness, and Readiness, when it comes to helping an employee deal with being fired.[3]

The best test for your mindset is not how well you can cope with the good times, but how you deal with the great tests of human life:

- children,
- old age, and
- death.

> The greatest attainment of identity, autonomy, selfhood is itself simultaneously a transcending of itself, of going beyond and above selfhood. The person can then become relatively egoless.
>
> **Abraham Maslow**[4]

How quickly we manage this journey of learning, from denial to acceptance, is up to our inner attitudes and the resilience of our spirits. Are we embracing change as the agent of learning (being neophilic) or merely spending all of our time and energy preventing loss and the growth that comes with it (being neophobic)? The trick to the whole game is to arrive at the stage of acceptance as quickly and painlessly as possible.

Taking care of unfinished business brings real peace.

John Donne, one of the greatest metaphysical poets, confronts death itself in his sixth Holy Sonnet, which is well worth memorizing:

> Death be not proud, though some have called thee
> Mighty and dreadful, for thou art not so,
> For those whom thou think'st thou dost overthrow,
> Die not, poor death, nor yet canst thou kill me.
> From rest and sleepe, which but thy pictures be,
> Much pleasure then from thee, much more must flow,
> And soonest our best men with thee do go,
> Rest of their bones, and souls' delivery.
> Thou'rt slave to Fate, Chance, kings and desperate men,
> And dost with poison, war and sickness dwell,
> And poppy or charms can make us sleep as well,
> And better than thy stroke; why swell'st thou, then?
> One short sleep past, we wake eternally,
> And death shall be no more: death, thou shalt die.

Or even better for beating a culture-induced death phobia, try a piece written by a 17–year-old, William Cullen Bryant, in 1814, *Thanatopsis*. The final several lines are included here:

> By an unfaltering trust, approach thy grave
> Like one who wraps the drapery of his couch
> About him, and lies down to pleasant dreams.

Control existential angst: write a LifePlan

Imagine this situation. You have just undergone your full medical check-up. Your doctor calls you several days later and requests a meeting with you (and your spouse) to go over the results and options: "something funny going on." You spend one of your worst weekends in recent memory as you reflect over the upcoming discussion. The physician explains that although you only feel a little run down, in fact you are suffering from a certain medical condition that, while it will cause no physical pain, will certainly curtail your lifespan to less than 3 years.

Now you know that you have only 3 more years to live. Take a brief pause for reflection and write down the three most important things that you would like to do with your life, if the next 3 years were to be your last.

My LifePlan: for the next 3 years, I shall insist that I accomplish these things:

1. _____
2. _____
3. _____

The LifePlan is a game where we set goals, go for them, and achieve what we set out to accomplish. Happiness is a state of mind of being satisfied with what you end up with. Let's look at some of the typical things that leaders want to get done in terms of concrete goals:

- Get a pilot's license or get over my fear of flying.
- Learn how to control my anger.
- Fix things up with my son.
- Learn how to be spontaneous and joyful.
- Rediscover the lost "child" within.
- Learn a musical instrument or develop an appreciation of opera.
- Go sailing around the world or just learn to sail.
- Body surf at Kuta Beach, Bali.
- Spend more quality time with my partner/children.
- Learn how to juggle, learn a language, learn how to draw.
- Get to know my spouse/kids as people.
- Learn to manage a crisis, without escaping.
- Become a disconnected bum for a weekend: no family, phones, credit cards, money ...
- Meditate in a graveyard, and imagine the various life trajectories of those buried there. Get comfortable to the point of conversing with that someone. Point of exercise: demystify death and realize that life is never more alive than after death.
- Write a book, not necessarily for publishing, but for my self-expression.

As health workers, we are constantly struck by the peaceful serenity of terminally ill patients. Deep reflection and late night discussions ensue. Questions arise in the family, at the dinner table, that require more than prefabricated answers:

- Are we missing something here, as we rush around in a vain attempt to protect ourselves from that which teaches us?
- How did they do it, remaining dignified in their hospice beds, while I lose my temper at a traffic snarl or business deal?

- Is it possible to be as centered as these patients without having the diagnosis of terminal disease?
- Why does our Western culture have such a death taboo?

Be altruistically selfish: write for yourself a LifePlan and learn to manage your regrets intelligently.

Regain lost years by controlling anger[5] and guilt

Do conversations or situations in your life (incompetence, inefficiency, traffic, waiting, and expectations) make you angry or cynical, or distrustful or depressed? If those are words you might use to describe your personality, your problems will not be restricted to isolation from family and friends. Every life situation that pulls you "off centre" and results in negative emotions will predispose you to a heart attack, a stroke or even cancer.

Remember these key points about anger:

1. It's OK to get angry once in a while.
2. Know the "trigger points" for anger.
3. Communicate anger before it smolders into hostility.
4. Never make important decisions while angry.
5. Never eat or make love while under tension.
6. Unwind between work and home to prevent "overflow."
7. Humor is the best antidote for over-seriousness.
8. Living well is the best revenge – fine dining, wine tasting.
9. It's not worth it.
10. Anger is a tempest; it will pass.
11. Seek distraction – a jog, a movie, go see some friends.
12. Communicate with your spouse/friend/partner – share the burden.

There is a very clever way, in the Zen sense, of extending your life, and not just your chronological life (though that's certain to be enhanced also). This is even better. The best idea is to increase those years of your life that are the happiest, the most serene, where your children and friends actually want to visit you to glean most wisdom from you.

> After all, what greater misery in life than to live a long sad life.

As we have all experienced, there is a sort of time lag between the actual life experience and wisdom. Do this mental exercise: when some type of change or loss happens to you, how long is the time lag until you grasp the lesson within the experience (i.e. wisdom)? This lag, which for some can be several decades, is strictly a function of attitude. Eventually, we all "get the lesson" of every experience, sometimes 6 months later, sometimes six decades later. The key to a regret-free life is to get wise as early as possible by milking every experience for a lesson. When you make learning about life the career, all time becomes "your time."

Given how short life is, are we spending our time well? Couldn't we be cramming even a little more into the time we have? Isn't there yet another ingenious way to cut finer and finer slivers of time? Are we unhappy when we cannot rush through things? In case you have forgotten, things do actually take time to do properly. Some things simply cannot be rushed; they have their own rhythm. Just go out into your garden and study it carefully. Nature will not be hurried into making roses bud or making the sky clear of clouds. Nature will, rather, make you synchronize yourself to her rhythm. The only way to know that rhythm is to study Nature (and people are part of Nature) and realize that everybody has their own rhythm.

We go to great unnecessary lengths to get wise. When will we realize that all the wisdom we will ever need to understand the life experience is within us already, just waiting to be discovered. We are born complete, listen to the wrong people, and convince ourselves that we need something or somebody to be complete. By quieting the noise or internal chatter of the mind, through, say, regular meditation and prayer, the mind's eye can see clearly. After all, we "see" the world with the mind, not with the eyes.

In most societies today, walls are constructed to keep "them" out (and lock ourselves in): artificial boundary lines are drawn and this fortress mentality is constantly reinforced. Paradoxically, we are surprised to discover that we have unwittingly made isolation and alienation an integral part of our lives. Being stuck in this survival mode, and never learning to loosen up and let go, can be a deep source of unnecessary worry to us. If human beings are ever to have a chance to evolve from this strict survival mode of behaviour to a living mode, we must learn to let go. Liberate yourself from emotional baggage, past autodestructive behaviour patterns and habits, and free your mind from the robotic software of action–reaction.

Paradoxically, worry now is the vaccine for worry later, as if it were a "dry run" for the real thing later. When we are forced back upon ourselves (the death of loved one, a natural disaster, a car accident or an air crash), we have the opportunity to reprioritize and avoid regrets. Don't miss these opportunities to eliminate regret. Stress really is about unfinished business. Stop wasting time. Carpe diem – seize the moment – or lose it forever.

To illustrate this:

Two monks were once travelling together down a muddy road. A heavy rain was falling. Coming around a bend, they met a lovely girl in a silk kimono and sash, unable to cross the intersection.

"Come on, girl," said the first monk. Lifting her in his arms, he carried her over the mud.

The second monk did not speak again until that night when they reached a lodging temple. Then he no longer could restrain himself. "We monks don't go near females," he said. "It is dangerous. Why did you do that?"

"I left the girl there," the first monk said. "Are you still carrying her?"

Now ask yourself, after an argument, what are you still carrying? How many heartbeats will be wasted?

REALIZE THAT THE HARDWARE DOES NOT ALWAYS SEE "REALITY" AS IT IS

The brain processes billions and billions of bit of data every minute. It uses incomplete data from the five senses (audition, vision, olfaction, taste, and touch) because those senses only are able to receive a minute fraction of reality. For example, take vision. The human eye is limited to the visible light part of the light spectrum, unable to perceive the ultraviolet and infrared parts. The result is that we have based our entire "reality" on potentially faulty data. Therefore, the *left* brain needs to be reprogrammed to relax (even if momentarily) long enough to let the *right* brain kick in with intuitive hunches.

Look carefully at the images below. Ask yourself several intriguing questions:

I wouldn't have seen it if I hadn't believed it.

Marshall MacLuhan

1. How many times have we used just sensory raw data and gotten into trouble in judging others? In traffic? With the family? At work?
2. How many critical decisions (health, business, politics) are based on faulty sense-based data?
3. How many times have we felt so convinced (to the point of violence) that our data are better than another's?
4. Why do snap decisions usually snap something good?
5. Does the Buddhist expression "Life is an Illusion" have a different meaning now?

If the doors of perception were cleansed, everything would appear to man as it is, infinite.

William Blake

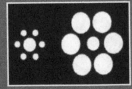

DEPERSONALIZE LIFE AS A CLASSROOM: EVERYTHING IS A MESSAGE

The following is a list of tried and true methods to take the first steps in centering the mind:

Concentrate on what you have and not on what you do not have

Our deeply materialistic culture has put us in a collective hypnosis that our material possessions (houses, cars, boats, mistresses) are a reflection of us. Note the ageless wisdom of this formula:

$$Happiness = \frac{Satisfaction}{Desire}$$

Your happiness will increase in *direct* relation to your inner satisfaction, and *inversely* to your desires. H = S/D. Imprint that.

Get off the work–eat–sleep treadmill for a weekend

Do something memorable, out of the ordinary:

- Visit a prison during a holiday: bring books, fruit or incense.
- Do a walkathon for a charity.
- Do a fast: just fruit, water, and Nature.
- Buy a musical instrument with your child.

Accept with enthusiasm any challenge that confronts you

Never push trouble away. Rather, study the opportunities within. There are many lessons to be learned, and a reputation as an effective troubleshooter is enviable. The most foolish action you could take when confronted by an angry dog is to turn and run. Life is that way, too. Make your mantra "Good news/bad news." The world rocks between the two. Go with the flow.

Do not yield to the charlatans of self-pity or doubt

These are symptoms of unmanliness. Mastering doubt is part of the offering of life's challenges. Negative feelings in a crisis are merely black clouds, whose transit through our lives can actually be slowed by our fascination with them. Ask yourself: would you be the person you are today if you had refused even one of life's lessons? Which of your difficult learning experiences would you send back? If you are defeated in this one battle, that should be lesson enough on how to escape the weakness, if escape is indeed the desired end. Face it, all of life up to now has been a series of contrived training sessions for taking risks. You have already done the most courageous thing anyone could do: in being born, you left the maternal ocean to explore this thing called life. Born naked and excessively curious, to die, inshallah, the same way. *Remove doubt in your abilities or die a smaller person.*

Embrace crisis

Within the Chinese character below, for "crisis" is two separate though inter-twined characters, first for danger, and second hidden opportunity.

危机

Crisis

Diplomacy and defense are not substitutes for one another. Either alone will fail. Great crises produce great men, and great deeds of courage.

John F. Kennedy, Campaign Speech, 1960

That's the mindset to work towards. Obviously, it's a good idea to recognize the inherent danger in change and to protect yourself from the imminent and real dangers (as opposed to the imagined sort) while keeping a keen eye on whatever hidden opportunity might be hidden for us within.

- Step 1: Find your breath.
- Step 2: Back straight, but relaxed.
- Step 3: Allow yourself to go passive by relaxing the muscles of your face – SMILE.
- Step 4: Just let go – breathe as the waves on the beach.
- Step 5: Create a modern mantra and repeat it three times a day. Examples include "This is my life and I am using this 5 minutes to get it right."

The "wait and see ... " approach to crisis management

A wise farmer's horse runs away. To offer their sympathy, his neighbors come over to lament the loss. "Wait and see ...," says the farmer. The neighbors leave, shaking their heads in bewilderment at the farmer's cryptic response.

The following day, the farmer's horse returns, trailed by three wild horses. The neighbors return to congratulate the farmer on his good fortune. "Wait and see...," says the farmer. The neighbors leave, more confused than before.

Later that week, the farmer's son breaks his leg trying to train one of the new horses, and the neighbors are back to offer condolences. "Wait and see ...," says the farmer again. The neighbors leave, discussing the man's mental stability.

The next day, the army comes riding through the village, conscripting young men for a battle the next day. The soldiers have to skip the farmer's son, since he has a broken leg. "Wait and see ...," says the farmer ...

So goes life, alternating between "good" news and "bad" news, like a giant fish swimming between the two banks of the river.

The past is never dead. It's not even past.

William Faulkner

WAYS TO REDUCE STRESS – THE "ILLNESS OF THE LITERATE" (IMMEDIATELY)

- Regain control of your diet, your health, and your mind.
- Learn to say "thanks," both upon awakening and upon going to sleep, for another shot at life.
- Practice the art of random kindness: it distracts the mind from your neurosis/self-pity.
- Spend a morning getting your life organized, nothing else.
- Learn to laugh it off: the joke of life may otherwise be on you.
- Spoil the child within from time to time: he's lonely and loveable.
- Develop a margin of time to move around the world: get up really early from now on.
- Simplify life: collecting "stuff" can't make you happy; less is really more fun.

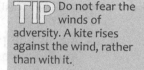 Do not fear the winds of adversity. A kite rises against the wind, rather than with it.

- Change your thinking: develop positivity and optimism. Defy cynical people.
- Avoid negative people, but when impossible, use negativity to help you get better.
- If it is your game, you make up the rules. If you are playing someone else's game (like your boss's), play by the rules until you can create your own game.
- Fail until you succeed.
- Practice the fine art of *letting go* of the ego-grasping that stresses you and family.
- Take a deep breath. Practice the art of dying: DABDA.
- Rest and relaxation play as important a part as exercise itself.
- Do not worry. All it does is gets you ready for negative outcomes.
- Think happy thoughts and there will be positive outcomes.
- Do not step back from the job at hand when fear subsides in you.
- Use your heart and not only your brain.
- Eliminate emotions by letting go of the past and thinking about the present.
- What has happened in the past will most probably stay the same: you can't change it. Instead focus on the present and live today instead of yesterday.
- Don't let time control you. You control time.
- Once again, forget the past and live it up in the present.
- Re-perceive stress in life as a "gift" to help you avoid living (and dying) foolishly.
- Learn to see with another set of eyes.
- Live your life with two principles in mind: first that you will live forever, the other that today is your last day.

HOW TO MAKE YOURSELF MISERABLE AND LIVE FOOLISHLY

When people, especially business people, experience difficult financial straits, the knee-jerk reflex is to prove their indispensability by working longer, harder days and weeks. Don't pay for several steps on the corporate ladder with your core asset: your mental and physical health. If you keep your health intact during the storm, there will be time and energy for other challenges. Don't forget, your kids are watching, not listening: how you handle stress will be how your kids will do so.

So, if that doesn't make sense to you, here are some tips to stay stressed out:

- *Work until you drop*, convinced of your invincibility and indispensability.
- *Pay no attention to the signs of stress and depression* – fatigue and withdrawal.
- When passing through a tempest of depression – colloquially known as the "blues" – ask yourself these three critical questions upon arising:
  - Am I in pain?
  - Are my bills paid?
  - Am I in reasonable health?

  If not, you are *way* ahead of most of humanity.
- *Develop an uncontrollable appetite for expensive toys* that will be obsolete in 6 months. Then go outside and watch a dog chase its tail without empathizing.
- *Make cynical and gratuitous comments* at exquisitely vulnerable moments of your adolescent's life choices.
- *Forget to laugh.* With that attitude, the joke of life is on you. Let the mask slip from time to time.
- *Forget to relax after making a mistake.*[6] These are the moments when we center the mind. Energize the body with a sauna.
- *Eat like the Chaplin character* in Modern Times. Just strap yourself in at meetings and conference calls and eat loads of fast foods and processed frozen meals: these can be high in sodium, calories, and fat.
- *Destroy your sleep patterns.* Get less than 6 hours, get irritable, and have difficulty with concentration, memory, and judgment until you finally crash or rear-end someone. Load up on caffeine and alcohol throughout the day, and get ready for tossing and turning until 3 a.m.
- *Forget exercise.* That's like throwing the parachute out of the plane *before* you jump out! Given that getting in a post-meal 15-minute walk plus a 4-minute work-out in the morning reduces the risk for nearly every major disease and reduces anxiety and depression, only the most disorganized person cannot find time to squeeze in some life-saving exercise.
- *Expunge the following marriage-saving expressions* from your vocabulary:
  - Thank you
  - Excuse me
  - Please
  - I love you
  - Help me
  - How was your day, dear?

YOGA OF THE EYES: HEALING THE BRAIN WITH SUN POWER

Yoga of the eyes, an ancient knowledge that is still taught at the School for Perfect Eyesight in Pondicherry, India, is a powerful tool to help you regain good vision, as well as teach you to relax and stay in the eye of the hurricane (your right brain).

These sun-powered exercises will also improve your concentration, memory, energy, and creativity.

Take a few minutes every day to do the following exercises and measure your improvement in vision by keeping a small print business card written in light print as your index of reference.

Breathing facing the sunlight (when the sun is there)

- Stand with your feet apart at shoulder width.
- **Inhale**, keeping your body weight on both feet.
- **Exhale**, shifting your body weight to your right side.
- **Inhale**, and come back to the center.
- **Inhale**, shifting your body weight to your left side.
- Repeat this five times each side.

Eye rotation

Standing or sitting (in a forest or city park at lunchtime, for example), with your eyes open, look up, then oblique right upward, then due right, then oblique right downward, oblique left downward, due left, and finally oblique left upward. Then change side. Repeat this five times each side.

Important note: Try not to move your head or grimace as you proceed.

Eye palming

Standing or sitting (at the seaside or while hiking in the mountains, for example), warm up your palms by rubbing them against each other (Fig. AIIa.1).

Without pressure, cover your closed eyes with your palms (Fig. AIIa.2). Look for total blackness. Breathe softly while relaxing the facial, neck, and shoulder muscles for a few minutes.

FIGURE AIIa.1

FIGURE AIIa.2

Bathing your eyes

Use a glass or an eye cup, and fill it with clean water. Place your right eye inside the cup and open and close your eyes 12 times. Do the same thing, with fresh water, for your left eye. Don't rub your eyes, but dry them very softly.

Tennis ball foot massage

This is a really fun exercise to improve your vision and lower limb tension.

Place a tennis ball under your right foot and roll the ball from front to back and back to front for a few times. Then make gentle circles with your foot on the ball to the right and to the left.

Repeat with your left foot.

NOTES AND REFERENCES

1. If there is a type A (aggressive. time-urgent, anger prone, all-or-nothing), there is, of course, a type B behavior pattern: passive, relaxed, good at listening, contented, not frustrated, cares enough, time-easy (everything in its time), easygoing. All of this leads to less adrenaline (high blood pressure) around in the blood, faster electrocardiogram responses to stress, less heart disease, and, naturally, a more balanced home life. If trying to evolve into a type B personality seems stressful, the other option is to understand and control the downside of the type A personality, especially anger and hostility. The risk factor status of type A is supported by three prospective studies: (1) a sample of middle-aged, predominantly white-collar men employed by various firms in California; (2) a population-based study of men and women in the ongoing US Framingham Study; and (3) three samples of employed men, white-collar and blue-collar, in Belgium and France (Yeung AC et al. The effect of atherosclerosis on the vasomotor response of coronary arteries to mental stress. *N Engl J Med* 1991; **325**: 1551–6).

2. Kubler-Ross, E. *On Death and Dying*. New York: Macmillan, 1969.

3. When you trigger the process of DABDA, as a manager you have to help the individual, at least as far as openness is concerned. At this point, managers knew that they were looking ahead rather than cycling stuck in the anger or depression loop. Social workers needed to be on standby in case an individual did not make it to this stage but was stuck in anger or depression, as that can be a very dangerous state, sometimes triggering suicide. See http://www.careertrainer.com/Request.jsp?IView=ViewArticle&Article=OID%3A107359

4. Maslow A. *Toward a Psychology of Being*. New York: Van Nostrand Reinhold, 1968.

5. Two major studies have shown that anger and stress produce physiological events that greatly increase the risk of heart disease and heart attack:
   - Researchers at Johns Hopkins' University (Maryland, US) have discovered that quick-tempered young men had triple the risk of premature heart disease and early heart attack. They followed 1,000 medical students between 1948 and 1964, and found that 35% of the "angry" men had developed cardiovascular disease with an average onset at age 56. Physiologically, anger causes a stress-related secretion of hormones that raises blood pressure, triggering inflammation, and constricts blood vessels,

putting extra stress on the heart, increasing the risk of heart attacks. University of North Carolina researchers showed that long-term anger and fatigue together form a type of "perfect storm" stress scenario that greatly increases risk of heart attack. From 1990 to 1998, 12,453 men and women were tracked. Those scoring highest on either "anger" or "fatigue" were 42% more likely to have a heart attack; high scores on both were 69% more likely to suffer a heart attack. (*Physician's Weekly* 2002; **XIX** (20)).

6. There is a downside to the unrelenting standards for high achievements, where often success is seen as failure. Perfectionism often amounts to an excessive hunger for approval, whetted at adolescence, which keeps these individuals vulnerable to criticism. They tend to avoid professional help as a sign of weakness and are more susceptible to alcoholism, depression, and suicide.

Most anxiety in modern life stems from the analytical *left* brain's mistrust toward the *right* brain, and the *right* brain's fabulous abilities to get us through a tough patch of life. You remember the right brain from Chapter 4? That's the side that deals with the present moment in all its infinity, not just through the prism of our material needs. It connects to all around it, without preconditions or prejudices. It could be compared to the innocent child within who projects peace and brings us back after a heated argument, always connecting, connecting, connecting ...

The *right* brain does all that by merely inviting us to let go of the grip of the analytical *left* brain. In fact, it was probably the analytical *left* brain that got us into this mess of anxiety or hostility, as it looks to new experience data and compares them to past data, then projects onto the future ... and then starts to worry. We say, "I just can't do it" or "That's impossible," but what we really mean to say is that "I cannot trust my *left* brain to find the solutions." So maybe the *right* brain has the solutions to the problem.

Unfortunately perhaps, the mind cannot be reprogrammed by simply reading black words on a white page. That's precisely why a university physics course has an experimental laboratory section, to test the theories discussed in the classroom. The exercises included here are designed to help leaders embark on their own journey of discovery, and plant their own seeds of awakening of the *right* brain and the present moment.

There are several general aspects of one's lifestyle that can help to maintain *right* brain health:

1. The easiest and most effective ways to reprogram the mind:
   a. Know your **psychosomatic symptoms**
   b. Learn to appreciate **silence**
   c. Become more **neophilic and expansive**
   d. Try **meditation**
   e. Seek out the **Grand Design**
   f. Check out the power of **mantra**
   g. Energize your sleep with **yoga nidra**
   h. Try the **leader's prayer book**
   i. **Alternate nostril breathing** (pranayama variation).
2. The top tips for beating chronic sadness (not quite depression):
   a. Know the **symptoms** of depression
   b. **Let go** of the past
   c. Make some **changes** to start the healing process
   d. Get back to **nature**

e. Develop a strategy to **ward off negative thinking**
f. Perform random **acts of kindness**
g. **Humor** yourself
h. Realize **we are all in this together**
i. Be **patient**
j. When all else fails, **take refuge**.

THE EASIEST AND MOST EFFECTIVE WAYS TO REPROGRAM THE MIND

Psychosomatic symptoms

First and foremost, take stock of *all* psychosomatic symptoms. Know your particular starting point stress-wise. The only way we can even tell if we have deep-seated conflicts as described above is by identifying the psychosomatic symptoms. These are direct messages sent from the body (somatic) to the mind (psycho-) which tell us that a conflict exists between past and present, and that it is time to clear out the software by reprogramming the mind. There might be:

- emotional lability: wide mood swings;
- sexual dysfunction;
- skin ailments (psoriasis, eczema or acne);
- hair ailments (alopecia);
- high blood pressure;
- diabetes;
- sleeplessness.

Silence

Learn to appreciate silence, not as an absence of sound, but as a presence. This, as musicians know, is as significant a "sound" as actual vibratory noise. Reflect on Aldous Huxley's 1946 essay "On Silence."

Become more neophilic and expansive

Allow more space in your worldview for less conformist ideas. Read the story of Nan-in, a Japanese master during the Meiji era (1868–1912), who one day, the story goes, received a university professor who came to inquire about Zen. Nan-in served tea. He poured his visitor's cup full, and then kept on pouring. The professor watched the overflow until he no longer could restrain himself. "It is overfull. No more will go in!"

"Like this cup," Nan-in said, "you are full of your own opinions and speculations. How can I show you Zen unless you first empty your cup?"

Your mind is like a cup of tea.
Empty your cup to make place for other ideas.

Meditation

Man's mind, once stretched by a new idea, never regains its original dimensions.

Oliver Wendell Holmes

TIP **Love and discipline**
One's thoughts are the children of the mind and must be managed as any child: *gently but firmly.*

What is meditation? Meditation is an invitation to understand the inner forces that influence our thinking processes and, in turn, our decisions and our lives. Through meditation, we can remove the stains of pride, anger, and fear on our soul that prevent us from reflecting on this cosmic wisdom. It is done through the development of the "witness" within. The witness can detach itself from the incessant "thought parade."

Now that you are cool with silence, and seek neophilic expansiveness, explore your thought parade with the help of meditation. In fact, if you have ever held a pencil or any simple object in your hands and drifted, you were

doing a sort of meditation. The best part is that you only need 3 minutes for this. Do it first thing in the morning before the thought parade begins.

This is very simple, yet very hard at the same time. In the simplest terms, you are going to use breathing as a tether for your mind as it is distracted by its own thought parade. Gaining detachment in this natural way is relaxing and builds confidence.

How to do it:

- Sit anywhere quietly and undisturbed, and imagine a hurricane, violent at the edges, calm at the center.
- Now, once ready, take five deep breaths with the intention of completely emptying the lungs of anxiety-causing carbon dioxide. *Important note*: with each cycle of breathing, allow the exhalation phase to increase.
- After these five introductory breaths, you should feel calm, as if at the hurricane's center. You will be aware of thoughts as they pass, but allow them to pass. Stay centered.
- Allow your breathing to go back to normal tidal breathing, like the waves, gently in and out, without forcing it: "in with the oxygen ... out with the carbon dioxide."
- Here's the *key* to the whole thing: every time a thought form (passion, anger, hate, joy, greed, worry or whatever) pulls you off center, remember to *gently but firmly* bring your attention back to your breathing.
- Back and forth: between thoughts that excite or sadden, and your breathing.
- For the entire time observing your breaths, treat your thoughts as you might treat your children (they *are* your mind's children): gently but firmly.

The goal of any meditation is to refine your everyday awareness and override any counterproductive hardware (alcohol abuse, addiction, anger). It could be enhanced by the attentive observation of an object, breathing, a symbol, a flame or incense.

Above all, meditation offers you peace of mind, a commodity hard to come by these days. When stressed out, before making the best speech you will ever regret or making any critical decisions, use your breathing to bring your mind over the center of the hurricane. You will know if your mind has been stabilized over the eye of the hurricane if you start experiencing the symptoms of peace of mind. When asked to report subjective or objective signs induced by a daily 3–4-minute meditation, participants in our Leader's Health Programme listed the following findings:

- An inability to worry for no good reason (which some may find a good reason to worry!).
- No more scapegoating, criticizing or judging others.
- A palpable sense of completeness, of no wanting or lacking.
- An enduring sense of humor, in all situations.
- A higher anger threshold: getting angry less, staying angry less.
- Freedom from time obsession, often confused with disorientation.
- Observation without commentary, freedom from conditioning/habits.
- A realization that you are pretty complete, and not really in need of being saved.
- Intense enjoyment in letting things happen and just witnessing them …
- A realization that the world is not so bad after all, deserving of our acceptance.
- The loss of the fanatical need to control everything, from the weather to the people in our lives.
- An irrepressible desire to converse with children.

You will find that once you have started to rewrite your mind's software, there will most certainly be perceptible changes. Keep an eye open for these changes as they represent the peace of mind that comes with the detachment that regular meditation brings.

Seek out the Grand Design

Whether you are aware of the Grand Design of it all is not important: it exists. The real fun comes from putting the bits of the puzzle together using and deciphering life experiences, buffing and polishing until the Grand Design shines through. For now, though, don't question the methods of this madness; just enjoy the ride. Modify the way that you *perceive* life: no hassles, just lessons. As discussed above, this type of engineering on the mind is one of the most effective. Converting life experiences into wisdom is the essence of life.

Check out the power of mantra

If you sing opera in the shower or hum while working, you are doing mantra. A mantra is a powerful way to reprogram the mind to act and react in a more controlled appropriate way. Everyone is constantly chanting their own mantra or mind chatter, as it were. That is, we are continually conditioning ourselves with the endless loop tape that represents a distillation of everything we have assimilated up to that point.

Alternatively, there are many mantras from every culture and religion (including Buddhism, Islam, Christianity, and Hinduism). Table AIIb.1 gives some examples.

Thought substitution through yoga nidra

This is an extremely powerful technique for developing a superior mind, with one great benefit over all the others: you can lie down and close your eyes. (Yoga nidra is the yoga of sleep.) Other surprising benefits that start to appear very quickly after a few weeks of earnest practice.

For reprogramming a dysfunctional mind, start slowly by reading through these steps. You can get someone whose voice you like to record these instructions:

First, set aside 10 minutes just before going to bed, for this starter session. Get relaxed before you go to sleep, and do some meta-programming.

- Lie down on the floor; turn off the phone.
  - Pay systematic attention to every part of your anatomy, progressively, from head to foot, silently whispering consciously to relieve any tension or frustration:
    - Head muscular, tighten, relax, let go."
    - "Neck muscular, tighten, relax, let go."
    - "Back muscular, tighten, relax, let go."
    - "Hand muscular, tighten, relax, let go," and so on.
  - The conscious mind gets stronger and nimbler, and thus better and better at avoiding external or internal distractions, as it goes around the body, until any residual tension is dissipated.
- Decide on a critical resolution (a sankalpa or a "wish") and send it into the depths of your subconsciouness.
- Ideas for sankalpa include:
  - becoming more intelligent;
  - leading yourself better;
  - developing optimal health and fitness;
  - improving your memory;
  - getting over your father/mother;
  - being a better father/mother;
  - I am the Buddha Nature, not my body nor my emotions.

TABLE AIIB.1 *Mantras*

SOURCE	MANTRA	ORIGINAL	MEANING	COMMENTS
Islam	La ilaha illa Allah	الا اله الا الله	There is no true god but God	Commonly known as the tahlīl (meaning rejoicing or jubilation)
Islam	(Surah Taha:114)	وقل رب زدني علماً	Our Lord Grant us increase in knowledge	Can be said any time
Sanscrit (Hindu)	The Gayatri Mantra: Aum Bhuh Bhuvah Svah Tat Savitur Varenyam Bhargo Devasya Dheemahi Dhiyo Yo nah Prachodayat	ॐ भूर्भुवः स्वः तत्सवितुर्वरेण्यम् भर्गो देवस्य धीमहि धियो यो नः प्रचोदयात् Rig Veda (10:16:3)	We meditate on the glory of the Creator; Who has created the Universe; Who is worthy of Worship; Who is the embodiment of Knowledge and Light; Who is the remover of all Sin and Ignorance; May He enlighten our Intellect	The Gayatri mantra is one of the oldest and most powerful of Sanskrit mantras
Christian	Lord, make me an instrument of your peace, Where there is hatred, let me sow love; where there is injury, pardon; where there is doubt, faith; where there is despair, hope; where there is darkness, light; where there is sadness, joy; O Divine Master, grant that I may not so much seek to be consoled as to console; to be understood as to understand; to be loved as to love. For it is in giving that we receive; it is in pardoning that we are pardoned; and it is in dying that we are born to eternal life	The Prayer of St. Francis of Assisi		
Tibetan	Om Ah Hung Vajra Guru Pema Siddhi Hung	ༀ ཨཱཿ ཧཱུྃ་བཛྲ་གུ་རུ་པདྨ་སིདྡྷི་ཧཱུྃ༔	OM AH HUNG defeat the army of the five mental poisons VAJRA defeats anger GURU cefeats pride PEMA defeats desire/attachment SIDDHI defeats envy and jealousy HUNG defeats the armies of gods, demons, and humans	Vajra Guru Mantra
Buddhist	Om Mani Padme Hum		Hail the jewel in the lotus	The Mantra of Compassion
Shinran Buddhist	Namu Amida Butsu		Hail to Amitābha Buddha	Chanted or recited by Japanese Pure Land Buddhists in order to gain rebirth into the Pure Land after death

- Use endpoints to gauge success and adjust.
- Repeat the cycle deliberately every night with total conviction and sincerity, until it is automatic.
- What you are determined to happen, will happen. It's just a matter of timing. It cannot be otherwise.

Convince your thinking mind software to accept the following statements and then, without resistance, see what the confirming mind software does:

- Life is designed to make me wiser and happier, and everybody is helping.
- Emotion control. When it comes to anger control, be realistic. Perhaps you cannot get rid of anger, but you can decide when to bring it out.

A leader's prayer book

Here are some sublime examples of the kinds of extracts/prayers a busy executive could collect together.

One night a man had a dream. He dreamed that he was walking along a beach with God. Across the sky, he saw scenes from life flashed before him. For each scene, he noted two sets of footprints in the sand, his own and that of God. When the last scene of his life flashed before him, he looked back at the trail of footprints. He noticed that many times along the path of his life, especially during the toughest and saddest moments, there was only one set of footprints.

Confused by this, he confronted God: "God, you said to me that once I decided to follow you, you would walk with me all the way. But what I see now is that during the most challenging parts of my life, there is only one set of footprints. I do not understand: when I needed you most, you seem to abandon me."

"My dear precious child," God replied, "I love you deeply and would never abandon you. During those times of trial and tribulation, when you see only one set of footprints, it was then that I was carrying you."

Author unknown

Lord, I know not what I ought to ask of thee; Thou only knowest what I need. Thou loves me better than I know to love myself. O Father, give to Thy child that which he himself knows not how to ask. I dare not ask either for crosses or for consolations. I simply present myself before thee, I open my heart to Thee. Behold my needs which I know not myself, see and do according to Thy tender mercy. Smite or heal, depress me or raise me up. I adore all Thy purposes without knowing them. I am silent; I offer myself as sacrifice. I yield myself to Thee; I would have no other desire than to accomplish Thy will. Teach me to pray. Pray Thyself in me. Amen.

François de Salignac Fenelon, Archbishop of Cambray, 1651–1715

Do not stand at my grave and weep,
I am not there, I do not sleep.
I am a thousand winds that blow; I am the diamond glint in the snow.
I am the sunlight in the unripened grain, I am the gentle autumn rain.
When you awaken in the morning hush, I am the swift uplifting rush
Of quiet birds encircling flight.
I am the soft stars that shine at night.
Do not stand at my grave and weep,
I am not there, I did not die.

Mary Elizabeth Frye

Lead me from the Unreal to the Real
Lead me from the Darkness into Light
Lead me from Death into Immortality

Brihadaranyaka Upanishad

... and I shall follow without hesitation.

Jules McGannon

O Lord, make me an instrument of Thy peace.
Where there is hatred, let me sow love;
Where there is injury, pardon;
Where there is doubt, faith;
Where there is despair, hope;
Where there is darkness, light;
And where there is sadness, joy.
O Divine Master, grant that I may not so much seek to be consoled, as
to console;
To be understood, as to understand;
To be loved, as to love;
For it is in giving that we receive;
It is in pardoning that we are pardoned;
And it is in dying that we are born to Eternal Life.

St. Francis of Assisi

PRANAYAMA¹ (ALTERNATE NOSTRIL BREATHING)

This breathing program is perfect for energizing your brain after a long day.
Although it sounds a little weird, it is a very powerful technique for calming
yourself during times of intense stress. It is just another breathing technique
that can help you clear your mind and control the noise of your thoughts in
just 2 minutes. Try it out:

1. If you are in your office, tell your secretary not to disturb you for the
   next 4 minutes (always give yourself a couple of minutes margin) – no
   phone calls, no interruptions.

2. Sit upright with your spine erect and your head straight but relaxed.
3. Use your right hand for the exercise. Your thumb will control your right nostril and your middle and ring fingers will control your left nostril.
4. Close the right nostril with the thumb, and inhale slowly and fully through the left nostril (Fig. AIIb.1).
5. Hold your breath for 2 or 3 seconds only, *no longer*.
6. Close the left nostril with your middle fingers and exhale slowly through the right nostril (Fig. AIIb.2)
7. Inhale through the *same* right nostril while the left nostril is still closed.
8. Again hold your breath for a few seconds only.
9. Close the right nostril and exhale through the left nostril. This completes one round. Complete three rounds and observe.
10. When you are ready, open your eyes very slowly, stretch your neck, arms, and hands.
11. When you want, stand up and stretch your spine backward very slowly, while resting your hands on your lower back.

Repeat the whole process for about 60 seconds, and you'll feel like (because you will be) a new person. Now you are ready to continue your day with more positive energy.

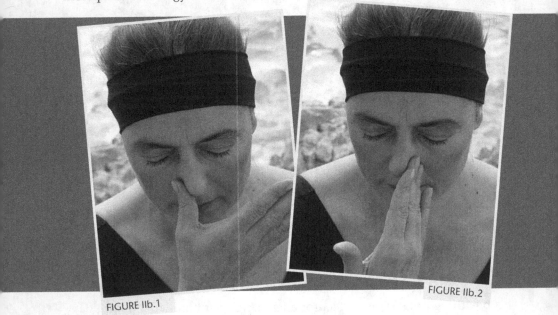

FIGURE IIb.1

FIGURE IIb.2

TOP STRATEGIES FOR BEATING CHRONIC SADNESS (NOT QUITE DEPRESSION)

Know the symptoms of depression

First of all, are you depressed or just down? Experts suggest that you seek professional help if you experience five or more of these symptoms every day for 2 weeks:

- Fatigue: decreased energy, fatigue, combined with insomnia, early-morning awakening or oversleeping.
- Withdrawal: loss of interest or pleasure in hobbies and activities that were once enjoyed, including sex.
- Persistent sad, anxious or "empty" mood.
- Feelings of hopelessness, pessimism, worthlessness, and helplessness.
- Difficulty concentrating, remembering or making decisions.
- Appetite and/or weight loss, or overeating and weight gain.

Let go of the past

Stop mulling over lost moments and get yourself ready for future ones. Forget old lovers, and get over your father or mother and what they did (or failed to do) for you.

Make some changes to start the healing process before going into life's tests and battles

Do not hesitate on this one. On days when your outlook is reasonable, get fit to fight another day. For starters:

- *quit alcohol* (or whatever brain chemical you are using these days) for a while. You have convinced yourself that the solutions are outside of you, and alcohol is no exception;
- do *BURST exercise* (see Chapter 1): after several sets, you are back in control;
- *eat clean*: consume a cleansing diet to purify the blood of depressing toxins;
- remember the *famous Frank Zappa quote* every morning:

  If you wind up with a boring, miserable life because you listened to your mom, your dad, your teacher, your priest or some guy on TV telling you how to do your shit, then you deserve it.

Get back to nature

Try this, in this order:

- Be shallow for once and stop thinking about you and yours. Thinking over your plight is exactly how you got into this mess in the first place.
- Tidy up your house or flat for 2 hours.
- Call up a friend and arrange to spend the day together.
- Go for a day trip to either the mountains, the sea or the forest.
- Refuse to engage in any self-description of your issues, just do "active listening" to your friend. Discover their humanity, flaws, and blemishes.
- After marvelling at Nature for a day, return home and run a bath or have a sauna.

- While drying off, put some Mozart or Charlie Parker on and give yourself a 20-minute foot massage with coconut oil.
- Do meditation before going to bed: detach from the drama.
- While lying in bed after an enjoyable day, whisper a sincere "thank you" for the slice of humanity and peace you have just partaken in.
- Be your own shrink: develop a unified mind, resolute and clear. Do yoga nidra as you fall asleep.
- The healing has begun and you are that much closer to wholeness.
- Repeat as needed.

Develop a gatekeeper to ward off negative thinking

By doing simple meditation, you can color or personalize your thoughts and emotions, which is the first step to detaching yourself from these "children" of your mind. That's right, your thoughts (including emotions, fantasies, fears, illusions, and phobias) are all the product of your mind. They are, therefore, your "children" in a very real way. What is the foolproof way to manage your children? Indulgence? NO way! That's how you got the blues in the first place by giving them full play in your mind. The answer is to *gently* (with love) but *firmly* (that's the discipline they need) address them: "Not just now, dear, a little later, perhaps."

Perform random acts of kindness

This will shift the focus of your neurosis from your ego to another's suffering. Visit a prison (with books and tapes), a retirement home, a hospice, a hospital for mentally challenged, an orphanage.

Humor yourself

Just let go of your melodrama. There is enough negativity in the world without adding to it. A sense of humor puts a new twist on life's challenges; it seems to even the playing field. Entertain this possibility: that life is an enormous joke, complete with all its absurdity. Just keep laughing to prevent from crying. At last, after a lifetime of laughing, the joke won't be on you. Humor may also help protect you against a heart attack, according to a recent study by cardiologists at the University of Maryland Medical Center in Baltimore. The study, which is the first to indicate that laughter may help prevent heart disease, found that people with heart disease were 40% less likely to laugh in a variety of situations compared to people of the same age without heart disease. Listen to a comedian on the Internet: try Monty Python, Bill Hicks or Will Ferrell. Or go to Google and type on the video section "bloopers," "banned" or "funny" and let go heartily.

Realize we are all in this together and that your sadness is not special (except that it is yours)

While travelling around northern India giving talks, the Buddha was approached by a women who was grieving at the loss of her son. The story continues: "I've been told that you once practiced medicine, and that you knew a cure for death. I beg you, sir, bring my son back to life. Please! My husband is amongst the city's wealthiest – I can pay you any fee. Please!" She cried. Still the Buddha was silent."Do you know the cure or not? I beg you!"

"Yes," the Buddha said. "I know the cure for death."

A collective gasp went through the crowd, and the Buddha's closest disciples gave him a suspicious look.

"Any price," the woman said, weeping. "Anything!"

"Very well," the Buddha said. "I require but a mustard seed – the other reagents I have. But it cannot be *any* common mustard seed. It must come from a family that has *never known death* or such suffering. If you bring me such a seed, I will be able to prepare your cure."

"Oh, most generous doctor! Enlightened sage! Thank you! Thank you!"

"Leave the child," the Buddha said, as the woman stood. "I can prepare the rest of the cure while you search." The woman went from home to home, and asking everyone the same question. "Can you spare a mustard seed?"

"I don't see why not."

"Thank you! But – *has your family ever known death?*"

"Yes. Only four months ago, my father passed away. You were there, remember?"

"Yes. My parents and their parents, and the brothers of them all are all dead and gone. I am alone in the world."

"My son was slain in battle."

"... killed by wolves."

"... executed ..."

"... drowned herself ..."

"... fell from a partition ..."

"... died from a cold ..."

"I am the only one left of my family."

The woman, battered and coated in filth, knelt in the mud of a long-due rainstorm and said to herself, "My son is dead." She then returned to the grove and found the Buddha, sweeping wood-dust from the construction site.

"Hello," the Buddha said in greeting.

"Blessed Sage," the women replied.

She was smeared over with the grime of the road, and old tears had carved paths through the dirt on her cheek. Despite this, the Buddha said, "Your wandering has done you well."

"Oh, Buddha, how selfish was my grief. I went from family to family, and pretended for two long days that there might exist some clan of immortals. Those wives alive who haven't already lost a son are bound to lose one someday. And if they never lose a son, then a son is bound to lose a mother. And how many parents lay buried beneath our feet!"

"Your observation is accurate in every way, Madam. Neither those wise nor those foolish are immune to death. However great a father roars, he can never waken a dead daughter. However much a mother begs the gods, a dead son will never cry again. One by one, Madam, we each die. This is but a greater disappointment among a thousand lesser ones, and just as a Sage does not mourn a broken pot, a Sage does not mourn death.

"Your tears painted trails down your face once, Madam, but those trails did not lead you to peace of mind. For four days, you suffered the elements as if you wandered a jungle instead of the heart of a great city. But your sorrow accomplished nothing for your son. Be prepared, Madam, for you will suffer many other deaths in your time, and some day, your own. Destroy the attachment that causes your grief, and you will lead a better life."

Thus the woman took her first step down the path of wisdom. And the Buddha finished sweeping the floor.

Be patient

You are closer to escape from the depths towards functionality and happiness than you think.

When all else fails: take refuge

When nothing else can stop the slide into darkness, take solace in these words from the Hindu sacred text, the Mundaka Upanishad:

Yea, this is the best of the worlds …
Thank the Lord, O moping man, O weeping man, Thank the Lord, O groping man, O thankless man,
That the world is not different from what it is! Here Karma works: you can do and undo.
Here mettle tells; good is valued. Here austerities bear fruit.
Self-application is rewarded.
Sincerity is understood, murder known. Here seeds sprout, flowers blossom, fruits ripen.
You cannot escape here blessings of virtue and burnings of sin.
Here the wheel comes full circle, without stopping anywhere.
Here the oppressor's head someday rolls on the ground.
Deferred justice is referred to and applied.
Here truth always triumphs, never falsehood.
Here hatred never succeeds, love never fails.
Here if you bring light, darkness everywhere disappears.
Here there is no dogmatism except in minds of perverted men.
Here no doubt that a sword-thrust brings forth flowing gush of warm red blood.
Again, here wounds are healed, tears are wiped, prayers are heard:
Here in God's world, you can die and be reborn.
Here God is seen. Aye, God is verily seen!

Where could you find, O foolish man, a better world than this world of cause and effect, of sowing and harvesting?
Moreover of grace?

NOTES AND REFERENCES

1. Effects of pranayama. The authors can testify that this type of stress-reliever is highly effective against *all* forms of severe stress, personal (grief, family issues) and professional (speaker's stage fright, deadlines or humor retrieval). It has been shown to contribute to a physiological response characterized by:
   - the presence of decreased oxygen consumption, decreased heart rate, and decreased blood pressure, as well as increased theta wave amplitude in electroencephalogram recordings;
   - increased parasympathetic activity accompanied by the experience of alertness and reinvigoration.

   Jerath R, Edry JW, Barnes VA, Jerath V. Physiology of long pranayamic breathing: neural respiratory elements may provide a mechanism that explains how slow deep breathing shifts the autonomic nervous system. *Med Hypotheses* 2006; **67**: 566–71.

Index

Printed in the United States
By Bookmasters